Star-Spangled Soccer

The Selling, Marketing and Management of Soccer in the USA

Gary Hopkins

palgrave
macmillan

First published 2010 by
PALGRAVE MACMILLAN

Palgrave Macmillan in the UK is an imprint of Macmillan Publishers Limited,
registered in England, company number 785998, of Houndmills, Basingstoke,
Hampshire RG21 6XS.

Palgrave Macmillan in the US is a division of St Martin's Press LLC,
175 Fifth Avenue, New York, NY 10010.

Palgrave Macmillan is the global academic imprint of the above companies
and has companies and representatives throughout the world.

Palgrave® and Macmillan® are registered trademarks in the United States,
the United Kingdom, Europe and other countries

ISBN 978–0–230–23973–9

This book is printed on paper suitable for recycling and made from fully
managed and sustained forest sources. Logging, pulping and manufacturing
processes are expected to conform to the environmental regulations of the
country of origin.

A catalogue record for this book is available from the British Library.

A catalog record for this book is available from the Library of Congress.

10 9 8 7 6 5 4 3 2 1
19 18 17 16 15 14 13 12 11 10

Printed in the United States of America

*To my wife **Paula**, who encouraged me to put pen to paper and whose endless patience love (and cups of tea) got me through it. My children **David**, **Lindsay** and **Veronica**, who simply make me proud every day I am their father, and my mom and dad who have loved and supported me since the day I was born … what more can you ask for? Also to my brothers **Paul**, **Graham**, **Mick**, sisters **Julie**, **Mandy**, and nieces **Kelly**, **Sophie** and **Lucy**.*

*Finally to **Doug Hamilton**, **Keith Heyes** and **Michael Forte**, friends I met through soccer in America who sadly never made it to full-time. I had some great times with all of them*

CONTENTS

LIST OF FIGURES AND TABLES

Figures

Tables

Acknowledgments

Star-Spangled Soccer could not have been written without the support of friends and colleagues in the American soccer world, many of whom have been there from the beginning. For the early days Alan Rothenberg, Hank Steinbrecher, Chuck Blazer, Sunil Gulati, Scott Parks LeTellier, John Guppy, Dan Flynn, Matthew Wheeler, and Edward Leask were all generous with their time and insights. For the past decade and the rise of MLS and Soccer United Marketing, Don Garber, Mark Abbott, Ivan Gazidis, Doug Quinn, Tim Leiweke, Joe Roth, Nick Sakiewicz, Clark Hunt, Jonathan Kraft and Will Chang along with Doug Logan all allowed me repeated – and, sometimes, I am sure – intrusive requests for "just one more thing". Agents Richard Motzkin, Mark Levinstein and John Langel all gave hours of time without sending a bill, for which I thank them!

Much of the story about soccer on American television was written and lived by David Downs and John Skipper who, despite World Cup bids and ESPN's push to South Africa 2010, made themselves available whenever I asked, as did Seth Ader at ESPN. I speak little Spanish but an afternoon with Mal Karwoski at Univision unveiled the true grass-roots story of the role soccer played in building a network from someone in the trenches from day one, while Dermot McQuarrie (Fox Soccer) provided a great view into soccer's 24/7 network.

Continuing with television, Mike Cohen (MLS) educated me on the important influence of television production, commentary and digital playbacks. If it's been "sold" in soccer over the past decades, chances are Randy Bernstein and Kathy Carter were somewhere around it and their sponsor stories were greatly appreciated, as were those of current sponsors from Russell Sargeant (MLS). Perennially buying such sponsorships was Bruce Hudson, a great soccer man whose dollars (from Budweiser) paid a lot of bills. No one knows more about buying soccer than Bruce.

At the youth level, Larry Monaco, Bill Sage and Lynn Berling Manuel all brought a perspective born of decades of involvement at the very core of the sport. At the team level, my thanks go to Tom Payne (Galaxy) and Gary Wright (Seattle Sounders) for their perspective from the "sharp end", along with Dave Kasper (D.C. United) who talked me through the complexities of player recruitment and development. Charlie Stillitano (CAA) as ever provided colorful insight into a sport that runs through his veins. Joe Cummings (NSCAA) and Joe Quinn (ex-WUSA) helped enormously with my understanding of professional women's soccer, while Chris Price (Xara), Antonio Zea (Adidas) and Ken Chartier (ex-Adidas) assisted with the perspective of brands that make a living from getting it right. And Garry Cook at Manchester City gave an international viewpoint. The game is of course all about players and thanks are due to Marcelo Balboa who provided solid soccer perspective.

For his research, I would also like to thank Jack Gidney – someone who knows more about soccer around the world than just about anyone I know. Thanks also to Sue Bridgewater, Director of the Center for Business in Sports at Warwick Business School, for not only helping me secure a publishing contract, but also her support and guidance throughout the process; and to Keith Povey my copy editor at Palgrave Macmillan who defines the word "patient"!

Finally, to all my friends and colleagues in American soccer ... many, many thanks.

Star-Spangled Soccer

As the trains started to arrive, it was clear something special and momentous was happening. Painted faces, flags over their shoulders, banners waving, thousands upon thousands of soccer fans singing, laughing, chanting, roaring their support and proudly stating their presence. Hour by hour the streets, bars and restaurants filled with these marauding masses: songs echoed, cheers went up, the banter and laughter was non-stop: to and fro with the opposing fans, standing their ground, giving better than they were getting, fearless and proud, passionate and fervent, friendly yet watchful. At 1pm the roar that went up was a deafening and almost surreal wall of sound: USA!... USA!... USA!... – not necessarily original but stirringly powerful.

It started outside the station where fans had gathered and journeyed along the narrow palisade that wound through the town center. It flooded walkway cafes, restaurants, and bars, it echoed through tight alleyways and overhead balconies, it drifted through open shop windows and market stalls, drenching the air with the fervent sound of unfailing patriotism that only soccer fans can deliver. Locals stood in amazement, Czechoslovakian fans stood back in begrudging respect. For on 12 June 2006 in a small town called Gelsenkirchen, American Soccer came of age. The thousands of fans, many of them fresh out of college, who flooded the streets of Gelsenkirchen that day, out-sung the Italians in Kaiserslautern five days later and "took over" the Nuremberg stadium a week after that, made a statement missed by the soccer world: a statement that reflected everything that had been happening for the past 20 years on soccer fields and in boardrooms from Los Angeles to New York. For at the 2006 FIFA World Cup in Germany a sleeping soccer giant awoke, "the American soccer fan", putting the world on notice that everything they thought they knew about "football" in the USA was about to change forever.

Star-Spangled Soccer takes it lead from a single premise, that the granting of the 1994 World Cup to the United States by FIFA set in motion a chain of events that has led to a soccer explosion in America and provided the catalyst for its now unstoppable march forward. For make no mistake in America today a live game between Real Madrid and Barcelona would out-draw the National Football League, decimate Major League Baseball and fill NBA arenas four times over. Why so confident? Well in the summer of 2009, over 94,000 came out to see Barcelona play the LA Galaxy, 72,000 bought tickets to see Real Madrid beat D.C. United and 79,000 poured into Giant Stadium in New York to watch Mexico defeat the USA. These were attendances that no soccer nation in the world could ignore and made it clear to anyone with an unbiased eye and a calculator that the USA is already a soccer nation and one that is at the tipping point of incredible growth. Many will say they have seen it all before, with the glorious but ultimately failed North American Soccer League, led by the legendary Pele and the incredible crowds at World Cup 94, but they would be wrong. Soccer in America today bears little resemblance to past times with 2010 bringing a much stronger array of players, fans, stadiums, and investors underpinning it, a rampant media and internet world connecting it and a new soccer educated generation embracing it.

In America today a new breed of young players see soccer as much a part of American culture and lifestyle as baseball, basketball and football. Exposed to World Cup, Premiership, Italian, Spanish and Champions League soccer aired daily on Fox Soccer, ESPN and Univision, American soccer kids are as likely to know Messi, Ronaldo and Rooney and the star power of "United, Barca and Real" as they are the pitcher for the LA Dodgers or the running back for the New York Giants. Their idols and role models are just a click away on their computer, a dial away on their television or ticket away from a summer tour. Equally a new breed of American soccer fans are rebelling against the slumber of the seventh-inning stretch in baseball and the obligatory "Mexican wave" at a NFL game. Instead, they are taking their lead from the throng of singing masses on the Kop at Liverpool, the chaos of the Bombanera at Boca and the all-encompassing passion of the Catalans at the Nou Camp. For soccer is not only the "beautiful game", it is also the global game, and the shrinking media world is allowing soccer to encircle and infiltrate America with its stars, its teams, its cultures and its passion, and with teams that are bigger and wealthier than the Dallas Cowboys or the New York Yankees and stars that are globally more powerful than A-Rod and Kobe Bryant. It takes a certain naïvety to think American society is not changing and that kids today are prepared to accept the status quo of American sports and together with the simple fact that 25 percent of the American population will be Hispanic by 2050, and 50 percent will be of ethnic origin by the same date, it should send shock waves through the American sporting world and have soccer salivating at what can be achieved.

The road ahead is still a tough one with many challenges to overcome and barriers to break down. The entrenched American sports are certainly not going to roll over and play dead as soccer seeks to steal its future fans, its sponsors and its TV time. And it must be causing great concern to them that ESPN will soon unleash on America the largest promotional campaign, for any sport it has ever broadcast, in support of its coverage of the World Cup from South Africa – exposure that could represent the tipping point for soccer in the USA and the moment from which it will never look back. Why? Because for the first time in American soccer history there now exists a sustainable infrastructure and, if you like, "operating system" for the sport in the USA, a structure that can truly take advantage of the developing "perfect soccer storm" appearing on the horizon. This infrastructure, both physical and human, consists of nine new soccer-specific stadiums in the ground with more to follow, a powerful group of some of the wealthiest and most sports-savvy investors in the country underwriting the professional game, 16 million kids playing it, major television networks airing it (including one dedicated to 24-hour coverage) and some of America's biggest sponsors supporting it. Equally there are 35, and soon to be 50, million soccer-mad Hispanics, who call America home, passionately in love with it.

In my opinion it will be the next decade that will decide the future trajectory of soccer in the USA and whether it kicks on to truly compete with the majors or tapers off to become a "nice" alternative "also ran". There are opportunities to grasp, hurdles to overcome and potential missteps to take. Can Major League Soccer capitalize on the 30,000 crowds in Seattle, the "sell outs" in Toronto and the profitability of an LA Galaxy to build a sustainable quality league to compete with the best? Can the US National Team develop players capable of winning a World Cup and populating the world's best teams? Can the sport create enough economic prosperity to entice the country's best athletes to choose soccer over "football" or basketball, for when it does the soccer world will change forever? Can America turn a nation of soccer players into a nation of soccer fans? Can American soccer embrace the global game without it consuming them? Can the American coaching system in all its forms and diasporas let go of its often insular instincts, protectionist outlook and political positioning, to come together to develop American players fully prepared and capable to play in the best leagues and for the best teams in the world – even if this entails losing control and money? Can soccer in America become a viable TV sport generating the millions that will underpin its economics, expand its professional league and allow it to compete for the world's best players?

There are many misconceptions about the game in the USA, most driven by a condescending international media and entrenched American sports writers or fans that fail (or refuse) to understand that their country is changing, their kids are changing and their sports are changing.

It's very easy to bemoan the lack of quality in MLS, the media coverage in national papers or the lack of perceived interest from entrenched (read old) American sports fans, but smart investors look to future earnings and growth, not the past and the fundamentals for soccer's exponential growth over the next decade are firmly in place. Nothing however will propel and fuel this growth more than the return in either 2018 or 2022 of the FIFA World Cup. It has nothing to do with economics, nothing to do with the financial impact, nothing to do with elevating the status of US Soccer with FIFA and around the world. It has everything however to do with turning America into a nation of soccer fans, a developer of top-class talent and cementing forever the future of the sport in the USA. For if the impact was huge in 1994 it will be stratospheric and unstoppable if it returns.

Soccer's journey to respectability in the USA has been a long, exciting and often troubled one filled with tremendous highs, stomach churning lows, Vegas-style gambles, dramatic elections, strong personalities, incredible commitments, huge mistakes, necessary

U-turns, and of course last-minute victories and extra-time heartbreaks. It is a story of how an insolvent Federation convinced FIFA to grant it the 1994 World Cup and how a "whip round" among friends paid for it. How Brandi Chastain tore off her shirt and sent the world into a media frenzy. How Phil Anschutz saved Major League soccer from collapse by purchasing five of its teams and how it then went on to become the greatest sports turn-around story of the decade. How the US National Team made an unexpected run to the World Cup quarter finals to lift a soccer nation and instill hope in the future of the game. How David Beckham shocked the world, and I mean world, by signing for the LA Galaxy, and how American soccer has transformed itself from a recreational participatory sport into a professionally run soccer business and industry that today challenges the major American leagues and excites the international soccer community with its growth and promise.

I hope that by the end of the book you will have an understanding of the great strides soccer has made in the USA over the past 25 years on its road to becoming a soccer nation, and the tough challenges and competitive forces it still has to overcome. I equally hope you enjoy my depiction of soccer's journey for while *Star-Spangled Soccer* is a business book, it's also about the events, the people and the players who made this great journey; personalities, great victories, crushing defeats, and heroic fight backs and trust me, soccer in America has had them all.

CHAPTER 1

You're Playing the World Cup Where?

It hardly caused a ripple in the American public psyche on 4 July 1988 when the announcement was made that the USA was to host the 1994 World Cup. Media coverage was tepid and sparse and American sports fans were uncaring and oblivious. Today's news, tomorrow's fish and chip paper as they say in England. To those that did care, i.e. the rest of the world, it was nothing more than a corporate sell out: FIFA had lost its mind ... how could it be hosted in the States? ... what did they know about "Football"? ... it's all about money, a farce, a joke, but I suppose at least a joke with benefits ... we get to go to Disneyland and Las Vegas.

To Werner Fricker, the President of the United States Soccer Federation, and a few USA visionaries it was the Holy Grail, and the catalyst for everything they wanted to achieve for soccer in the United States. To FIFA it was a huge new market to expand the beautiful game and an economic powerhouse they were desperate to harness, but for 95 percent of the American population they could not have cared less. In a country where they proclaim the winners of NFL SuperBowl World Champions the fact that an event of true world inclusion and stature was coming to the USA held no interest, offered no appeal. The fact that it was also soccer doubly compounded the issue. Who the hell plays soccer? Only wheezy kids that cannot make the football or baseball teams at school or those crazy Latins and Europeans that play in the parks at weekends. Oh and by the way, aren't their fans always rioting and killing each other? Probably all true at the time.

But, however it was achieved – like it or not, interested or not – America was going to host the 1994 World Cup, the promise of which and its ultimate success, underpinned everything good that was to happen to soccer over the next 20 years. As the history of soccer in the United States is written it will be seen that

4 July 1988 was the day that the sport entered the modern era and began its march towards international respectability. Respectability founded on the improbable idea that the world's greatest sports event would be hosted in the land of Mickey Mouse and John Wayne.

Tremendous cynicism abounded as the world's media questioned why a country completely lacking in any soccer credibility was awarded such a glittering prize. A country where the collapsed North American Soccer League (NASL) and circus-like commotion of the New York Cosmos, Fort Lauderdale Strikers and Los Angeles Aztecs with their gaudy shirts, fireworks and crass half-time promotions, represented everything glitzy and Hollywood that the soccer world, at the time, was not. This was a place where Pele and Beckenbaur went to see out their final years and take their last hugely rewarding pay checks, a fun diversion, maybe later a movie – but not serious soccer. The media were convinced that the World Cup would be turned into some Spielberg-inspired production that would tarnish and trash its image for ever. Surely the Americans could not possibly understand the nuances and fineries of the "beautiful game" or treat it with the reverence and subtlety it deserved – Americans after all do not do subtlety! And they are notoriously not high on reverence!

So just how did it come about? How did the USA manage to convince FIFA to hand over the keys to soccer's crown jewel risking the ire of traditional soccer nations and cynical soccer press from around the world, particularly knowing full well that 95 percent of the country had no idea what the World Cup was and cared even less if they thought it involved soccer. The answer, as with many things in life, came down to a mixture of luck, preparation, hubris, vision and personal commitment. It started as most things do with the vision and commitment of a few people who believed in soccer and ultimately felt that an event of this magnitude might just be the catalyst for the sport's explosion. There were soccer people such as Werner Fricker, a Yugoslavian American, who arrived in the USA with nothing, played for the US National Team, built a highly successful construction company and then went on to be President of the United States Soccer Federation. There was also Chuck Blazer, now General Secretary of Concacaf, Scott Parks LeTellier who would go on to be the Chief Operating Officer of World Cup 94, and Sunil Gulati now President of the

United States Soccer Federation (US Soccer) – people who were attracted to the game, administered or coached and had a passion for seeing soccer develop in the USA and thought hosting a World Cup would help. None however, I can guarantee, had any idea just how big and how much this single decision would change the face of soccer and indeed to a degree, culture in America.

It sounds like a great idea on paper but how do you go about bidding for the world's biggest sporting event when it was clear you would need to use "air miles" (if they were around then) to visit Zurich to convince FIFA you could do it! Basically insolvent, US Soccer were forced to move from their Empire State Building Offices to three "subsidized" rooms at an airport hotel near JFK provided by a friendly patron of the sport and move its remaining staff to free space in Colorado Springs. (No one mentioned this to FIFA of course.) If this was not bad enough, its Olympic Team was close to being evicted from its training camp hotel when it became clear the Federation could not afford to pay for the extra pot of coffee, morning paper or indeed (and more importantly) the rooms the team were staying in. Only a last minute check provided by sponsor, Budweiser (and delivered coincidentally by the now General Secretary of US Soccer, Dan Flynn), saved the day and of course the Olympic spirit! Suffice to say, times were tough and US Soccer clearly had no right even contemplating bidding for an event of such magnitude and gravitas.

From the outside, every ounce of business school and real-world smarts would scream they were out of their depth and woefully incapable of executing such an event and that FIFA would be crazy to even entertain a meeting let alone a bid. But if twenty years of living and working in the USA has taught me one thing, it is that Americans are never afraid to punch above their weight and have unflinching confidence in their ability to pull off the impossible. It may not always work out but there is always an unfailing belief that somehow it will, and because of this, it invariably does – and in the World Cup 94 case, it did!

In fairness, despite its financial shortcomings soccer in the USA had some strong headwinds helping it along, not least of which was the very strong desire of FIFA to "crack" the American market. They had been shocked by the success of soccer at the 1984 Los Angeles Olympics where it had outdrawn track and field events in attendance with 102,799 turning up to see France beat Brazil 2–0 for Gold, and 100,374 to see Yugoslavia beat Italy 2–1 for Bronze, both staged at the Los Angeles Rose Bowl. Sitting in the expensive seats the proverbial light bulb went on and the realization dawned that they might just might be witnessing the birth of the next great soccer frontier. As such, when the time came for bids to be accepted for the 1994 World Cup, the USA was gently "encouraged" to apply. A few other things were at play here during this time as it had not gone unnoticed by FIFA that a watershed moment in world sports had just occurred. Usually a loss making financial "white elephant" for host cities, Peter Ueberroth had transformed the Olympics from a city-backed tourism brochure into a financially profitable marketing, sponsorship, licensing and television-driven property that had American corporations lined up at the door to partner and Angelinos devouring every ticket they could get their hands on. Witnessing all of this first hand was FIFA salivating at the prospect of replicating this and understanding immediately what the financial impact of turning American Corporations onto soccer might mean.

The reality of the success of soccer in Los Angeles was however a little different. I was living in LA during the Olympics and tickets were near impossible to get, with those for gymnastics, swimming and track events almost impossible and being scalped for ridiculous dollars. Compelled to get their Olympic "fix" Angelinos grabbed on to any ticket they could. This is not to undermine soccer and certainly soccer fans turned up but with Carl Lewis and the USA track and field team sweeping all before them it would be wrong to draw the conclusion that soccer was more popular, because it was not. In truth it mattered little as impressing FIFA was all that did. It reflects however a more a cautionary note that was to be born out in later years to costly effect. Drawing conclusions and spending millions based on Americans showing up for "big events" can be a very expensive mistake. I will introduce my own word here for a disease prevalent in American sports, a disease often misdiagnosed with disastrous consequences. "Big Eventism" defined in the medical dictionary as "the uncontrollable compulsion to attend any big sporting event irrespective of overall underlying interest" … watch for its appearance throughout the book.

Apart from the incredible crowds and potential financial windfalls, FIFA also bore witness to the great organizational and operational skills of the Americans and in particular those people involved in staging the soccer events. Commissioner of Soccer, Alan Rothenberg, would go on to be the President of US Soccer and World Cup 94, Organizing Committee. Scott Parks LeTellier, Chief of Staff in 1984, would play a pivotal role in securing the World Cup bid and go on to be the Chief Operating Officer of World Cup and Hank Steinbrecher who worked on the Boston venue for 1984 would go on to be General Secretary of US Soccer. These were all people who impressed FIFA, had established personal relationships at the highest level and had instilled in them the confidence that should the World Cup ever arrive on US soil it would have the personnel and skill-sets to execute it.

So FIFA were interested in the USA making a bid, but it still did not mean that US Soccer could afford to do so – not something however that was going to get in the way. Like all good soccer fans around the world, when looking to buy some new uniforms or a new ball, the first instinct is to have a quick "whip-round" among the lads to see what can be raised. Well, US Soccer raised $500,000 from 100 soccer "lads" who happily contributed $5,000 each with the promise of good seats and a hot pie should they succeed (and membership in US Club 94) and with another $750,000–$1,000,000 secured in the form of a loan from Werner Fricker's Savings and Loan Bank they were set. Lobbyists from DC were hired to woo various governmental agencies and Ronald Reagan engaged to send a video message expressing the full support of the Presidency and the US Government (but interestingly no money). Ultimately US Soccer submitted a professional, on the point, bid document that covered all bases and could not have failed to impress FIFA.

It's an interesting note that US Soccer, along with the old NASL, actually bid for the 1986 World Cup after FIFA decided that the chosen site, Colombia, while making great coffee had not quite mastered the art of building soccer stadiums yet and were, as such, not ready to host. Looking for a quick alternative site, the USA were invited to bid but submitted a document that even the architects admit was decidedly amateurish, underwhelming

FIFA on every level, who granted the rights to Mexico, doing the USA a huge favor.

So America's bid was in, funded by a private initiative of an insolvent Federation, a line of credit from a local bank and a "whip round" among the "lads". Compare this approach to those of its main competitors, Brazil and Morocco, both of whose bids arrived with the full backing and political influence of their national governments, the full support and involvement of their media outlets and the passionate support of their entire population who really, really, really cared if they won or not. Morocco could even call upon King Hassan 11 while Brazil of course had the incomparable Pele, decades of World Cup heritage and the fact that they had not hosted the event since 1950. To make matter worse for the USA, the President of FIFA, Joao Havalanche, was Brazilian, which had to help the Brazilian cause. As decision time drew closer, the USA, keen to know where they stood, casually approached FIFA at a meeting in Toronto for a sense of the direction of the prevailing wind (or simply, "do we have a chance?"). Clearly unable to answer, FIFA did however let it be known that in their opinion, and completely unscientifically, if a poll was taken that day among member nations it was likely that Brazil would get 80 percent of the votes, the USA 10 percent while Morocco and Chile (who pulled out in support of Brazil) would get 5 percent each. A body blow to all involved and visions of some very tough discussions with a local Savings and Loan Bank pending.

Sometimes however when you're brave enough to start down a path, events can conspire to work for you – events you could never have predicted or planned for, yet ones that can turn failure into success or of course success into failure. In the US Soccer case it was fortunately the former. With scenes eerily similar to the current financial meltdown, word was leaking out in the financial press that some leading countries were about to default on substantial loans issued by American Banks, which if true could send the issuing banks into bankruptcy. The biggest culprit was Brazil, the USA's main and only real competitor. This was bad for the banks but great for US Soccer. It's a little tough to claim poverty and "stiff" American banks for billions in loans and then go ahead and build 12 new soccer stadiums and nice new motorways to connect them all! The President of Brazil seeing the writing on the wall and a potential phone call from Reagan in his future decided to remove his government's support for the bid and consequently any hope the Brazilian Soccer Federation had of winning. Morocco, with just one stadium built and a lot of sand where the other 11 would go, soon fell out of favor and so when FIFA then announced that the decision on who would host the 1994 World Cup would be made on American Independence day, 4 July 1988, it was clear to all that the world's greatest sporting event was heading Stateside.

With tears all round, Fricker and LeTetellier stepped out to meet the hundreds of flashing light bulbs, thrusting microphones and probing questions of the world's media. Stunned by the enormity and ferocity of the exposure, Fricker had his first taste of the media circus that surrounded the event. Never comfortable dealing with an aggressive and often cynical media, he would one day pay the ultimate price, for the man whose vision and money helped bring the World Cup to the USA would not be the man to lead it.

Back in the USA, however, the world just went about its way. No live camera shots from the steps of FIFA, no jubilant flag-waving public from cities around the country, no countdowns to the announcement on CNN or ABC. After all, it was not like the Olympics were coming or anything the USA really cared about. On the flight home LeTellier explained to a fellow American passenger that they had just secured the World Cup of Football for the USA who excitedly responded "I love that sport ... those scrums sure look like a lot of fun". Politely explaining he was confusing football with rugby, LeTellier returned to his seat, dwelling on just how much work they had to do and wondering if, after all the struggles, they might have bitten off a little more than they could chew!

Winning the World Cup bid was one thing, convincing the soccer millions around the globe they were justified winners, quite another. To the rest of the world soccer in America was still viewed as an interesting experiment, a summer's diversion from the real "football" taking place in the NFL. Confident that it was all glitter and fluff and no substance, no one was either surprised or disappointed when the old NASL collapsed. Soccer was just not an American sport. It was not a sport they were any good at and actually not a sport anyone was necessarily interested in them becoming good at. The world did not expect soccer from America; it expected great Hollywood movies and iconic stars, great westerns, rock and roll, Motown, *Happy Days* and corvettes. All over the world people's lives were touched and excited by these icons of American culture, that were embraced, absorbed and envied. (Who didn't want to ride out of town heading a posse, beat Billy the Kid to the draw, or ride into the sunset with John Wayne and just what teenage kid did not want to be the Fonz ... as kids growing up in England, we all did.) These were our images of America, distant, untouchable and inspiring: no one however thought soccer when they thought of America. No one in the 1980s actually thought "soccer" at all; it was "football" – soccer was something the Yanks called it (or saacer as Brits with lousy American accents termed it), a lazy irreverent term that smacked of American marketing. Simply put, the world's expectations were that America might ruin the World Cup, might turn it into an over-hyped fiasco with cheerleaders, cowboys and Disney characters clambering through the stands. The world's media made no secret of their fears and would spend years questioning the validity of the decision. Come 1994 however, they would be here in their thousands, downing hot dogs and coke and sneaking off to Disneyland and Vegas! (Never underestimate the hypocrisy of the European press.)

The world's expectations were one thing, but the expectations of the American soccer community quite another. For every home-based US soccer player, coach, administrator and fan that had toiled in relative obscurity on playing fields across the country, the World Cup represented a momentous opportunity. To those that had suffered the derision and condescending cynicism of American football, baseball and basketball aficionados it was a chance at payback. To those that had battled and fought to get soccer played in schools and colleges, funds allocated, fields appropriated and kids engaged, it was a chance to show how big the sport really was. To every group of parents and coaches that fought with local councils and cities to build new soccer fields, or allocate even 10 percent of a budget scheduled for baseball to soccer, it was to strengthen their arm. To every expatriate and ethnic group that had grown up in a country where soccer was life it was to be a chance to say "this is why we love it". To the few true soccer writers who toiled to get column inches printed, or television presenters fighting to get a spectacular goal "aired" this was their moment, for when World Cup 94 arrived they would be the "go to guy", the one with the knowledge, the understanding of the game and the contacts for tickets and access. It was their chance to say "I told you this sport was big". In fairness though, most had no comprehension of what was about to hit them and the impact the event would have on their soccer lives.

Arriving back in the States, with proclamation in hand, US Soccer was immediately faced with a couple of pretty significant and pressing issues, issues that if not handled could easily see FIFA issuing a quick U-turn. Firstly they were still broke, in fact less than broke, they were still in debt to the tune of $750,000, further compounded when the Federal Government raided the Savings and Loan Bank carrying the note and quickly requested it be repaid. (Loaning money for World Cup "bids" sort of explains the 1988–89 Savings and Loan crisis really.) In fact, the new company set up to execute the event, World Cup 94 Inc, was penniless! A situation that was temporarily resolved when LeTellier, the new CEO, funded operations from a private $125,000 line of credit on his home. It was clear however that this would not last long and a significant influx of cash would be needed for the company and the event to survive. A white knight did appear on the horizon in the form of Steve Caspers and Phil Woosnam, two ex NASL executives who "generously" offered to loan the company $2m in return for being allowed to control all of the in-country marketing rights for both World Cup 1994 and the United States Soccer Federation. To make the offer even more tempting they were also bringing NBC to the table (in the form of Sportschannel America) who would agree to fund and broadcast the entire tournament.

For an insolvent federation and penniless World Cup 94 Inc, it must have been tempting and a seemingly obvious and easy way out of their current dilemma. Had LeTellier accepted however, it would have signaled the end for World Cup 94 and a financial meltdown that could have crippled the sport. The devil is always in the details and in this case it was most certainly was.

In return for providing a $2m line of credit and agreeing to guarantee the $70m minimum payment due to FIFA from ticket sales the new group would have the right to sell all the sponsorship and marketing categories for US Soccer and all the television advertising inventory on the local broadcasts. The strategy was to acquire these rights, wrap as much World Cup equity around them as possible and seize the market. As an added bonus they would receive a 50/50 share of all ticket revenues above the $70m guarantee to FIFA. You can't blame a man for trying and after all this is America, but while a great deal for the white knights, it was a lousy deal for everyone else.

Had they achieved what they wanted, the world of soccer in the USA as we know it today would not exist. There would have been no $60m legacy, no professional league and a group of wealthy marketers playing golf in the Cayman Isles. Fortunately, LeTellier fought this off acquiring an $8m line of credit from Hanover Bank secured against the unencumbered ticketing and sponsorship income the event would surely generate. With his home equity line replenished and boarders repelled, World Cup 94 Inc could concentrate on the task at hand, or so it thought!

The premise of this book is that securing World Cup 94 and executing it successfully changed the future course of soccer in the USA and directly shaped what it has become today. Much of what was achieved however had its roots in the tumultuous times, both on and off the field, surrounding the 1990 Italia World Cup for during this period four momentous events took place in US soccer that in isolation were exceptionally influential, but in combination changed the face of American soccer forever.

Trinaaadad ... we want a goal!

On 19 November 1989 at precisely 4pm a speculative 30-yard volley from Paul Caliguiri rattled the back of the net at the National Stadium in Port of Spain, Trinidad. Lost in a sea of red, no more than 50 ecstatic US soccer fans (including yours truly) leapt from their seats and celebrated as only soccer fans know how. The unbelievable was taking place; the result the USA could only dream of was unfolding before the eyes of the "massed"

USA ranks! Unfortunately for the real massed ranks, the 35,000 bedecked from head to toe in red, things were not going the way their President had promised. The program notes had made no mention that they might actually lose this game. Sunday had already been declared "Red day" for the people and Monday a national holiday in anticipation of a great and surely certain victory – a victory that would send little Trinidad and Tobago to their first ever World Cup Finals. It wasn't as if they needed to do much: just a single point against a faltering USA team that had struggled in every game towards qualification; just a single point to crown the greatest day in Trinidad's sporting history; just a single point to reward the smiling, always hospitable and fun-loving "Tico" fans who turned every corner of the stadium and every street in the country into a sea of patriotic brilliant bright red. Today would surely be their day, how could it not be!

True soccer fans however know not to tempt the soccer gods for fear of severe and painful retribution. Their ability to turn a goal-bound shot onto the post or wicked deflection into the net is legendary. Their decision that day to send a dipping 40-yard volley over the keeper into the Trinidad net was cruel in the extreme. The soccer gods however are not to be messed with, take them for granted, as the whole of Trinidad did, and you will usually pay a humbling and soul-destroying price. Against all the odds, against 35,000 screaming fans praying for victory, and because the President of Trinidad took his team on victory tour *before* the kick off, the gods led the USA to a stunning 1–0 upset victory, and shattered the dreams of a nation. It was certainly a surreal feeling having 35,000 pairs of eyes focused entirely on you as you celebrate the abject despair, desperation and utter disbelief of a country: dreams shattered, hopes crushed, grown men crying and children heartbroken. But as we all know that's the beauty and tragedy of the game.

"A Gift from the Soccer Gods" as Grahame Jones, editor of *Soccer International Magazine*, announced to the world (well the USA), the USA's first qualification in 40 years. America's best soccer writer had got it right of course but missed one important thing; it was not a gift everyone wanted. In truth it wasn't just the fun-loving Ticos who were suicidal over the result, the world of soccer was not best pleased either. The international press lamented the fact that the "Ticos" with their carnival of color and smiling faces would not be gracing the cafes of Italy, replaced sadly by the young fresh-faced rich kids from America. It was a much better story had the small Caribbean island humbled the mighty USA that day in Port of Spain and sent home a country where soccer was only an afterthought in the sporting landscape condescendingly tolerated by a nation brought up on the other "football". It was a much better story for the cynical international soccer press if they could point to the USA's failure to qualify as yet another reason why they should not have been granted soccer's richest prize and that at the end of the day it really was all about money.

Although of course neutral, I am certain FIFA breathed a huge sigh of relief. The USA under their own steam (though assisted by the fact that Mexico had been banned for fielding ineligible players in an under-20 tournament) had qualified for Italia 1990. It could now claim, rightfully or not, that soccer in the USA was on the rise and that great strides were being made in its development, strides that would be given an enormous boost by the granting of a World Cup. The USA's qualification softened, if not quieted the doubters, but gave FIFA the breathing room it needed to justify its decision. For US Soccer it meant they would be arriving in Italy with their heads held high as qualifiers and participants rather than just interested observers, looking to learn how to stage a World Cup: an important distinction as they sought the international approval of their peers.

As a side note, Grahame Jones wrote in Soccer International that Paul Caliguiri had only scored one other goal in 5 years and 24 games playing for the USA team. This came in a World Cup qualifier four and half years earlier to the day. The opposition (yes you have guessed it) Trinidad and Tobago, the goalkeeper, the same Maurice who was to wander just a little too far off his line as Caliguiri swung his left foot that day. Let no one doubt the soccer gods!

Italia 90: nine men, no goalie

There was nothing good about being beaten 5–1 by Czechoslovakia in the opening game of your first World Cup for 40 years, a result that clearly highlighted just how unprepared and naïve the US National Team were to the scale and intensity of "big time" international soccer. There was equally not much to shout about when finishing 23rd of 24 in the overall tournament (with just goal difference separating you from the last placed Arab Emirates). There was however something very heroic about being expected to wilt and crumble against the hosts Italy in front of 80,000 of their most fanatical fans but instead putting on a performance that let the soccer world know you were not as pathetic and hopeless as they were portraying you. A gloating media had reveled in predictions varying from a 5–0 to 10–0 and that would be only if the Italians played with nine men, no goalie and agreed to kick with their least favored foot. The press room was full of witty condescending jokesters plotting their next "yanks are planks" headline. But as they were to do many times over the next four years, the media underestimated the true metal and resolve of the American players and in particular the group that stepped into the cauldron of the Olympic Stadium in Rome on the night of 14 June 1990. Up stepped Doyle, Balboa, Harkes, Ramos and to a man the USA fought, hustled, and battled to keep a rampant "azzuri" and 80,000 fans at bay, falling to a late Giannini winner, with only a late goal-line clearance preventing Peter Vermes giving the USA what would have been a monumental draw. This game however was not about whether the USA won or lost, it was much bigger than that. It was about whether the USA players had within them the courage and pride to battle to the very end, to fight and scrap for every inch of ground, to represent with pride and respect the badge of United States of America. This game had gone beyond tactics and systems; this was now about just one thing, character! Did the USA players have it or not? That night in Rome they proved to the soccer world they did. Lessons were learned, bonds formed, character forged and pride restored; the performance was the bedrock on which, over the next four years, some of the greatest victories in US soccer history would be achieved.

I walked out of the stadium that night with Tab Ramos, delayed from a lengthy press conference, still slightly in shock and "coming down" from the adrenalin of the game. For the first time I got the impression he truly felt he and this team could compete with the "big boys" and actually "belonged" at this level. It was a mindset that was critical if the USA were to have any hope of competing with the world's best when they arrived on US soil four years later.

A very Swiss coup

If on-field results were a disaster (leaving Rome aside), off the field they were worse! Relations between the United States Soccer Federation and FIFA were deteriorating rapidly as Werner Fricker and his team battled with both FIFA and their marketing agents ISL. Equally unskilled and unsuited to dealing with the scrutiny of the international media, Fricker alienated and upset many, with a very foreseeable end result: articles that seriously questioned the USA's ability to stage the event. (The Germans, apparently circling, were letting interested media know they were ready and willing to step in and save the day.) To make matters worse, with an election to choose the next US Soccer President in just two months, both Fricker and his main opponent Paul Steihl, decided to air their grievances and fight their campaign on Italian soil and in full view of soccer's body politic, rather than quietly and respectfully in Florida where the judgmental eyes of local youth administrators would be less penetrating: as the somewhat amateur bickering and petty squabbles undermined the credibility of an already under scrutiny Federation. Very serious doubts were emerging in the minds of FIFA that maybe, just maybe, they had made a monumental mistake!

Just when it seemed it could not get worse (a common phrase when writing about the early days of soccer in the USA) it of course did! While the world's eyes were on Italy, back in New York, Soccer USA Partners, a British Sports Marketing Agency, announced it had signed a multimillion-dollar eight-year agreement with Werner Fricker and the United States Soccer Federation to control all of their marketing, sponsorship, licensing, game day events and television broadcast rights. A decision that at the end of the day proved very profitable for US Soccer but one that caused palpitations within FIFA and its marketing agents ISL. If it wasn't before, Fricker's fate was now most certainly sealed and in true

Shakespearean fashion plans were afoot to overthrow the king. Plans initiated, orchestrated and executed from within the secretive walls of FIFA headquarters in Zurich, Switzerland; plans that would result, just six weeks after the final ball was kicked at Italia 90, in a new President sitting atop US Soccer.

During the weekend of 2–5 August 1990, in one of the most conspiratorial US Soccer elections of all times, and with FIFA playing puppet master and orchestrator, a late entry was announced on the US Soccer Presidential ballot and swept to victory in a tidal wave of euphoria and support. Alan Rothenberg, a no-nonsense Los Angeles attorney who had acted as Commissioner for Soccer at the 1984 Los Angeles Olympics, and as such a known and trusted friend of FIFA, assumed control. Supported by Hank Steinbrecher (at the time a leading Gatorade executive and later to become the General Secretary of the Federation) and, operating a hit-and-run campaign that would have made Washington Lobbyists blush, votes were secured, promises made and "behind the scenes" deals done. One thing was certain, Rothenberg had not lifted his head above the parapet and entered a very public election to lose. Using a sophisticated (by 1990 standards) computer system to track support, he hosted lavish cocktail receptions, schmoozed with delegates and charmed and cajoled all with promises of a new tomorrow. Criticized as a "newcomer and opportunist" by the opposition, Rothenberg refused to get drawn into the petty acrimony between long-term candidates Paul Steihl and Werner Fricker, each accusing the other of a variety of irregularities. It was indeed desperate stuff but on the final day, maybe recognizing the threat they faced, they combined to turn their focus on the usurper Rothenberg. On the morning of the election, Julie Cart reported (in Soccer International Magazine) that delegates awoke to find a 1986 newspaper article critical of the way the NBA's Los Angeles Clippers were being run, all references to Rothenberg (a member of the Clippers management group) had been underlined in red. Hardly Watergate in scale and all very high-school politics, but symptomatic of the desperation beginning to set in as it became clear that some very powerful forces were lining up against them.

Rothenberg had after all not arrived alone or unarmed. First, there was FIFA, not a bad friend to have, particularly when they were to bring an army of fellow "friends" with them including: Peter Ueberroth, the charismatic head of the Los Angeles Olympics and now a board member of FIFA's official sponsors Adidas and Coca-Cola; Pele, the world's greatest soccer star and still the only player most Americans had ever heard of; and, in case that wasn't enough, Dr. Henry Kissinger, the man who brought the Vietnam war to an end – one of the most powerful men in world politics – who let it be known he would "quite like" Rothenberg to win. This was complemented by an array of US-based companies and organizations that were equally insistent that change should take place. Hank Steinbrecher, a Gatorade executive at the time, was highly critical of US Soccer's inability to support sponsors, a view echoed by Bruce Hudson, a senior sponsorship manager at Budweiser, whose concern reached further, stressing that without change there was every chance the World Cup would be "yanked". The Soccer Industry Council of America, an amalgam of soccer industry companies representing everything from shoe companies to ball manufacturers, were the least politic of all, stressing simply "it had lost faith in the US Soccer".

As the weekend unfolded it became clear that anybody who had any commercial or political "skin" in the World Cup being a success lined up alongside Rothenberg: and behind the scenes was FIFA, orchestrating like Fabregas – Arsenal's mercurial midfielder – at the Emirates. They wanted change and change they would get. Just to cover their bets they even took the extraordinary step of apparently offering Paul Steihl a World Cup job should he pull out of the election and throw his support to Rothenberg. This was clear intent of their seriousness and the reality that with millions of dollars on the line they had no desire to see the Cup moved. Steihl, unfortunately for him, mistook this offer as a sign of panic and weakness and went on the offensive. Claiming FIFA was in the midst of orchestrating a hostile takeover of US Soccer, he portrayed Rothenberg as nothing more than a FIFA puppet and stooge. In a "we will fight them on the beaches" and "never, ever surrender to FIFA" moment, Steihl proclaimed that he and Fricker had patched up their differences and were now best buddies working together for all that was great in US Soccer. To reinforce the point the two former foes embraced in a friendly hug in front of the voting masses as the orchestra broke out and the lights faded. Unfortunately for Fricker and Steihl no one was buying it and while they might have been willing to fight FIFA on the beaches, no one else was. Rothenberg prevailed in a landslide victory gaining 59 percent of the popular vote, Fricker 29 percent and Steihl just 12 percent. The truth was that both had been outmatched by a new professional business and political reality that was to sweep across the sport over the coming years. Understanding that the key to success was splitting the youth vote, which they did, and then ensuring the vote of the professional leagues went their way, Rothenberg was in the envious position of simply needing the support and 30 percent voting block of his long-time friend and former fellow NASL owner Earl Foreman to secure victory. Needless to say it was delivered and the rest is history.

Controversy and rumor surrounded the involvement of FIFA, a matter put to rest when they openly admitted that its press secretary, Guido Tognonoi, had placed the mysterious call to Steihl. They stopped short however of making an apology, simply stating that it was in the best interests of FIFA and US Soccer that Alan Rothenberg be elected! No more to be said, mission accomplished, change initiated and the 1994 World Cup, in their minds, back on track.

The Orlando election represented a clear turning point in US Soccer on almost every level. First, and most importantly, it clearly let the US know that the sport of soccer belongs in the global not just national arena. FIFA and in particular the World Cup are bodies and properties that offer a wealth of opportunity and riches to those that embrace it. The privilege of hosting a World Cup is offered to few and those few must play by FIFA's rules. Any hint of potential embarrassment or failure cannot and will not be tolerated. If that means assisting change, then so be it. FIFA sensed both of these were possible with US Soccer prior to the 1990 election and stepped in to act. Second, FIFA had made it clear that they were committed to "cracking" the very lucrative US market – why else spend so much effort initiating change? Some of the largest corporations on the planet either resided or wanted to do business in the USA and FIFA wanted to ensure that a World Cup event could deliver the market to them, turning on 250 million plus Americans to soccer was just too much to resist.

Third, US Soccer was being dragged kicking and screaming into the commercial, professional and, some would say, mercenary world of professional sports business. Rothenberg was not the man you asked to put up soccer nets, cut up oranges or make T-shirts for the annual Thanksgiving Soccer Shoot-outs. He didn't mire himself in the bureaucratic nightmare of youth player registration, state association politics, or Labor Day tournaments which, while being the building blocks of grass-roots soccer and home to committed and loyal soccer people, were distractions that impinged on the bigger picture now required. It was time for soccer to elevate itself above the amateur enthusiast and into the arena of professional executives, savvy marketers, tough lawyers, aggressive sales people, experienced event managers, accomplished TV broadcasters, astute financial directors and creative entrepreneurs all committed to moving the business of soccer to a higher level. Soccer in the USA was clearly entering a new professional and commercial era. Its ability to embrace it would determine whether it was to truly compete with the NFL, NBA, MLB and NHL or forever remain in the shadows, a mere fun pastime for suburban kids.

In Rothenberg, soccer had a leader who epitomized the new way forward: a man who had never played the game and carried no political baggage from years of youth soccer administration. Foremost a lawyer and businessman he got his first introduction to soccer as an attorney for Jack Kent Cooke, then owner of the Los Angeles Wolves and later famed owner of the Washington Redskins. Rothenberg's baptism of fire in soccer was being given $400,000 by Cooke, put on a plane to England and told to buy an entire team of players for his LA franchise. With no ability to choose good from bad he did what any smart man would do and found a man that could. Put in touch with Ray Wood, the ex-Manchester United goalkeeper and Munich air disaster survivor, he signed Wood to a contract and told him he could use the rest to buy his outfield! (Even in the 1970s however $400,000 did not buy a lot.) The team arrived in LA but did not last long. Rothenberg however was hooked and soon became an investor in the Los Angeles Aztecs, (George Best and all) in the burgeoning NASL. Free spending New York Cosmos however soon pushed everyone to the brink of bankruptcy and teams folded under the unsustainable financial demands of trying to compete on the field, knowing full well the economic returns off the field would never compensate. These were lessons learned that would ultimately shape the underlying single entity structure of Major League Soccer. In 1984, Rothenberg had acted as Commissioner of Soccer for the LA Olympics, staging a tournament that ultimately played a huge role in convincing FIFA that soccer had a future in the USA and making a personal impression that six years later would convince FIFA he was the man to deliver World Cup 94. He had years of sports business experience, advising and running the NBA Los Angeles Clippers and the National Hockey League Los Angeles Kings and came with a wealth of powerful political connections and a cadre of well placed and influential friends. Soccer was entering a new era of professionalism and it was clear Rothenberg was to lead it.

Just like a camera

In July 1989, the match USA versus Trinidad and Tobago in Torrance, California, a World Cup Qualifier for Italia 1990, had barely 3,000 people in the stands. The game was not well promoted, the junior college stadium hardly befitting the event, with a snack bar dispensing tepid coffee and donuts. The game was unremarkable but a very meaningful 1–1 draw on the way to qualification for Italia 90. It also marked the beginning of a business relationship that was to transform the commercial landscape of soccer in the USA forever. For strolling around the stadium that day was an ex-Kodak Senior Marketing Executive, and the youngest ever person to make Vice President at the company. He was a man with a wealth of consumer marketing experience, an inventive and creative mind and an understanding of corporate America that over the next five years was to see soccer infiltrate some of the most important boardrooms in the country. Michael Forte was a diet-coke drinking, cigar-smoking maverick of a man: not a soccer aficionado, had never played the game, never watched the game and never really understood the game. He certainly would not have made anyone's list of the soccer people you need to know. He couldn't have named five past World Cup winners if his life depended on it, but in Michael Forte the sport had found a man who had a tremendous skill. He had the ability to translate the "beautiful game" into the beautiful dollar. A man who analyzed the sport like he analyzed a camera, a soda drink or a car – features and benefits, needs and wants. He spoke the language of the boardroom, thought with the psychology of an advertising agency and sold with the enthusiasm and empathy that only the few possess. Unfortunately, Michael was to die of pancreatic cancer in 2005 but his legacy lives on in the tremendous commercial success of the sport.

Forte had been recruited by an English sports marketing agency headed by former British Olympian Alan Pascoe and his partner Edward Leask. Known for their strength in track and field events and sailing, API had become one of the leading sports marketing agencies in Europe. Neither of the partners were particularly interested in soccer but made the decision in 1990 to acquire the marketing and licensing rights to the United States Soccer Federation, the financially impoverished organization that had miraculously pulled off the World Cup bid, promising them $1.2–$2m per year for the privilege for the next four years. It was a stretch to understand how a company with little interest in soccer led by an ex-Kodak marketing "hotshot" who knew next to nothing about the game was going to succeed where everyone over the past decades had failed. But in 1990 maybe this was the best that soccer in America could have hoped for. The big traditional sports agencies had completely ignored the sport and why not? Their clients were hardly screaming "bring me soccer": on the contrary they would not have recognized a soccer ball if it bounced down the boardroom table, knocked over their coffee and hit them square between the eyes.

Although a deal that finally sealed Fricker's fate, Soccer USA Partners (SUSAP), would go on to generate millions in revenue for the Federation and deliver a level of professional sports marketing expertise that the amateur organization could not have replicated at the time. SUSAP also took a huge amount of risk in staging and broadcasting games that often drew small crowds and lost very serious money. There is no doubt Rothenberg and Steinbrecher would have liked the deal to disappear and start with a clean sheet of paper in the USA, but without it US Soccer would have struggled mightily to replicate its achievements.

As a result, as 1990 came to an end, the soccer landscape in the USA was taking shape.

Alan Rothenberg was the new President of US Soccer and while not yet CEO of World Cup 1994 (a post he initially gave to Chuck Cale, a political friend and a significant influence in his election run, but took back in 1991) he was the "defacto" personality and leader of all things soccer in the USA. There were no arguments and no lack of clarity. You either agreed with his vision and methods or you did not – if you did not you were out. LeTellier, the legal architect of the World Cup bid and a man who literally put his house on the line, was justifiably given the role of Chief Operating Officer while Hank Steinbrecher, one of the key players in the election "coup", was made General Secretary of the United States Soccer Federation. Soccer USA Partners, having paid a sizeable guarantee to US Soccer, were ready to hit the road running and knock down the doors of corporate America: it's financial success and indeed very survival resting on the tenuous belief that corporate America was ready to buy soccer and hopefully buy big. The USA national team players bloodied and battered from Italia 90 were home and smarting to prove that despite their overall poor performance, the result in Rome was not a fluke and that they were made of better stuff than the statistics portrayed. Reputations needed to be built, careers fashioned and big money transfers secured. FIFA was content it had its man, the World Cup was on track and their decision to come to the USA justified.

Everyone in soccer realized that the next four years culminating in the World Cup Final on 17 July 1994 were to be the most important in the history of US Soccer. Some people would make fortunes, some would launch careers, some would get the big transfer and some would fall by the wayside. Whatever happened, this was soccer's time and everyone knew it.

CHAPTER 2

Selling Soccer to America, the World Cup Years!

There's an old and well worn saying in US sports: Question: "How do you make a million dollars in American Soccer ?".... Answer: "Start with $10m" – ominous and scary but unfortunately pretty true. The American soccer landscape is littered with the bodies of entrepreneurs, investors, passionate hobbyists and serious business minds who had failed to make a dime in the sport. People who had given their all, formed leagues, staged exhibition matches and pounded the corporate corridors, but to a man failed and often spectacularly so. How then was a British Sports Agency, with no background in soccer, led by an ex-Kodak marketing executive who knew even less, to succeed where all else had failed? The answer at the end of the day was a pretty simple one that gave SUSAP a clear advantage over all those that had come before it: it was the advantage of being able to treat the business of soccer as just that, a business. SUSAP was not interested in trying to get more kids to play the game, not interested in preparing and developing players to win matches or creating coaching curricula. These things were someone else's responsibility and purview. Edward Leask, the Financial Director and part owner of the Agency, had little interest in soccer as a sport and despite living in England, he could probably not name one England National Team player, let alone an American one. Michael Forte, his newly appointed CEO, knew even less, barely understanding there were 11 players on each side and that the game lasted 90 minutes.

This seemed sacrilege to many whose blood boils at the very prospect of the "beautiful game" being placed in the hands of such commercial heathens, but the truth of the matter was that the sport needed people like this in the early 1990s. Forte looked at the sport from a different viewpoint than most before him, that of a buyer not a fan or soccer enthusiast. He clearly understood that companies did not buy offside traps or 4–4–2 systems; they did not buy long throws, goal kicks or the "diamond" midfield formation. Corporations are only interested in "buying" what the sport can do for them on their playing field and where they are measured and evaluated: namely the cash register. Forte and his team understood this and understood it very well. They also had a pretty good idea that the corporations they would be selling to knew even less about the sport than they did, living by the adage that "in the land of the blind the one-eyed man is King"!

Soccer to most American corporations, and indeed Americans at the time, meant just one thing: PELE: he of the great bicycle kick and star of the New York Cosmos in the days when New York's finest and richest would beat a path to Giant Stadium to watch the great man perform; he, who adorned the cover of Sports Illustrated and filled the column inches of the New York Times; he, who for one brief moment along with his compatriots Beckenbaur, Carlos Alberto and Steve Hunt gave the USA a glimpse of what might be possible. The balmy atmosphere laden nights when 70,000 fans would come to pay homage to his silken skills, soaring headers and of course, the unmistakable Pele party piece, the overhead kick. These were heady days for soccer in the USA but eventually even nights like this were not enough to ward off the grim reaper of financial reality whose repeated appearance would eventually bring the league to its knees and the grand experiment crashing down around soccer's ears.

Pele went home, Sports Illustrated photographers stopped clicking and New York's elite returned to the upper east side, the opera and the latest Broadway shows. Like the rubic cube or pet rock, soccer had been an exciting diversion, the latest "hot thing" and place to be seen. It had flickered brightly, some would say very brightly, and nearly forced its way through the American sports psyche to briefly challenge the NFL, NBA and Major League Baseball, who quietly could not have failed to be impressed by the size of the crowds flooding to Giant Stadium. Conspiracy theories abound as to how these leagues conspired and colluded to bring down the league, so worried of its potential that they convinced the TV networks to boycott coverage – accusations that were almost certainly unwarranted and unfounded. The harsh reality was that soccer in the 1970s and early 1980s was just not ready to capitalize on the exposure the glittering Cosmos circus, with its star performers, was delivering, which aligned to the fact that the overall business plan itself was unsustainable to all but the Cosmos, meant the league had little chance of survival. When it did come crashing down it simply added more fuel to the fire of public opinion that soccer would never catch on in America and that it was just a game for "ethnics" or high school wimps that could not make the football, baseball or basketball team. This was a game that belonged on the Spanish channel they flicked past on their TVs and the inner city parks they sped past on their way to anywhere but there. Ultimately the league failed and critics everywhere joined in the chorus that soccer would never "sell" in America, an opinion SUSAP had to change quickly or face financial ruin.

Before passing from the demise of the NASL it would be unfair not to praise the incredible part it played in shaping the future of many great US soccer players and the role it played in enticing kids around the country to start kicking a ball. US Youth Soccer went through an incredible growth spurt during the late 1970s and 1980s, rising from just 100,000 players in 1976 to close to 2 million by the end of 1989. Thousands of young kids got their first fan experience by attending NASL matches and in particular at Giant Stadium, home of the incomparable New York Cosmos: the American Manchester United, Real Madrid or Barcelona of its time. Three of these young kids, Meola, Harkes and Ramos, who would go on to be stalwarts of the successful 1994 team, grew up just a goal kick away from Giant Stadium. Harkes's dad, Jimmy, would coach them by day and then take them to Giant Stadium to complete their education by night. Exposed to the floodlight nights of superstar players, rabid fans and stirring football they were to absorb the emotional DNA that drives all fans of the game: a failed league, yes; a failed experience for many, no. When Harkes, Ramos and Meola stepped onto the field at the Rose Bowl in front of 90,000 partisan US fans in their opening game of World Cup 1994 … it all came together … the cold New York nights, the Peles, Beckenbaurs and Chinaglias, the huge crowds. This time however they were the stars: American soccer stars with 90,000 pairs of eyes glued to their every move, absorbing the excitement and passion of the overwhelming spectacle unfolding in front of them, visions of Giant Stadium past and the incomparable Pele! The NASL has a special place in the hearts of many people who still work in, or support, US Soccer and without its existence the sport would have been much the poorer.

Winding through the Lincoln tunnel on his drive home from NFL's New York office and coming out onto an almost "Close encounters of the Third Kind" vision of a floodlit Giant Stadium, Don Garber, now Commissioner of Major League Soccer, could not help but be intrigued at the sight before him and amazed by the atmosphere oozing from its rafters, little knowing that one day his destiny would lead him into the heart of the Mother Ship.

Does anyone care?

Setting up their office on 1533 Broadway, Soccer USA Partners plugged in the phones, unpacked its desks and hired its first employees – purposely locating in the heart of New York City, the sports business capital of the world, and announcing to the soccer world and all who cared that it had arrived. Its goals were simple and unambiguous: to make money off the investment they had just made in US Soccer. There was no room for failure, no margin for error, and little time to lose. To do so however would require every ounce of sales and marketing, sports business, event management, and client service skills that Forte and his new team could muster, and then some.

The challenges ahead of them were immense and the US National Team program they inherited was sparse and under-funded. Following the 1990 World Cup, just two main sponsors remained: Budweiser, perennial supporters of soccer and sports in general and Adidas, the team's uniform supplier, between them providing no more than $250,000 per year in revenues – certainly not enough to fund any comprehensive or meaningful programs. This went a long way to explaining why its teams were not far off invisible on the American sporting landscape, with the men's team drawing just 3,000 fans to the important World Cup quali-fier against Trinidad I mentioned earlier and the women's team attendance measured by the amount of family and friends in town that day who didn't have anything more exciting to do. All of this had to change and change quickly if SUSAP was to have any chances of recouping and hopefully profiting on the significant investment they had made. It was no wonder Forte would take the 5am train into New York each day contemplating just how he could convince corporate America to spend its marketing dollars on a sport few grew up with, even fewer understood and even fewer still actually liked.

As with most things in business, it is the quality of the product that ultimately dictates its level of success. This simple fact however posed a huge problem. The USA Men's National Team was hardly a global force, having just come a last but one place finish at Italia 90. While not a laughing stock, they were treated with condescending acceptance around the world but more worryingly, with complete indifference in the USA. Its players were not great, the team were not winners, and its public profile was non-existent. How then could this group of individuals sell product, increase brand share and motivate a consumer? The answer was of course, it could not. Most Americans could not have cared less if Harkes drove a "Cadillac", Doyle wore "Right Aid", or Ramos sported a "Swatch watch" – good for them but retailers would hardly be backing up the trailers to support demand. SUSAP however had to convince corporate America that soccer could be used to "sell" their product or they faced financial ruin, for without doing so they were dead in the water. It would not be an easy task! Soccer was faced with the very tough challenge of carving out a niche for itself in the already crowded American sports psyche at both the corporate and consumer level. Just where did soccer fit in the American sports landscape? What set it apart from other sports and why should advertisers care? Why should TV Networks give up valuable airtime to broadcast soccer? Just why should American sports fans give up their seventh inning stretch and three hours of slumber to attend a soccer game? All questions SUSAP needed to work out or see millions of dollars evaporate.

Equally, there was little point in working out all of the above if they could not deliver the sport to a place where people could buy and consume it, a huge problem in the early 1990s. Most other sports had their spiritual homes, the place where their fans came to worship at the altar, their Yankee Stadiums, Wrigley Fields or Redskins Parks, the places where each week loyalties are reaffirmed, prayers answered and hot dogs bought. Soccer however had none of these cathedrals of homage, no soccer stadiums to call home, and their abode was wherever cheap rent could be found and a crowd mustered. The US National Team in the late 1980s was at best nomadic: roaming the country looking for a place to pitch their tent and put on a show, just like the circus or the Harlem Globetrotters, rolling into town one day and out the next. Americans love the Globetrotters, but do not treat them seriously or lose sleep when they lose (which of course they never do) and they also love the circus but would not follow one abroad to watch it. For soccer to gain meaning and importance it had to distinguish itself as more than just a touring sideshow – it needed identity, it needed structure, it needed meaning and it needed people to care if it lost, go crazy if it won and understand if it gained a hard fought and valuable draw. Off the field, it also needed a clear identity and marketing position. In a straight shoot-out with the NFL, NHL, MLB and NBA for the corporate dollar, soccer needed to give a clear and compelling argument as to why boardrooms should change years of entrenched spending habits and choose soccer over what has always worked in the past. In the American marketing world no one had ever got fired for buying a National Football League or Major League Baseball sponsorship but might be escorted from the building by "security" if they ventured to cancel the boss's luxury suite at the SuperBowl or World Series in exchange for two tickets to USA versus El Salvador in New Haven. This could be a dangerous and potentially suicidal career move!

So just what did soccer have that could be packaged and sold? It did of course have the World Cup but that was still four years away and just a three-week event at that. Soccer needed traction now, needed identity now and needed games now and it needed something sponsors could latch onto and market. It had no chance, at the time, of competing with the major sports who had entrenched fan bases, television ratings, press coverage, leagues, and star players along with decades of storied history. As such it had to look for something new, something it could sell, something that would set it apart from its competitors and make corporate America sit up and take notice, or at least take a meeting! In the end Forte would do what every other smart marketer would do, he looked for the things his competitors did not have, their weaknesses and gaps, areas that could be exposed and exploited, positions they could not defend or protect. It was not easy and sometimes difficult but ultimately a strategy emerged and a marketing position established that would differentiate soccer from their competitors. The obvious however would not work. Sure, soccer was a global game and the world's biggest, but with less than 7 percent of the US population holding a passport at the time, this was not going to fly. Equally the Marketing Directors that needed to be impressed were looking to sell product in Minneapolis not Moscow. Certainly, soccer was a fun game for kids, but so too was baseball, basketball and football. Sure, the World Cup was arriving but as already said, that was four years away and would not pay the bills today. Ultimately Forte combined three major forces of the American psyche to crack open the corporate vault and wallet. Patriotism, Feminism and "Big Eventism" (while not a real word you get my meaning!). In a majestic piece of positioning, soccer called on America to get behind it as it battled world powers, embrace it as it recognized the emerging strength and power of the American female, and support it as it demonstrated once again, to the entire watching world, that when it comes to big events, nobody does it better. Let's look at these three positions.

The most powerful and emotive feeling in all American sports and indeed American life is that of patriotism. Deemed hokey and sometimes overbearing to many around the world, the Pledge of Allegiance recited every morning at schools and the Star-Spangled Banner sung at the beginning of every major sports event are constant reminders of the emotion and passion Americans feel for their country and which form the fabric that binds the multicultural society as one. David Beckham has openly expressed the view that one of the major reasons he finds America so appealing is the unashamed pride the people have in the Red, White and Blue, and their unapologetic willingness to openly express their allegiance. Soccer's first move was to take ownership of this emotion and quickly position itself as the only sport (outside of the Olympics) that could legitimately allow sponsors the rights to wrap their brands around the flag of the USA. An offer the "majors", for all their economic power and media reach, could not match. For while these sports had Detroit versus New York and Los Angeles versus Boston, Soccer could deliver USA versus Mexico, Russia versus Czechoslovakia and West Germany versus England. Soccer had the stuff of wars and global power, marauding armies and single minded fanaticism all wrapped up in centuries of politics and culture. It's pretty hard to get excited about the history of Kansas, the trials and tribulation of Tampa or the struggles of Toledo but the *azzuri* of Italy evokes images of the Romans, Mussolini, tragic operettas, *The Godfather* 1 and 2 and the Coliseum. The St George flag of England and Union Jack encapsulates the Battle of Britain, the Queen, fighting back the Germans (twice), Shakespeare and Henry VIII (plus of course the birthplace of soccer). Russia, dark and sinister, represents the true enemy, communism, spies, drop boxes and the Kremlin and of course vodka. These may all be very stereotypical and flippant but they underpin a key advantage soccer had as it looked to set itself apart from the rest of American sports: patriotism.

Take the Olympics for example, millions of Americans tune in to watch the USA out-tumble Russia at gymnastics, out-swim the Germans in the pool and out-run the world on the track. Millions stay up late into the night to watch their weightlifters out-lift the Bulgarians or their table tennis players out "ping pong" the Chinese (it doesn't happen but they still watch). Whatever the sport, whatever the time of day, if it's the Olympics and the flag, Americans will watch and watch in big numbers. Three weeks of flag-waving fervor and expert analysis on the "triple backward somersault" after which most would rather watch repeats of *Lost* than tune into a track and field event from Oregon or swim meet from Omaha. But without a doubt, the one thing you can take to the bank – and the Olympics does every four years – is that the American flag sells, and sells big!

Soccer as such had found its key differentiation, found the one thing that it could sell that could not be ambushed. It wasn't power hits or touchdowns, it wasn't three point throws or home runs and it wasn't cracker jacks or popcorn. How could it ever dare to compete with these bastions of American culture? Instead it was to hijack for its own use America's most prized possession, the Star-Spangled Banner that was the American flag. Soccer was smart enough to ask America to not just support Harkes, Doyle and Lalas but to support Harkes, Doyle and Lalas take on the world: take on the global soccer powers that had ruled over them for decades and were now coming to American shores to rub it in. Along the way it was to latch onto soccer moms, soccer kids and reluctant fathers. It was to make believers and supporters of Americans that had never played, watched or read about soccer but who, draped in the flag, came out to ensure those Russians never got the upper hand or those Mexicans handed us another soccer humiliation. Never bet against the power of American patriotism, the strategy was to work like a charm!

With the first pillar of its positioning in place, soccer turned to the second most powerful attribute it possessed: its ability to reach and influence the all-powerful American mother and her kids. With a buying power dwarfing most European nations the soon to be infamous "soccer mom" was to play a critical role in convincing corporate America that soccer was the next "great" thing and opening up previously unreachable budgets.

The prevailing corporate wisdom about soccer in the early 1990s was that only ex-patriot Brits, Europeans and Hispanics were interested in playing soccer and as such sponsorship (if any) should come out of their multicultural or ethnic marketing budgets. What almost all had missed and needed much convincing of, was the fact that over the past two decades a groundswell of grass roots involvement in soccer had been developing throughout the country. City by city and state by state, hard-working volunteers, passionate coaches and supportive parents had been toiling almost unnoticed in the sporting shadows to bring soccer to the masses. Soccer programs were being expanded daily, additional fields requisitioned, and thousands of clubs and teams formed. With no great fanfare or media coverage, state and national champions were being crowned at all age levels for both boys and girls alike. Unbeknown to most, millions upon millions of kids and their families were swarming over the fields of America, enjoying being involved and playing the great game of soccer. The sport was organized at a level that would shame many so-called sophisticated soccer nations, run by thousands of passionate, enthusiastic and committed volunteers. It was equally run, as no other was, by women. Long before "soccer moms" became a political catch phrase for the Clinton Presidential election, there were "soccer" moms. While dads were engaged in bulking up their kids for American football or stretching an extra inch of height for basketball, moms were ferrying their kids to soccer practice, organizing schedules, planning fundraisers and running tournaments. With over 45 percent of all participants in the sport being young girls, soccer represented a gender equity that mirrored the increasing power that women were asserting in society.

Soccer had discovered its second significant differentiating point and advantage it had over every other sport: the American female. The girls that flooded the fields to play the game represented tremendous current buying power but also represented future mothers and parents who would go on to control and influence household spending for decades to come. Brands are built on the allegiance of the young and soccer had millions of young girls (and their mothers) engaged every week. While dad was off coaching football, helping fielders stay awake at baseball or organizing a hockey fight, mom was on the soccer fields with her kids and in particular her daughter: a daughter who had no place on the "football" field, the baseball diamond or the hockey rink for these were the domain of alpha American boys and fathers urging them to "skate tougher", throw stronger or hit harder.

American soccer fields in comparison were places where a parent could often watch their sons and daughters play the same sport, with the same intensity often at the same location. Throughout America the inclusive sport of soccer was quietly becoming the family bonding event of the weekend, with minivan-driving suburban soccer moms, grandparents and siblings in tow, gathering to watch "Johnny's and Jenny's" latest games – gatherings that represented the wholesome values and disposable income level "brands" cherished. It took a long time convincing but once corporate America caught a glimpse of what was happening the check book opened and the first stage of the economic boom that was to embrace soccer began. Soccer was to become the "sport de jour" for companies looking to reach middle-class suburban America (read soccer mom) and the sport of a new young family demographic, throwing off its age-old stereotype of being a game for ethnics and wimps. (Although in fairness, most

American football fans still think it a game for wimps, but that's a whole different story.)

Two of the three pillars of differentiation were now in place with the Red, White and Blue unfurled and soccer moms and young girls wrapping it around themselves. The final pillar played into the unwavering love Americans have for the "big event". Everyone loves a parade, as the song goes, but no one more than Americans. Whether it's the Olympics, the Super Bowl, the Oscars or the World Series, there is something in the American psyche that draws them to the flame, throw in the Red, White and Blue and it's doubly compelling. While most in America had little idea of the size and scale of the event that was about to land on their shores, corporate America and the professional marketing executives they employed in the most case did, or at least knew enough to pretend they did. Afraid to miss what might be a great "show", corporations soon recognized that the US National Team represented a great vehicle for reaching down to grass roots America and the millions of soccer families that lived there and if the team just happened to win the World Cup well …!

America goes to war

A strategy that required the USA going to war against the world's greatest soccer powers waving its flag and singing its battle songs was exciting and saleable, but useless if no one came out to watch, no one tuned in on television or no one bought a bottle of beer or bar of chocolate because of it. The USA had to find some fans and find them quick.

No disrespect, but a diet of games against Costa Rica, Guatemala, Finland and Malta, all opponents in the 1989–90 season, was not going to generate the excitement and media coverage required to build a nation of rabid fans living and dying with every win or loss. Bigger plans and bigger games were needed and for this SUSAP needed a knowledge of soccer that at the time they did not possess. Forte was a smart man however and while he recognized he knew very little about the game, he knew a man who did, hiring Kevin Payne from US Soccer. In Payne, SUSAP had found what it was missing: a diehard soccer man who understood the sport at the player, administrative and business level and who could talk the language of soccer, a language Forte could not. Payne knew a good team from a bad one, which was just as well as they were contracted to bring 12 of them to the USA each year! They equally could not be just any old teams, they had to be ones that excited spectators, intrigued the media and generated exposure, there was little to be gained in lining up a schedule of whipping boys the US could "hammer", if such whipping boys could be found in the early 1990s! Equally, there was not much joy in setting up the USA for a series of depressing defeats, nothing would dampen the ardor and enthusiasm of the American public quicker than a series of public humiliations. Winning is after all a national pastime in America. So a very difficult balancing act was required: one that could make or break the commercial success of the National Team program and if wrong could jeopardize the overall success of the World Cup itself.

So just how popular was the men's team and exactly what did SUSAP have to work with? Well if Italia 90 was any indication, the answer to those two questions was: not very and not much.

The "road to Italy" send-off tour celebrating the country's first appearance in a World Cup in 40 years and designed to whip the country into a frenzy of uncontrollable soccer passion, was nothing short of tepid. Probably a function of the desperate financial state US Soccer found itself in, games against Iceland in St. Louis (3,200), Colombia in New Jersey (8,500) and finally Poland in that metropolitan hotbed of soccer Hershey, Pennsylvania (12,000) were hardly going to set the American soccer world on fire or send our boys into battle with the country's cheers ringing in their ears. The truth of the matter was that the team crept out of New York unnoticed and unappreciated by the vast majority of America as it headed to Europe to take on the world.

The Russians are coming

Amidst all of this however there was a hint that things might all not be lost: that should SUSAP create the right program, the American public might rally around the team and support them in big force. For on 10 February 1990, the USA played the Soviet Union in

Palo Alto, California and 61,000 of them turned up to watch. Why 61,000? Well it was simple, the game had meaning! Sure it was just a "friendly game" but since when had anything between the USA and the Soviet Union ever been deemed "friendly". While relations were obviously much improved, the Soviets had always been America's nemesis and bitter cold-war foe, fueling decades of mistrust and suspicion, with most Americans convinced the communists were out to get them. While the Berlin Wall had come down, opinions were not going to change overnight. The Soviets were now here on US soil, in the shape of their soccer team, and this was America's chance to give them a beating. The US Ice Hockey team had done it at the 1980 Lake Placid Winter Olympic Games, immortalized forever as the "miracle on ice". Now it was soccer's turn – the "overthrow on the grass" or "triumph in the turf" if you like. But whatever it was to be called that day and probably for the first time in years (maybe ever) the USA team was engaged in a game that really mattered to the American people. A people who were convinced that losing would somehow be a "slight" against their sense of being American, evil would have prevailed over good, dark over light, communism over democracy. All somewhat flippant but also true, for this is exactly what international soccer is all about, a potion of sporting, political and social history played out between two nations with "history" between them. It should never be more than a game but always is! (By the way, maybe the Soviets were "out to get them" after all. They handed the USA a comprehensive 3–1 beating.)

Meaning and relevance is everything in sport and while the 1990 World Cup in Italy may not have captured the imagination of the American public, trying to beat the Soviet Union had. This however had to change. The World Cup had to gain importance and relevance in the minds of America or risk an embarrassing failure in 1994.

I attended the Soviet game in my capacity as Publisher of Soccer International Magazine and was horrified at the post-game reception to see the USA team turn up in jeans and sneakers in a show of disrespect and unprofessional behavior that could not have gone unnoticed. It wasn't meant to be a "slight", it was just symptomatic of how the US program was run during that period and how out of touch the US was to the fineries and protocols of

international soccer. I did publish an editorial on it and in fairness
the Federation made changes. It was a small thing, but important.
One has only to look at the impeccable attire of the team in the
present day to see how far they have come.

As mentioned earlier, the USA hardly set the world alight at
Italia 90, finishing 23rd out of 24 teams. Poorly prepared, they had
not bothered (or could not afford) to have their first-round opponents physically scouted and were to pay the price as the daunt-
ing Czechs outmatched them in every area, handing them a more
than comprehensive, "could have been eight" 5–1 hammering. Not
a good day for American soccer. Shrewdly however, US Soccer
officials had hedged their bets and pre-booked flights home,
assuming the team would fail to progress, so all was not lost!
The US fan base in Italy numbered family and friends and a few
die-hards, but in numbers were probably the worst supported
team there. The team performed poorly (aside of Rome), looked
what they were, young inexperienced college kids and returned
home to anonymity and indifference. But this was to all change
and change quickly.

With Rothenberg and Steinbrecher on board and a World Cup
just 48 months away the US National Team had to be improved.
It was a critical element in the overall plan for both US Soccer
and the 1994 World Cup that the US Team be competitive; in fact
not just competitive, it had to win. To achieve this, radical and
unpopular surgery was required.

A foreign coach: are you kidding?

In what I would call the fifth crucial development in the growth
of soccer in the USA, Rothenberg and Steinbrecher incurred
the wrath and fury of American coaches everywhere when they
fired Bob Gansler and decided they needed a foreign coach
to lead them to World Cup glory. Having met with both Franz
Beckenbauer and Sven Goran Erickson, US Soccer ultimately
settled on Bora Milutinovic (Bora), a Serbian coach who had
lead Mexico to within a hair's breadth of the semi-finals in 1986
and who came with a track record for achieving exactly what the
USA needed: creating a team that would qualify out of the first

group stage of the 1994 World Cup Finals. No host nation had ever failed to achieve this and the USA did not intend to be the first. Bora equally had a reputation for playing intelligent attacking soccer, the sort necessary to excite educated fans as well as create new ones. Engaging, quotable and humorous with a strong personality, he spoke seven languages, knew everyone in soccer and walked with the air of a confident man who knew exactly what he wanted and expected from his teams, perfect credentials for managing a team of young and inexperienced American players. He had the Hispanic press "eating out of his hand", holding almost iconic status for his achievements with Mexico, guaranteeing column inches and desperately needed media coverage. In Bora, US Soccer had found its Pied Piper, its leader and its talisman. He would not disappoint!

Rothenberg and Steinbrecher were to make many multimillion-dollar decisions during the four years leading up to the World Cup Final in 1994. None in my mind were as influential and important as the selection of Bora Multinovich as coach. They could have chosen another American and placated the masses, but it would have been a mistake. No one could have come close to the experience Bora possessed and the respect he commanded. A successful US National Team was critical for the success of World Cup 94 and for this they needed the best coach possible. At the time that ruled out American coaches. Over the next four years, under Bora, the US National Team morphed from a group of naïve college kids lacking that belief that they belonged on the world stage into a group of solid, confident professionals that on their day felt they could beat anyone in the world. Bora proclaimed "I will work with the Team with love in my heart and teach them to think as one about the game. I will teach them tactics and in 94 when the results are important we will get important results". How right he was to prove to be. Any coach that talks about soccer with love in their heart clearly understands why we play, watch and follow this great game. He was to impart this enthusiasm to the team, the fans and, dare I say, even the media during his time with the US and played a significant and important role in building a sustainable fan base for the US Team and international respectability for its team and players. (Under Bora the team was a fun place to be around. Go to any hotel or restaurant in

America with Bora and the Mexican and Hispanic staff working there would leave their jobs to shake his hand, take a photo or get an autograph, such was the reverence and regard with which he was held. It always meant your food got cold though.)

Build it and they will come: the World Series of Soccer

Some focus and shape had to be bought to the games the USA would play over the coming years and to be commercially successful they had to appeal to sponsors and fans alike. Sponsors usually like to know what they are buying and with the 3-pillar pitch outlined earlier supplying the demographics and meaning, it was now left to deliver the nuts and bolts: the games, signage boards, television commercials, player appearances, logo rights and promotions they needed to justify their spend. To be successful, soccer needed a clear message and clear understandable deliverables, hence the creation of the "World Series of Soccer". Leaving aside the fact that as with most things in US sports the word "World" is used when it should be "American", in soccer's case it at least had a semblance of truth. Over the next three years some of the top teams in the world would compete on American soil. While the World Series of Soccer became the umbrella title for the games the US played each year it was the creation of the US Cup, a small summer tournament designed to replicate the opening group stage of the World Cup in 1994, that grabbed most of the attention and best competition, including Brazil, Italy, Germany and England (see Table 2.1). Setting up matches of this quality however did not come without its risks. A diet of international humiliations was not going to satiate an American public that "prefers" to win or impress sponsors looking to align with the best. Fortunately US Soccer need not have worried for Bora's team was to perform well beyond anyone's expectations.

By all measures 1991 was a good year on the field for soccer in the USA. Beating Uruguay 1–0 before losing narrowly to Argentina 0–1 were good results, with both games attracting respectable crowds of over 30,000 such as, when 51,000 fans flooded in to Foxboro Stadium in Boston on 1 June to see the USA take on

Table 2.1 Key games and attendances for US Cup 1991–93

The Irish in Boston 1991			USA win Cup 1992			Beating England 1993		
Against	Score	Crowd	Against	Score	Crowd	Against	Score	Crowd
Uruguay	1–0	35,772	Ireland	3–1	35,696	Brazil	0–2	44,579
Argentina	0–1	31,761	Portugal	1–0	10,402	England	2–0	37,652
Ireland	1–1	51,272	Italy	1–1	45,000	Germany	3–4	53,549

1991 was not an official US Cup

Source: Compiled from US Soccer Media Guides.

Ireland and soccer could feel with much justification that something special was happening. Fans were treated to a tremendous game of soccer with an atmosphere to match. There was huge Irish support, huge USA support, a fun, colorful party atmosphere and one of the best days in US Soccer's history. A credible, action packed 1–1 as "good as you get" draw. Yet the next day, in the Sunday Boston Herald, players, fans and officials awoke to the headline "Soccer needs a swift kick out of here". It went on to say "I don't think the Patriots want to share their field with a bunch of guys called Felipe who just hijacked a 747 from Tunisia" and "the coach of the USA team last night could not even speak English". Staggering in its condescending vitriol it unfortunately reflected many of the stereotypes that were to dog soccer throughout the build-up to World Cup 94 and underpin just how much work still remained to be done. In 1991 it was by no means a "racing certainty" that America would take to the World Cup and more columns like that in the Boston Herald would not help, especially coming after such a tremendous success. Clearly the writer could not have been at the game. By the way, how many Mexican/Irish Felipe O'Boyle's wrapped in the tricolor, wearing a silly hat and drinking Guinness do you know? And as for that foreign coach, Bora speaks seven languages fluently, including very good English (when he wanted). The journalist that crafted that article probably spoke one language, vacationed every year in Florida and had his fill of international culture satiated by a couple of trips on the "it's a small world" ride at Disneyland!

The Irish Team was paid a customary appearance fee of around $25,000 that day plus of course all expenses. Arriving at the stadium they were stunned to see the size of the crowd and in particular the numbers of Boston Irish that had left their pubs to make the pilgrimage to Foxboro Stadium. Realizing this was a decent "payday" for US Soccer they let it be known that they expected a little more "compensation" if they were to perform that day. US Soccer, unwilling to be held hostage and to make a point, politely handed the Irish a microphone that would allow them to explain to their fans why they would not be appearing today. Sense of course prevailed and the not uncommon ploy rebuffed. Afterwards over a couple of pints of Guinness an equitable agreement was reached. The message however was clear: while new to the "game" the USA was not going to be pushed around. Over the next four years many other teams tried but none succeeded. Remember this was a Federation that secured the World Cup when $750,000 in debt and operating in rented hotel rooms at JFK airport! It was not afraid to call anyone's bluff.

The gringos to the north

A month later, the USA would take a monumental leap forward as a team when it won the inaugural Concacaf Gold Cup, securing a huge "upset" win over Mexico 2–0 in the semi-final before going on to beat Honduras 4–3 on penalties in the final. Bora in just three short months had led the USA to its first International Trophy and put everyone around it on notice that a new sheriff was in town. The Mexican press, not surprisingly, were in an uproar. This was after all their sport, the last thing they wanted was the gringos from the north becoming any good at it.

The USA were already the dominant political and financial power in the region and Mexico could do without them becoming the dominant soccer power as well. For the past 50 years Mexico had ruled soccer in the region, losing only twice in 27 games to the US (with one of those being in 1937!). The thought that this might be coming to an end hurt and the fact it was being orchestrated by their hero Bora made it even more possible. In reality the balance of power was indeed shifting and the easy ride Mexico had enjoyed for the past decades was over. Winning the 1991 Gold Cup put Mexico on notice that a new day was dawning on the field for American soccer and that everything they took for granted in past years was over and a whole new era of fierce competition was in front of them. Over the next two decades the 800lb gorilla in the Concacaf room would not be Mexico!

As hard as the US National Team had been competing on the field, Forte and his Soccer USA Partners' colleagues had been competing off it. Traversing the country through remote airports and Sheraton Hotels, long days on the road and evenings away from their families, it felt like they had presented to, or been thrown out of, just about every major corporation in America. The effort however paid dividends (as it usually does in sales) and by the end of 1991, Coca Cola, Sprint, Mastercard, American Airlines and Chiquita had joined perennial sponsors Budweiser and Adidas in signing long-term sponsorship agreements. Seeking to ride the coat tails of this new emerging sport, the wholesome family demographic it delivered and of course the soon to be arriving 94 World Cup, they were spending anywhere from $200,000 to $400,000 per year for the privilege. American Airlines took its involvement one step further and signed on as a sponsor of the English National team in a cheeky shot across the Atlantic that upset British Airways. (Until the English failed to qualify that is.)

In a further sign of the professionalism that was starting to seep into the sport, SUSAP was to organize its first ever "sponsor summit", an event designed to bring together those partners that had entrusted their millions to the sport. Leading executives from each of the companies gathered to share ideas, listen to marketing plans and develop the contacts. Forte, Payne, Steinbrecher and Rothenberg, along with their team, working the rooms in a full court press to convince partners that their investment in soccer would be incalculably improved if they would develop sales, marketing branding and PR programs that utilized soccer as its core vehicle. Between them these companies controlled millions of dollars in marketing and advertising spend and could take soccer into the homes of every American should they choose, SUSAP was desperate to make sure they did. Despite the fact a high-ranking Coca Cola executive fell off the tee box and broke his leg in the customary end of event golf tournament, the summit was deemed a resounding success and a clear indication that the sport was becoming professional. This was a critical development if soccer was to maintain the trust of the companies that had risked their brand equity on this newly emerging sport.

Unfortunately, someone had thought it would be a great idea to end the summit by taking everyone to the USA versus North Korea match being held in Washington DC, just a short bus ride from the summit. A good idea on paper, but a 2–1 loss to our communist friends did not end the event on a high note. Fortunately most of the new sponsorship contracts ran through the end of the 1994 World Cup. You can only control what you can control!

As sponsors left with promises of great marketing programs to come, one of the simplest yet important reflections to come out of the summit came from Peter Priner, President of Adidas America, the most soccer savvy of all sponsors – a comment that was to foretell the future of the sport. "We see soccer as, after many false starts in the USA, finally getting a solid ground level support among young players. We see it today as being a pretty hip sport. The hip kid at school today is a 'soccer player'". This somewhat conversational reflection depicted a change the sport was undergoing throughout American society. Soccer was moving out of the domain of the "wheezy boys" and "ethnics" and into the psyche of mainstream sports. Soccer was no longer the catch-all sport for those not tall, big, or good enough for the football, baseball or basketball teams. This change was to gain incredible momentum over the next decade and ultimately result in the acceptance of soccer as being as much a part of the American sports landscape as any of the other traditional American sports. To kids in 2010, soccer has always been an American sport, for they have known no other time when it wasn't! It's also deemed a cool sport! Priner was right.

Three thousand miles away the Red, White and Blue adorned the sports pages of every newspaper in England as John Harkes became the first American to win a Cup Final medal when his Sheffield Wednesday team beat Manchester United in the 1991 League Cup Final. He had also scored a wondrous 35-yard volley in an earlier round against Derby County that would go on to win the goal of the season and elevate him to status of hero worship with the Wednesday faithful. America had its first international media soccer star. Good looking, charismatic and quotable, the British media and soccer audience lapped it up, giving rise to the possibility that, just maybe, something exciting was happening in American soccer. It made cynical managers and fans rethink their opinions of the US game. Maybe these Yanks can play after all; maybe the World Cup won't be so bad. While in 2010, the American player is a respected and valuable member of the English soccer scene, in 1991 it was far from it. Harkes was a pioneer and talisman and earned US Soccer much needed respect and awareness when it needed it most.

And, thirteen thousand miles away the USA Women's National Team was, in almost total anonymity, about to put the women's soccer world on notice that it had arrived. Led by one of, if not the, greatest women players of all time, Michelle Akers, the USA were crowned World Champions at the first ever Women's World Cup in China. More later, but the true significance of the victory would not be felt for many years when the girls that laced up their cleats in China would go on to change the sport of soccer in America forever and create a tidal wave of national pride that would prove unstoppable and expensive!

1991 was a great year for US Soccer.

Never go up against Michael Jordan ...

The 1992 US Cup proved a couple of important points. One, the USA was improving and international teams would underestimate them at their peril. Two, it is a mistake to go up against the greatest basketball player in the world. The event itself represented a great victory for the US as it claimed the title against three strong European powers, Italy, Portugal and Ireland. The product on the field was clearly improving, helped by the fact the USA had scoured the world looking for potential players who may have some claim to US citizenship. Not quite as bad as the Irish policy under their legendary and immensely popular coach Jack Charlton, where anyone drinking a pint of Guinness might be deemed eligible to wear the green, the USA found legitimate players in Roy Wegerle, Thomas Dooley and Ernie Stewart, all experienced professionals earning their living in Europe with the potential for US eligibility. Having Henry Kissinger on the World Cup Board could not have hindered the speed at which green cards were acquired.

(Roy Wegerle's, eligible through his American wife, may just have been one of the quickest in immigration history.) The 1992 US Cup got off to a good start with 35,000 fans turning up in DC to see the US beat Ireland. Four days later however, less than 10,000 showed for a midweek game against Portugal in Chicago: a game that highlights the perils of staging international soccer in the USA and an insight into just where soccer stood in the pecking order of American sports. The US game unfortunately ended up coinciding with a NBA Finals game between Chicago Bulls and LA Lakers, a game everyone, and I mean just about everyone, wanted to see. "Big Eventism" was rampant that night in Chicago and USA versus Portugal was simply not on the radar screen. The timing was un-avoidable due to the international commitments but it hurt none the same. (I published the game "program" for that night's game so if anyone is looking for an extra 5,000 copies?)

Order was restored three days later at the same stadium when 45,000 turned up to see the USA and Italy battle to an exciting 1–1 tie. According to Europeans there was a time in years past when you could have picked the first eleven healthy males of any Air Italia flight landing in America, given them a uniform, a half time "orange" and a quick rub down and they would have beaten the USA. These stereotypes were now over. This was a new era, a new time and, under Bora, the USA team offered a whole new set of challenges for the world's best to face. However hard or not the opposition were trying, however unimportant in the grand scheme of things the US Cup was in world soccer, to soccer in the USA these games were critical. SUSAP could walk through the doors of corporate America and say: "hey we beat Portugal, we beat Ireland and we tied with Italy and by the way we are reigning Concacaf Cup Champions, you need to jump on this bandwagon". Remember in the "land of the blind the one eyed man is King"? Well America loves winners and in 1991 and 1992 America was winning.

The Boston soccer party

The front pages of the English tabloids in June 1993 had a picture of the then England Manager Graham Taylor superimposed over a turnip! Not a very flattering image, but it sold papers and vented the nation's despair as they struggled, and eventually failed, to qualify for World Cup 94.

If that image ruined his breakfast as the paper landed on his doorstep, those that appeared on 10 June, the day after England crashed to defeat against the USA in Boston, must have had Taylor wondering if it was safe to head back to England at all and if he did, would it be the "Tower" and a quick beheading: the fate of many who displeased the Monarchy. Losing to Holland was no shame, losing to Norway disappointing, losing to the "Yanks" unthinkable and in all ways unforgivable. One team's despair however is usually another team's glory and on a rain-slicked pitch on the night of 9 June 2003, the glory lay with the USA.

England had been invited to play in US Cup 93 along with powerhouses Germany and Brazil, the event billed as a prelude to World Cup 94. This was an opportunity to test how far along the US was in its logistical preparations, how enthusiastic were its fans and how competitive was its team, and with just 12 months to the "real thing", the answers needed to be positive. Fortunately in the most part they were. By the end of the 2-week tournament an average of 47,000 fans per game would have poured through the turnstiles, with close to 62,000 alone showing up to watch England play Germany at the Detroit Silverdome (the first ever "indoor" encounter between the two teams). This clearly highlighted that FIFA need not worry about fans turning up for games that did not involve the USA, which considering 95 percent of the games at the World Cup would not, was a comforting thought.

The most significant moment of US Cup 93 delivered a victory that was to elevate the US men's soccer team to the front pages of almost every major newspaper in America and the highlight reels of every sports show on television. For on 9 June 1993 the USA beat England 2–0 sending shockwaves through American sports, the impact of which should not be underestimated. To Americans this result represented one of the greatest sporting upsets since the famous "miracle on ice". Every newspaper led with the startling result and of course references to the infamous "Tea Party", the last time the British got slapped around in Boston. You see for most Americans and certainly those suburban families, soccer was an English game. Their kids were typically taught by English coaches, went to English soccer camps and took their lead (for better or worse) from English coaching methods. How was it possible for the USA to beat them? How could the pupil now be better than the master? It just didn't make sense. We all know that one result does not make a team but beating England that day did. There was a different "swagger" about the team – a swagger they carried forward to 1994. Off the field, the result was immense and garnered incalculable branding and PR for the team and the World Cup. "Maybe the USA was not that bad after all? Maybe it could win this World Cup thing?" Great for ticket sales and great for exposure! (No one needed to know that Brazil had given them the run around or that Germany had stormed into a 4–1 lead before realizing they were "guests" in the country.) It mattered nothing because the USA had beaten England and therefore must be good, which they were, of course, just not good enough to win a World Cup.

The event itself was a tremendous financial success and with over $10m in ticket sales and a $3m profit achieved, was enough to convince the Federation that after World Cup 94 it should go into the game promotion business for itself.

The lessons learned from US Cup 93 were huge. First, it was clear that American soccer fans would turn out to watch games between two non-USA teams, a big relief to FIFA and confirmation of what they witnessed at the Los Angeles Olympics. Second, that logistically the USA could, as usual, stage a phenomenal event and third, that a winning American team could capture the attention and hearts of a nation. The key word here of course was "winning", because without a winning American team in the years leading up to 1994 and the World Cup itself, the odds were very high that the event would struggle. Fortunately Bora amassed a group of players that to a man knew the importance of the moment and their role in it, and of course the potential exposure it provided them. The Mission Viejo residency camp the players were brought into created the club-like experience and controlled environment the coach wanted and developed a unified focused group of players with one goal in mind: qualification from its first round group at World Cup 94. It had shocked the world once by beating England and planned to do so again in 1994. The team had few shrinking violets when it came to character. John Doyle was a tough, no-holds barred center half, and goalkeeper Tony Meola growing in stature every game with sharp reflexes and confidence to match. Tab Ramos was now an impact player over 90 minutes with the ability to glide past opponents at will and John Harkes, hardened from seasons of English soccer, was rugged and competitive with an engine to match. These players were complemented by the arrival of the silky Wegerle who plied his trade weekly in the English League; Tom Dooley, a tall, steely, strong midfielder from Germany and Fernando Clavijo a level-headed experienced Uruguayan who exuded professionalism and class; Wynalda playing and scoring freely in Germany was growing up from the petulant youngster who was naïvely sent off against Czechoslovakia in Italia 90; Brian Quinn, the energetic and feisty Irishman; experienced and demanding Balboa, who though injured for the US Cup had matured into a fierce and accomplished defender, who would not suffer fools gladly and expected much of himself and his team mates. Coming through the ranks was Jeff Agoos with as good a left foot as the USA had had for a long time; the charismatic and rangy Lalas who drove the nail in the coffin of the English team with his off the bench header to secure the second decisive goal and Cobi Jones, the speedy combative winger who would go on to make over 150 appearances for the national team.

The USA team in 1993 was full of strong characters, experienced professionals, blended with talented and confident youth. Bora put together the ingredients for a team designed to qualify from its group in 1994 and anything less would be deemed a failure. Nothing in US Soccer was as important as the product on the field during the early nineties and fortunately the team delivered. It would have been easy for the USA to have been wrapped up in the commercial "hoopla" that was the World Cup and seduced by the new found wealth corporate America was heaping on it. Thankfully they realized from the very early days the importance of creating a winning team and when it mattered most, delivered one. That's not to say there were no problems and issues along the way, many surrounding the salaries and bonuses paid to players, but it never seemed to influence the performance on the field. Ultimately the moment, the event and the opportunity was just too big to let anything get in the way. Ultimately, all sports marketing begins and ends with the product on the field.

No home advantage

Research undertaken after US Cup 93 highlighted the importance of staging such an event and gave rich understanding of the soccer audience that existed in the USA. Of those surveyed 40 percent stated they were attending an international game for the very first time. While 85 percent said they were US citizens, 50 percent stated they were not born inside the country, which seemed logical. Interestingly (and for MLS maybe an insight they might have learned from), fans were not the young suburban kids who were flooding the fields at weekends but older educated and professional people, aged 25–54, 75 percent of whom held college degrees. Interestingly, close to a third of the fans were women (27 percent) which would have been a significant anomaly in world soccer during this period. Happily for World Cup 94 close to 60 percent stated they intended to attend a World Cup match (which meant 40 percent were not) and 27 percent said they fully intended to buy a Major League Soccer season ticket when launched, which if true meant the New England Revolution would have an average home attendance of 92,000!!! In another important bit of information, nearly all the fans were connected to the sport in some way as a coach, player or administrator, again logical.

Business and sports often live and die by the demographic they identify and deliver while marketing executives pour over reams of clever statistics, charts and focus groups to develop the latest hard-hitting promotional plan. For the sport of soccer there is more at play than just numbers, for these only reflect one dimension of what a sponsor needs to know about the American soccer fan. Understanding it all requires an empathy with the social, cultural and political history of the USA and how it relates to soccer. It helps to be a fan to explain it.

Just how far had the USA come in three short years in their quest to turn America into a fervent, singing, swaying mass that would drive the US to victory in 1994? The answer unfortunately was "not very". Fans did turn out in tremendous numbers but as yet were not passionately and fanatically USA centric or biased: most were still learning how to act and behave at matches and to fully understand the important role they could play in securing a result. At the Yale Bowl in New Haven, Connecticut where the USA took on Brazil, Bora bemoaned that his brave players needed more support, and that US fans needed to understand how hard it was for his team to play against the best in the world. "There is no advantage to us playing at home" declared Bora understanding that, unlike most American sports, home advantage is a huge deal. Yes, American fans were in the stadium in big numbers, but just did not yet know how to act or behave. Way too polite, they applauded great Brazilian plays and were in awe of the samba-beating drums and colors of the Brazilian fans. They were spectators of the game and the event but not yet ingrained with the DNA of what being a soccer fan was all about. In fairness, these events were about exposing and teaching the US what it takes to be a "fan", an apprenticeship and education in what was coming "down the pike" in 12 months when hordes of bedecked fans, with painted faces, draped flags and unwavering loyalty would land on US soil and put America to the test. Their goal was to do whatever it takes to give their team the critical sense of home advantage by dominating the stadium atmosphere, out-sing and out-shout the opposition fans, to win the game and move on. The US National Team fans in 1993, while patriotic, were "nice", that poison chalice of words no sports team wants to hear. This was all to change in later years with the arrival of Sam's Army, the fanatical US supporters group, but in 1993, US soccer fans were mere intimidated apprentices, afraid to react and way too respectful of their opponents.

Not "nice" thankfully were the millions of multicultural ethnic soccer fans that called the US home and it was these fans that led the way in creating the atmosphere so unique to soccer everywhere. To most of these groups following and supporting their teams when they arrive to play in the USA was rite of passage and cultural necessity.

There is a special sense of belonging and identity that comes with joining other fellow fans as you travel around the country, or indeed world, in support of your team. It's a special mixture of passion, pride and commitment in being one of the few, or many, that made the journey and shown support. It's tribal, it's family and it's addictive. The fan standing next to you singing, jumping and swaying is, for that day, a member of your clan, your tribe, your brother sharing the same love, fervor and passion for the team.

Often outnumbered and in "hostile" or "away" territory you are there to stand by your team, drive them to perform and let them know that they are not alone as they battle for supremacy on the field. These are your players, representing your club, your country and your heritage. Americans have little concept of what soccer calls "away" support, whether it is distance or tradition – NFL, NBA and MLB fans just do not travel in large numbers, only college "football" traveling in large numbers. This is not however true for many of the ethnic minorities in the USA that come from soccer-playing nations and still have strong nationalistic ties. Those that arrived with the Mayflower have long since lost their soccer roots but many first and second generation immigrants' families still have strong and emotional ties to their homeland and in particular their national and often club soccer teams. The fiercest and most loyal support seems to come from the first generation central-American ethnic groups who often came to the USA to seek a better life and as with all early immigrants they congregated in areas where their fellow countrymen settled and took whatever jobs they could, however dull or menial. Blending into the background they become part of the melting pot that is America. However come "game day" when their country, whether it be Mexico, Honduras, Guatemala or El Salvador appears in the USA, they have the opportunity to break out from the anonymity and daily grind, join fellow countrymen to celebrate their heritage and culture, announcing to everyone they are here and they are proud. The eleven soccer gods who wear their country's colors and fight their battles are a catalyst for an explosion of patriotic fervor. For one afternoon or evening they unite with others who made the journey to celebrate everything they are about and reaffirm, at the altar of soccer, the cultural ties that bind them. For though most are proud Americans they are also, as all Americans are, proud "something else". The beauty of marketing soccer in America is that no matter where you go and what team you bring there will be a community of fans that will come out to support them and often in huge numbers.

I have always loved traveling "away" to watch my teams whether it be Coventry City, England, or the USA national team. There is just a special feeling that comes with being a true fan supporting your team in foreign or hostile waters. In literature

I liken it to the great scene from Shakespeare's *Henry V* and King Harry's emotive St Crispin's Day speech. Outnumbered seven to one on the eve of the Battle of Agincourt, his troops weary and tired, hundreds of miles and the English Channel away from home, he exerts:

"If we are mark'd to die, we are enow to do our country loss: and if to live the fewer the men the greater the share of the honour" … he continues:

> And Crispin Crispian shall ne'er go by
> From this day to the ending of the World
> But we in it shall be remembered
> We few, we happy few we band of brothers
> For he today that sheds his blood with me
> Shall be my brother, be he ne're so vile
> This day shall gentle his condition
> And gentlemen in England now a bed
> Shall think themselves accurs'd they were not here
> And hold their manhoods cheap whiles any speaks
> That fought with us on St Crispin's Day

Any fan who has stood in stadiums, outnumbered, out-sung and often unwelcome will know what I mean. Any away fan at Hampden Park, Boca, Anfield, Old Trafford, or West Ham will know what I mean. Any USA fans that venture to Mexico City for a World Cup qualifier will know. Any US fan that traveled to Germany in 2006 and who were in the Kaiserslautern stadium when the USA overwhelmingly outnumbered, both out-sung and out-supported the Italians will know. It's the heartbeat of being a fan to follow your team away wherever they go and against what-ever the odds, either to victory or defeat. To stand up and say "you were there when …"

Come 2009, Sams Army and the American Outlaws have become the official flag around which fans who want to follow King Harry (if you can forget for a while Americans threw out the British Monarchy) and rally to live or die for the team. Traveling to all US National Team games, both home and away, this army replicates soccer fans you see around the world. They stand behind the goal, they abuse the opposing goalkeeper and they passionately sing for their team, and the Red White and Blue. Still small in number they are exactly what USA soccer needs. Their numbers will grow and over the next decades will become a potent fan force that will travel and shock world soccer. When thirty thousand US fans travel to Rio for the 2014 World Cup finals, the world will know, don't bet against it.

Paying the bills

The strategy of staging the World Series of Soccer and building fan support for both the US National Team and World Cup 94 had to be paid for by someone and this fell to corporate America. SUSAP underwrote and took the financial risk but it was, of course, always hoped that sponsors would cover the costs, and then some, hopefully leaving a profit that made all the hard work worthwhile. It was an interesting commercial landscape however with sponsors basically having three options: (1) sponsor the US National Team program, (2) Sponsor World Cup 94, or (3) break the bank and sponsor both!

Let's make one thing perfectly clear, without FIFA agreeing to give the World Cup to the USA, there would have been no commercial landscape for soccer in the USA (and no SUSAP). As I said earlier, everyone knew this was soccer's time and that included the marketers.

FIFA as usual arrived in the USA with a cadre of top-level international sponsors including Coca Cola, Adidas, McDonalds, Canon, Fuji, JVC and Gillette, all paying around $5m per year, but they were faced with a tough decision. Do they cover their bases and also sponsor the US National Team? Most did and paid an additional $250,000 to $500,000 to SUSAP for the rights. Interestingly, two major American corporations decided against it including McDonalds who used their sponsorship to develop international franchise expansion and Gillette who maybe thought 10-year-old soccer kids don't shave! This posed a dilemma for SUSAP who, looking to maximize their investment, needed to ensure every category was sold but was faced with the wrath of World Cup 94 and FIFA if they allowed partners to ambush the event. It is of course a problem that has plagued sports for decades and will continue to do so. The inevitable test case fell to Coke who as an official World Cup sponsor initially decided they would "pass" on sponsoring the US National Team. US Soccer General Secretary Steinbrecher, an ex-Gatorade marketer, made a call to old friends and cemented a $1m ($250,000 per year) four-year deal for the sports drink category. Probably rightfully assuming Pepsi might be next, Coke came to the table with a deal that worked for everyone and brought the US team under its sponsorship wing. It's not always about the "benefits", sometimes fear, protection and leverage play a significant part.

It was hoped that brands would spend heavily on promoting their partnerships with soccer in both the media and at retail, and the US National Team players certainly were hoping to be used as endorsees and "pitch men". In fairness, while soccer certainly got a huge lift, most brands were still reluctant to fully embrace the sport or throw their marketing assets at it. For the majority of the top level World Cup sponsors it had always been about the international impact a World Cup provided, preferring to focus their resources in markets where "soccer was life" and the impact of their marketing dollars most effective. Budweiser's move to become a World Cup sponsor mirrored exactly their global expansion as a company as it did McDonalds' thrust for international franchise expansion. World Cup Soccer was a proven product driver around the world with an unparalleled track record, its backers always eager to let you know that there are more member countries of FIFA than there are the members of the United Nations. Ask them to choose which to give up, and it would not be FIFA: such is the power of World Cup Soccer. In the USA however, it was still very much unproven.

Sponsors did however support soccer with some campaigns during the period. Gillette for example did little in the Anglo market but ran a major sweepstakes promotion in the Hispanic community, recognizing their love for soccer and the fact that adult Hispanics shaved.

Procter & Gamble undertook a gigantic Rolling Stones Tour-style series of soccerfests that included Rivellino, Geoff Hurst, Gordon Banks, Michelle Akers and more. Expensive, big and logistically challenging it was by far and away the most significant promotion any brand undertook during the period. Whether it moved product or sold a few more boxes of detergent is unknown but it was both impressive and ambitious.

Fuji created on-pack promotion giving soccer gifts and gear for points that ran at retail; American airlines sponsored camps and clinics; Sunny Delight gave away soccer balls. MasterCard signed Pele, utilizing him effectively throughout the country and world as spokesman. They also executed a significant program of US National Team player appearances with the only stipulation being that they be allowed to pay the players more than they were contracted to pay, raising it from $250 to $500 per appearance. A nice gesture but even at this level it was clear the players were not going to get rich any time soon. Under their US National Team contract even for a national advertising campaign they would only receive $500 – Tiger Woods wouldn't allow one of his golf balls to be used for this amount, but such was the lot of the American players during this time, World Cup or no World Cup. Meola with Upper Deck and Ramos with Snickers broke through the clutter a little but ultimately, until Alexi Lalas, Mia Hamm and Freddy Adu came along, corporate America had little confidence soccer players "sold". It had been hoped that the World Cup would blast American soccer stars into every household and across every billboard in the country, but in the most part, it did not happen. Only Alexi Lalas, guitar in hand, captured the attention of media and sponsors alike, garnering a host of valuable endorsement contracts. Lalas had that rebellious cavalier persona that set him apart from most in star-driven America. He would go on to be the most noticeable and marketable player in soccer and coax sponsorship dollars from upwards of a dozen or so corporations. Only Mia Hamm matched and probably surpassed his earnings, along with Freddy Adu the 14-year-old "phenomenon" who captured the heart of America, appeared with Pele and became the future face of American soccer. Unfortunately for him Pepsi had more faith in him than his coaches.

CHAPTER 3

World Cup 1994: Everyone's a Fan

The mandate from Rothenberg was simple: stage the best World Cup ever and leave a lasting legacy for soccer in America. Pretty simple really and easily tripped off the tongue when said quickly – and, by the way, we are going to launch a Division One Professional League on the back of it: not so easy!

It's hard to overstate the importance World Cup 94 had on US soccer and to over praise those that actually pulled it off. Sometimes in life you get one shot at greatness, one punch to knock out the "champ" and claim the title: well for soccer, this was it – get it right and the sport would explode, "screw it up" and it was over, the world once again retrenching into the position that soccer would never make it America. While 1994 would turn out to be a spectacular success, no one in 1991 had any sense, or indeed confidence, that it would be.

Headed initially by Chuck Cale and Scott Parks LeTellier, the original headquarters for World Cup 94 was established close to the nation's capital, Washington DC. With Rothenberg's election however the center of power was moved back to Los Angeles and new offices opened in the prestigious Century City Towers, just one block from Beverly Hills. This was Rothenberg's backyard, a place from which he could control every aspect and monitor every move, a place where he had a network of contacts and supporters stretching back to the 1984 Olympics and further. It was also the scene of American soccer's greatest success, the France versus Brazil Olympic Final and the 101,000 fans that convinced FIFA the USA was ready.

Staging "the best World Cup ever" was pretty much something the USA does for a living, there being little doubt that when it comes to running and operating major events the US has few equals. Of course, it had a head start: stadia were in place, plenty of hotels, airports nearby, infrastructure developed and security tough! So the real success of the events and the challenges faced centered on the "softer" elements of ticketing, sponsorship, marketing and broadcasting. Get these right and there might be a financial legacy to leave behind for the future good of the game, but get them wrong and there would be nothing. It would be little good to the USA if World Cup 94 made a healthy profit, but which left in a suitcase (a big one mind you) on a flight back to Zurich with FIFA. The USA had to ensure it developed a model that gave it every chance to secure significant revenue for itself. It was to start by staking out the patent office in Washington DC.

Kill the lawyers

Shakespeare once proclaimed "kill all the lawyers" – pretty strong words! Had we listened however, the US Soccer Foundation (recipients of a $60m windfall from World Cup 94) would have been left with about $20m less to invest. For it was a lawyer, Scott LeTellier, who recognized that important changes were imminent in US patent and trademark law, changes that if used to their advantage could secure millions in additional revenue for the World Cup Organizing Committee.

While in 2010, the legal ownership and delineation of marketing rights between FIFA (owners of the World Cup) and the local organizing committees (countries given the right to stage the event) is clearly set down in volumes of legal language and "line by line" contract definition, in 1990 it was not. In fact it owed more to the Wild West than efficient Zurich banking and LeTellier knew it. John Wayne movies taught us how the "West Was Won" and just who claimed it and from everything I saw it certainly wasn't a bespectacled Swiss banker with a pen and calculator in hand! (It also wasn't by LA lawyers but that gets in the way of the point.) The point being that the US took a very proactive, aggressive, "possession is 9/10ths of the law" approach to acquiring and securing marketing rights in a move it knew may be contentious. On the morning the legislation came into being LeTellier had a team of attorneys register with the Trademark Office every iteration available, in English and Spanish, of World Cup 94, including US 94, USA 94, USA 1994, USA World Cup 94 (you get the picture).

In all, by the end of the morning, 12 variations were secured, variations and ownership that paved the way to millions. LeTellier knew that once "Italia 90" was over negotiations would begin in earnest with FIFA and their marketing agency ISL to establish the ground rules for many of the undefined rights surrounding World Cup 94. If they owned all of the important names and trademarks it would certainly strengthen their negotiating position, which indeed it did. By the time ISL showed up at the table the dye was cast and the end result inevitable. Controlling 100 percent of the licensing income generated an extra $22m, creating and owning a whole new category: that of "Local Marketing Partner" another $15m and developing a new travel and tourism package added a further $10m – not a bad return for a morning at the Patent Office. The lessons for any major event are clear: pay attention to the fine print and don't kill your lawyer! While early morning "stake outs" at the Trademark office might not sound like exciting sports business practice, it was the difference between a good financial result and a great one. The dollars, as ever, are always in the details.

While the above provided the legal framework and foundation for generating marketing revenue there was still much to be done to ensure the overall event prospered. This could only be achieved by basically getting three numbers right. First, every ounce of ticketing revenue needed to be squeezed out of the event. Second, sponsorship and marketing revenue needed to exceed all expectations and third, costs had to be kept in check.

$1,000 a ticket

By the time Brazil hoisted the World Cup Trophy at the Rose Bowl on 17 July 1994, 3.6 million tickets had been sold to games generating $150m in revenue which accounted for 43 percent of the $350m revenues generated for the entire event. A stunning success and a World Cup Ticket sales record that still stands today. The secret to the record was: (1) being prepared to take a risk and (2) the belief that if it's worth doing it's worth doing "big". When the World Cup was first granted in 1988 the feeling was that the event should be staged in smaller, college-based stadia that could house the 20–30,000 fans per game US Soccer thought might attend. With Rothenberg's election this all changed and buoyed by what he had orchestrated at the 84 Olympics, he set about preparing everyone for the fact that he intended to play the games, for the most part, in 70,000 seat NFL Stadiums, a major, and in 1991, highly risky decision. It could of course have backfired with 32 billion global viewers being treated to half empty stadiums and echoing chants. Had it done so the USA's reputation as a potential new soccer market would have been "shot" and the business plan for a new professional soccer league returned to the filing cabinet. Ultimately, the plan did not backfire and the professional league in 2010 is entering its 15th season.

The strategy however still meant there were a lot of tickets to sell and huge stadiums to fill and to do so would require a huge grass-roots marketing effort. A clever five-stage approach ensured every ticket was sold.

Phase one in March 1993 was a "private" offering to the internal USA soccer family consisting of coaches, players and administrators, all given an early opportunity to buy strips of tickets to stadium venues. The key, of course, was that you had to buy a "strip" of tickets to all the first round games in the venue you chose, which, as it was still 1993, meant you had no idea just what games you might be seeing, and if your venue was scheduled for a round of 16 games you bought that as well. There were some expensive tickets of course but overall the prices for category one tickets were fair, priced at $25–$180 per game. Maybe too fair, with requests for 650,000 tickets over-subscribing the 450,000 made available. Scheduled to coincide with US Cup 93, the second phase of the ticketing plan was unleashed, this time a public sale resulting in an additional 300,000 tickets being snapped up. This was followed up by a highly publicized random lottery for the later stages, quarters, semis and the final itself, which again was massively over-subscribed.

The fourth stage took place in April 1994 with a second "Friends of Soccer" round. Billed as a three-day "invite only" opportunity the 1-800 number was leaked to the press, causing overwhelming backlogs on the ticket sales phone lines, bad press, angry callers and masses of free publicity, generating 100,000 tickets sales just three days. The fifth and final stage took place

1 May 1994 when 450,000 extra tickets arrived in the USA from tour operators, federations and sponsors around the world; again all snapped up by the ravenous soccer hordes. The soccer hordes however were not the millions of kids and their parents running to soccer practice and games each week. The biggest purchasers were referees, officials and coaches followed by the amateur adult soccer community (with strong ethnic ties), only then by the newer youth-soccer families ready to support the Red, White and Blue, even if they had no idea who was in the team. A tremendous grass-roots guerilla marketing campaign ensured there was not a major youth-soccer tournament around the country that did not have a World Cup 94 presence supported by a direct mail campaign utilizing the three million members US Soccer purchased for 75 cents a name from State Associations (a nice bonus considering some states have 100,000 plus members).

Getting the ticket sales strategy correct was obviously vital to the overall success of the event and considering 70 percent of tickets were sold domestically it was clear they hit a home run. When the TV cameras turned on, viewers witnessed packed stadiums and spectacular images, with 95 percent of all seats to all games being filled – even the "lesser" matches, crucial to broadcasters that had spent $275m globally to air matches and more so to FIFA who had charged them for it. The genius of course was that, unlike previous World Cups where tickets were sold on a game to game basis, the US introduced the concept of "strip" sales. If you want Germany versus Spain; you need to buy Korea versus Bolivia. It stopped people cherry picking, created full stadiums for TV and added millions to the bottom line.

The above added millions to the revenue line, but it was the introduction of the "unheard of" $1,000 VIP hospitality ticket that sent the profit margins soaring. Rothenberg knew there were many Americans who were quite willing to splash out for the best seat in the house, especially if it came with some "inside the ropes" extras such as parking and a little food. FIFA baulked, feeling $1,000 was too high a price to pay to see the "game of the people" and worried about reaction from the world's media. The headlines were easily written in British tabloids,"Mickey Mouse gouges soccer fans". The fact of the matter was that "touts" were already charging and getting $1,000 for key games.

Rothenberg's idea was to take them out of the market, offer a $1,000 high-end ticket and satisfy the demand from those who could afford it – it was America after all. Ultimately Rothenberg got what he wanted, fans got a ticket and a sandwich and World Cup 94 got millions in "found" revenue. Adding to the ticketing "icing on the cake" was an innovative hotel and ticket package that allowed fans to follow their team wherever they played and to whatever round they progressed, even the final, commonplace now but invented in 1994. Between these two initiatives World Cup 94 added a staggering $25m–$30m to the bottom line.

Make Brazil travel

Under the heading, saving money is just as relevant as making money, World Cup 94 managed to find a way to cut $30m from its costs by simply reducing the number of venues in which the tournament was held. FIFA were reluctant, feeling 12 stadiums allowed more people to watch the event while LeTellier had worked out that nine stadiums would accomplish the task just as well and save them a fortune along the way. Twelve stadiums also meant that some venues might be perceived as less likely to get the big matches and hence hurt ticket sales. It was better to have nine venues, each with guaranteed "big" teams and each in major media and population markets. By the way, he also wanted to do away with the age old practice of the "seeded" team staying in one location. Fans being asked to buy tickets to venues "site unseen" needed to be sure they would see a top team. For this to happen, seeds needed to travel, and travel they would. There was still the issue of FIFA however, and their insistence on 12 stadiums. As it worked out, it was actually just one person in FIFA rather than FIFA itself who had a real issue with the numbers and he unfortunately passed away prior to 1994, so nine stadiums it was, and $30m in savings.

It was now time for LeTellier's strategy of staking out the Patent Office to pay off. Controlling almost every iteration of the term "World Cup 94" gave them the ability and flexibility to maximize every ounce of marketing and sponsorship revenue from the event. Six levels of partnerships were designated: (1) Official Sponsors;

(2) Marketing Partners; (3) Official Products and Services; (4) Official Supporters (regional); (5) Equipment Suppliers; (6) Official Licensees.

Under the agreement, ISL Marketing had the exclusive rights to sell all international sponsorships and kept all of the revenue, (though a small portion did go to WC 94), while World Cup Marketing was allowed to create a whole new level of sponsorship category called "Local Marketing Partners" and retain the revenue. This included exclusive rights to eight key categories including airlines, hotels, entertainment, insurance, telecommunications and computer information systems, charging between $750,000 to $1,500,000 per year, while also insisting they provide budget relieving services. It wasn't long before major corporations signed up for these with Sheraton, EDS, Sun Microsystems, Sprint, American Airlines, Adidas, Budweiser and Upper Deck stepping up to the plate, generating a combined $8–$12m along the way. Another $20m in revenue was secured from Time Warner who became the master license holder (using the rights secured in DC) and a further (though ultimately disappointing) $2m from the launch of the World Cup coin, which bombed. All other rights were thrown into a joint-venture company with ISL and profits shared equally. These included official products and services, equipment suppliers, regional supporters, national and international licensing, official films, books, music and more. The Joint Venture Company also provided much of the overall marketing services to the Organizing Committee and ultimately some of the sponsors.

No hooligans – no terrorists

One of the biggest line items in the World Cup budget for 1994 was security. Hooliganism was still rife with England fans rampaging through Europe (joined by German and Dutch fans, it must be said). The political landscape was still fraught, with relations between Iran, Iraq and Libya as tense as ever. American police forces and FBI security do not come cheap. As luck would have it, England, Iran, Iraq and Libya would all fail to qualify for the World Cup in America and the threat of lager-fueled skinheads or middle-eastern terrorists as such removed and a quick $20m was slashed from the budget.

It seemed that everything was going their way and as such the decision to gamble on hosting the World Cup a good one. There was, however, one embarrassing and potentially catastrophic omission: no English language television.

Unfathomable around the world, but none of the major television networks in the USA had put a bid in to secure the television rights and so soccer fans were faced with the prospect of having to brush up on their Spanish. (Univision had already stepped up to air all 52 games live!) As ever when it came to soccer in the USA, it would take someone with a belief in the game and the willingness to gamble to make a difference. David Downs, now Executive Director of the USA 2018/2022 World Cup bid, but in 1991 a senior executive at ABC, was charged with exploring how the network might profitably secure and air the event. He knew ABC could do a better job than TBS who carried and some would say "butchered" the event in 1990, but his advertising guys were less than convinced and certainly not willing to give up the revenue surrounding their afternoon "soaps", while his bosses had little appetite for any financial risk. This was certainly not a recipe for success in the TV rights business. At the end of the day the approach was simple: ABC approached all the World Cup sponsors with a fait accompli – you commit to buy "x" amount of advertising time, upfront, guaranteed and we will go to FIFA to acquire the rights and broadcast the games. If you don't, we won't. Left with the possibility that they could have spent millions on acquiring the rights to a World Cup no one would see on television, the sponsors willingly stepped up to the plate. ABC counted $11m in commitments and offered FIFA $11m for the rights, it was that simple!

One final hurdle, however, had to be overcome before everything was wonderful in the World Cup 94 television world. With no commercial interruptions, how were they going to fit in the advertising they had just sold?

Viewers were furious in 1990 when TBS would switch to advertising during the match, missing goals, corners and free-kicks, creating a backlash they could have done without. Univision took a different tack running "crawler adverts" under the broadcast which, while better than cutting to commercials, looked a little amateurish. Somehow the sport had to work out a way to convince its broadcast partners and sponsors to give up some of their traditional 30-second commercial time and let the game run advertising free through each half. The solution devised by ABC or SUSAP (both laying claim) was a clever one. Instead of commercial interruptions, sponsors were given five minutes of logo time placed directly on the screen, and in-game announcements and recognition from the commentator. Games were wrapped with a 10-minute pre-show, a 15-minute half-time show and a 10-minute post game, during which commercials would be aired (crammed) in. It was not perfect and not what sponsors were used to but it worked, and today, this is the preferred route for all soccer broadcasts. SUSAP claim that their broadcast of the USA versus Germany game on 18 December 1993 on Sportschannel America was the first ever commercial free, English-language broadcast of a soccer game in the United States, while ABC claim that its broadcasts of World Cup 94 represented it. Only two things are fact here: (1) that it doesn't really matter and (2) that the Germans won!

Live long enough to collect your pension

What was little known in the run-up to the World Cup was that Rothenberg and his team actually gave serious thought to broadcasting some of the key matches, certainly those involving Mexico, Brazil, Argentina or Italy on Pay-Per-View. With the knowledge of the revenue being earned by major boxing events, Rothenberg estimated that World Cup 94 might be able to generate $160m, which after paying the local operators 50 percent, would leave $80m to be shared between the English language and Spanish language broadcast partners. Convinced it could work and figuring it worth a trip to Mexico City to visit with Univision's owner Televisa, Rothenberg jumped on a plane. While $40m sounded attractive, he was smartly made to understand that forcing the Hispanic fans to pay to watch their beloved teams in the most important soccer tournament in the world was not a clever move for anyone looking to be around to collect his pension. There are some things you just do not mess with and Hispanics and their World Cup coverage is certainly one of them. This was sound advice, duly accepted.

The World Cup arrives

The stadiums were ready, the tickets sold, the sponsors on board, the media accredited, broadcasters scheduled, dignitaries and kings were en route. President Clinton was to grace both the opening ceremonies and the first game between Germany, the 1990 winners, and Bolivia at Soldier Field in Chicago. His presence required 50,000 plus fans to single file through just two metal detectors.

It was commonly felt that the future of soccer in the United States rested on how well the USA competed and played at World Cup 94. The players knew it, the media hyped it and the pundits and cynics claimed that it was the single shot the sport had to capture American hearts. Brad Friedel, in *Soccer International Magazine* stated "We feel like we are ambassadors for the game and we want to try and get the people excited the way they got excited about the USA Hockey Team in the 1980 Olympics". Derek Armstrong followed up with "if we don't get out of our group we will have done nothing to help the progression of the sport in the USA. No host country has ever failed to get to the 2nd round and the USA did not want to be the first".

Well, if early 1994 games were an indication, the team would be lucky to get a point in its group, let alone qualify out of it. With just a month to go before its first appearance, the USA had played 14 games, winning just three, tying seven and losing four. A 1–1 tie with Moldova, a 2–1 loss to Iceland and depressing 2–0 loss to Chile were not instilling confidence in the powers that be. Could all the money they had spent on preparation, putting players under contract, building national training centers, traveling the world to seek competition be about to blow up in their faces! Well, it wasn't looking good! Bora however remained consistent; judge us at the World Cup, not now. He had never deviated from his 1991 statement "when we need results we will get them". He knew that many of his foreign-based players had been missing for most of the year and that, once back, his team would improve. They returned in time to play Mexico on 4 June, two weeks before their opening World Cup game against Switzerland, helping the US to a 1–0 victory in front of 91,000, mainly Mexican, fans: a new sheriff, a big game and a confidence inspiring win.

As the World Cup neared, much had to happen for it to be deemed a success. The USA team had to be successful; the event had to make money, fans needed to not just have tickets but actually turn up and television ratings had to be good. If these were achieved, the lasting legacies should fall in place. Equally though, World Cup 94 had to make lifelong fans of the millions of people that would attend live games, and the tens of millions that would be watching on television. It had to establish heroes, American Soccer heroes: Wynalda, Lalas, Balboa, Harkes and Ramos had to break through as major sports figures, idolized and adored by fans everywhere, fans that could not wait to see their stars again in a town near them once MLS was launched. Because above money, above media, and above all else, the legacy of World Cup 94 had to be a nation of fans baying to see more soccer, lining up to buy season tickets, proudly walking down streets wearing their new MLS team jersey. World Cup 94 had to turn America into a nation of soccer fans.

They certainly turned out in unprecedented numbers to support the Red, White and Blue, who, despite being burdened with gaudy stars and stripes uniforms, gave their fans a set of incredible performances, just as Bora had predicted. There were 73,425 crammed into the Silverdome in Detroit to see them draw 1–1 with Switzerland; 93,194 to see them stun the strongly favored Colombians 2–1 at the Rose Bowl in LA and another 93,896 to see them lose 0–1 against Romania at the same venue. These were stunning sell-out crowds, considering that just five years earlier only 3,000 fans turned up to see their 1990 World Cup qualifier against Trinidad and Tobago in the same city. A little un-American really, but all anyone in US Soccer hoped for at the time was that the team would qualify out of its group. In the grand scheme of things this could be deemed a success, particularly as Colombia led by Carlos Valderama was quietly being tipped to possibly win the whole thing. It was beyond anyone's hopes that results would conspire to create a 4 July

Independence Day showdown between the USA and eventual winners Brazil: a game that was broadcast live to a vacationing America – 84,177 fans showed up and 13.6 million viewers tuned in, easily surpassing ratings for the NBA Finals and Wimbledon that year. The narrow 0–1 loss was softened by the standing ovation and ringing cheers as the players left the field battered and tired but proud of their achievements.

For the US team, the tournament was over but this did not stop the event steamrolling on with record attendances and powerful viewership. The final game, Brazil versus Italy, in truth a cagey, dull affair, drew 92,000 fans to the Rose Bowl and 14.7m viewers to their sets, making it the most watched soccer game in US history. (This was enough to make ABC quickly pay $22m for the rights to the 1998 World Cup in France, a decision they were to come to regret.)

With typical World Cup confidence, Rothenberg had promised Downs great ratings, which coming in 1992, had the wizened hard-nosed ratings executives at ABC and ESPN politely smiling. When the dust had settled and the ratings released, it would be seen that the numbers were far beyond anyone's expectations, and anyone's logical calculation. Bora had done his job, the USA team had done their job and the World Cup had once again proved itself as the most exciting and watched sports event in the world.

Financially the event was an overwhelming success, generating $350m in revenue and returning a profit to World Cup 94 Inc of $60m, significantly more than anyone had predicted or could ever have hoped for. The money was placed into an independent not-for-profit company called the United States Soccer Federation Foundation Inc, formed for just such a purpose. Over the next 15 years, the Foundation was to invest millions of dollars in worthy soccer causes and issue grants to build facilities and programs throughout the country. Controversially, it also loaned Major League Soccer $5m to fund its delayed start up, which caused some controversy among the rank and file. Not quite the purview of a not-for-profit organization but as launching a new professional league was one of the main demands that FIFA exerted when it gave the US the World Cup, there is an argument for saying it was the right thing to do. (Considering the league would go on to lose $250m in its first four years, it ended up being a drop in the bucket.)

As World Cup 94 came to a successful conclusion amidst fanfare and accolades from around the world soccer, the USA was basking in the glory of what had been achieved. When the media went home and offices closed down it was time to reflect on the reasons it had been successful.

Here are ten reasons that I think were critical:

1 **The US national team and its players**

   At the end of the day it's all about players and teams and winning. It was critical for fans, sponsors, and the success of World Cup 94 itself that the USA were not embarrassed or blown away on the field. Fortunately for all concerned from 1991 to 1994 the USA was blessed with a group of players and a team that are in my mind the best this country has produced, either before or since. Not only did they compete, they competed well, won frequently and fought hard when they lost. To a man they understood the game, its history and the importance of what they were doing. They arrived battered and anonymous from Italia 90 but by 4 July 1994 were playing against Brazil in the round of 16 in front of 82,000 fans and 13.6m TV viewers (Table 3.1 illustrates the increase in attendances). Along the way they had claimed the Gold Cup, beaten Ireland, Portugal, Mexico and, famously, England and as promised, qualified out of their first-round group to keep the US dream alive and the Americans excited. (The decision to put the team into a Residency Camp the Federation could not afford (insisted upon by Gulati) and to treat them as a Club Team paid huge dividends.) Many would go on to play a significant role in the sport in later years but soccer owes a tremendous debt of gratitude for what they achieved during the early 1990s. (An end of tournament bonus check out of the $60m might have been a nice gesture.)

2 **Bora**

   He delivered exactly what he promised. Hiring a foreign coach was an inspired and necessary move. This was a tough decision with a lot of negative political consequences for those that made it. Bora promised a lot, delivered a lot both

Table 3.1 USA national team attendance 1990–94

A "Club team" home schedule

Year	Games played	Total crowd	Average crowd	US Cup crowd	v. Mexico crowd
1990	11	198,385	18,035	n/a	5,261
1991	14	292,951	20,925	39,503	45,261
1992	12	233,618	19,468	24,324	no games
1993	28	418,863	14,959	45,250	23,927
1994	22	648,276	29,467	86,173	92,216

Notes: The USA played a lot of smaller games over the four years to give players much needed experience: this drove the averages down. Meaningful matches such as US Cup averaged over 40,000 during the period. Considering my first match was a critical World Cup qualifier against Trinidad in 1989, with just 3,000 fans in the stadium, it was clear just how far the sport and Team had come.
*World Cup Final Games.
Source: US Soccer.

on and off the field and played a style of soccer that excited crowds when it was needed most. US Soccer went out on a limb and won.

3 **Alan Rothenberg**
The right man at the right time. The sport needed to become professional and needed a leader with a strong vision, personality and strength. He provided all of this and while many of the constituent members of the sport were not big fans, he elevated the professionalism of the sport and everyone around him. (He was paid a reported $7m plus bonus that many resented, but was worth every penny. I would have done it for $5m however.)

4 **Soccer USA Partners**
They risked millions to stage and broadcast US national team games when no one was interested in watching or corporations sponsoring. They changed how the sport was sold in America and created packages that sponsors could understand and buy while delivering the "soccer mom" and "Red, White and Blue".

5 **Legal "smarts"**
LeTellier wrote a professional bid document and also secured control of the trademarks and licenses for World Cup 94. This allowed them to generate millions of dollars in incremental revenue underpinning the $60m legacy. The decision to play in nine instead of twelve stadiums: priceless!

6 **FIFA**

Their vision to grant the World Cup to the USA: the sense to interfere with the election in 1990.

7 **Werner Fricker**

He fought with FIFA and ultimately lost. But he had the courage, vision and belief in the first place to attempt to bring the World Cup to the USA, without it there would be no reason for the book.

8 **Television**

David Downs going cap in hand to sponsors bringing the games to television and allowing 32 million to watch USA versus Brazil live on 4 July. And Univision for showing all 52 games live.

9 **Ticketing program**

It was critical that stadiums were full. A cleverly orchestrated and creative ticketing program ensured this. Providing $1,000 VIP tickets was brave and lucrative.

10 **US soccer fans**

They purchased millions of tickets and attended every game, whoever was playing. Seventy percent of all tickets were sold in the USA. Thirty-two billion fans around the world witnessed full stadiums and a glimpse of what might be. Whatever their ethnicity, whatever their demographic status, they embraced and celebrated the event making it the most successful World Cup in history.

CHAPTER 4

Soccer goes Professional: The Launch of Major League Soccer

In the summer of 1994 there was no other place to be, or sport to be associated with, than soccer in the USA. Basking in the glory of an incredibly successful World Cup, fans were primed, players motivated, media intrigued and the names of Lalas, Meola, Harkes, Balboa and Ramos tripped off the tongues of sports fans and media pundits nationwide. The timing was perfect, the country ready with FIFA and the world waiting for the sport to explode.

In the perfect world, America's top players would have rolled out of World Cup 94 with long-term contracts to play in Los Angeles, New York, Chicago and Washington DC. The 3.5 million tickets sold at World Cup 94 would have translated into packed stadiums and waiting lists for season tickets, every newspaper would have a dedicated soccer writer, every TV station covering the great plays and goals of the day. FIFA of course had made it an almost mandatory condition of granting the World Cup that a new Division 1 professional league be formed: a great mission, but easier said than done. Hosting a World Cup was one thing, building and sustaining a new professional league, particularly in a country that was an economic graveyard for most new professional sports ventures, quite another. One thing was certain however, the confidence and hubris that had allowed US Soccer to stage one of the greatest World Cups ever was now to be diverted to launching Major League Soccer and come what may, they would.

True to their word, a league would launch in 1996 amid great fanfare and hype. By 1999 it would be on its knees hemorrhaging cash in a death spiral of falling crowds, plummeting viewers, sponsor defections and a "fight to the death" legal battle with its players. Each on their own would be enough to bring the league crashing down, but in combination this was almost fatal! By 2009, buoyed by a new commissioner and business plan, the league would be ready to announce its 18th team, have nine new soccer stadiums either open or being built, see the Seattle Sounders draw 30,000 fans per game, see two million fans attend a "summer of soccer" that included Barcelona and Real Madrid and be sitting on a television contract that actually paid them money! This was the equivalent of being 3–0 down at half-time, a man short and kicking uphill (against the wind) in the second. Major League Soccer mounted one of the great off-field comebacks in American sports business history. It has a few tired legs, some experienced heads and two or three young players exciting the crowds. It has a strong substitute's bench and a few irons in the fire for expanding the roster. The manager is street smart, the owners have invested heavily and the fans are beginning to believe. But enough of the soccer metaphors – Major League Soccer's greatest achievement over the past 15 years has been that it survived at all!

To examine and measure the successes and failures of MLS we have to look at the steps it willingly took, the steps it was forced to take and the compromises and choices it had to make to stay alive and prosper. To do so we need to go back to the very beginning. Fortunately for readers, that beginning was barely fourteen seasons ago but for all those involved, including investors, management, marketing executives, ticketing sales, coaches and general managers, people in the trenches, every day each season left its "mark". Cut open those that were there from the beginning and you will see a ring for each poor crowd, lousy television rating or lost championship hopefully matched (depending on the team) by the great years of play-off victories, unexpected crowd surges, sponsor acquisitions and ultimately Championship rings. But for most in MLS it has been a long hard road.

Major League Soccer was incorporated as a limited liability company in Delaware on 24 July 1995, so clearly it was never going to be ready to pounce on the euphoria of 1994. It's not certain what impact (if any) this delay had on the League's ultimate success and while not perfect it was simply too ambitious to expect that the USA could stage a World Cup and attract 12 investors to launch a new risky professional soccer league at the same time. FIFA had actually wanted the league to start in 1992 to seed the ground for the World Cup, as leagues do everywhere else in the world. This however was the USA and the newly elected Rothenberg, a veteran of professional sports leagues and who, as an owner of LA Aztecs, had witnessed the collapse of the old NASL, soon realized it was just too much to take on. Rothenberg informed FIFA of this before putting the launch on the back burner, to be revisited at a later date when the World Cup was on track and looking like it actually might succeed. This was certainly not the case in 1992.

After the success of US Cup 93 however and the World Cup tickets sales program, it was becoming pretty clear that 1994 was going to work just fine and actually might "blow the roof off". Sleeping easier, Rothenberg let it be known within his law firm that he was looking for "volunteers" to help write and construct a business plan for the launch of a new professional soccer league. Mark Abbott (now President of MLS) and Ivan Gazidis (now CEO at Arsenal) stepped up. Beginning in one office and a sequestered broom cupboard, they set about what must have been an exciting diversion from corporate litigation and the requirement to review "what's his name" versus "what's his name" in some landmark but ultimately deathly boring case. Their days were now to be filled with "soccer" – what could be better?

A clean sheet of paper

The seeds for what is now the business and operating structure for Major League Soccer were sown as far back as the early 1970s. Rothenberg acting as an anti-trust lawyer and involved in various NBA and NHL lawsuits, as well as owning a team in the North American Soccer League (NASL), coming to the conclusion that there must be a better and more efficient way for professional leagues to operate. Experience with the 1984 Olympics and then the 94 World Cup cementing in his mind that, given a clean sheet of paper, there was only one way any league should be structured and that was as a single entity with centralized control of players along with many of the key revenue streams and costs. Instead of twelve individual franchises (which experience had shown often acted with extreme self interest and could be leveraged in a myriad of ways detrimental to the overall league) investors in MLS would be asked to purchase one twelfth of a "single" company that owned all 12 teams. Each investor would then be given the rights to operate a team in a given protected geographic area. It was new, it was contentious and it was borne out of experiencing the challenges faced and mistakes made by the current "Big" American Leagues and those that paid the ultimate price and failed – including, of course, the North American Soccer League. This simple structure has been at the heart of the League's success and, more importantly, its survival ever since. It equally has been the catalyst and breeding ground for a battle with its players that could still yet bring the league crumbling down.

While criticized as a way to control player wages and restrict free movement, which of course it did, the structure was not devised with this sole purpose in mind. Controlling wages was certainly an issue but not the only and certainly not the over-riding one. At the very core was the belief that MLS wanted all of its investors to be working together sitting around the same table when important decisions regarding the league's future were made. It did not want a maverick owner outspending every-one else or another deciding to downgrade the team to part-time or minor league status. It wanted to be in control of whether it could move failing teams to new markets (without the fear of lawsuits). It wanted to be able sign national television agree-ments without fighting with local owners and wanted to be able to package and sell national sponsors without being ambushed by its own teams. In short, it wanted to be able to make the big decisions, ones that impacted the success and failure of the league, around a table with investors who were true business partners, rather than independently motivated franchise owners. While new and innovative, the "structure" became a critical part of the investment pitch and instantly appealed to owners who liked the control it afforded while providing the "we are all in it together" approach to building a league, particularly when that league was in a sport they didn't really understand. It would mean leaving a few egos at the door and the approach did seem more suited to a 1970s Soviet league (where of course everything was shared) but overall the structure brought experienced and successful businessmen together in a collective partnership unlike any other league in America and laid the foundation for its survival and ultimate success. It wasn't perfect of course and was challenged almost immediately by a group of a players filing a "restriction of labor movement lawsuit", an attack that while unsuccessful nearly brought the league to an end. More about this later, but the issue of player movement was to dog the league throughout its first 14 seasons and as the parties enter a new 2010 collective bargaining agreement, still does, with those dreaded words "player strike" looming.

With a structure in place it now needed an investment pitch that would excite. The value proposition was straightforward: with the huge number of kids playing, the increasing growth and importance of the Hispanic community and the fact that millions of tickets had been sold in the World Cup, now was the time to jump on board the soccer bandwagon and secure an ownership stake in a new Professional League that was set to capture this explosion. It sounded good, but in early 1994 not good enough – they wanted proof. It became very clear that before committing serious dollars, investors wanted to really make sure that soccer had actually "arrived". They wanted to see a successful World Cup 94 but more importantly they wanted to see a successful US National Team and the emergence of American stars that would fill stadiums, drive television ratings and excite sponsors. Fortunately, the event and US Team were to exceed all expectations and investors could not have failed to be impressed by the crowds, the performance and the stratospheric television ratings. The three-and-a-half million fans that attended would surely translate into attendance for MLS making World Cup 94 the best interactive sales brochure any new league could have dreamed of? So far so good!

Thanks for the tickets and goodbye

While the league was out presenting to investors, the World Cup 94 sales group, many of whom would go on to form the nucleus of the MLS sales team, were out searching for the corporate partners whose commitment the investors would want. Taking advantage of the fact that every soccer sponsor in the country would be at the World Cup Final, MLS hosted a gala presentation to America's corporate elite. Anticipating that "drunk" on the exposure and overwhelming success of the event, they would arrive, checkbook in hand ready to buy the next great step in soccer's inevitable rise to the top. They gave a slick professional presentation highlighting that this was just the beginning: the touch paper lit, they stood back and waited for the onslaught of marketing executives, pens in hand, fighting to be the first to sign on the dotted line. Remember the soccer gods? Well there also exist equally cruel "marketing gods". Just when you think the stars are aligning and a deal imminent it "blows up" and vanishes (I speak from a wealth of experience on this). Well on the eve of the 1994 World Cup Final, Major League Soccer's sponsorship dreams were "blowing up" everywhere as corporate giant after corporate giant rejected the offer to "come on board" – a huge setback. It was to be the first indication to those involved that there was a world of difference between hosting and marketing a "must see" world class event and launching a weekly soccer league. It was also to be a telling insight into the harsh reality of the American sports sponsorship world. Paraphrasing it goes something like this: "Hey this World Cup thing worked out really great, we got a lot of exposure and sold a lot of stuff, my boss loved the tickets by the way and those US boys were fantastic". Coming back for 95? "No, we're allocating our budgets elsewhere next year, the Olympics are coming in 2006 and NASCAR is really getting big … thanks though". In reality it was an easy decision for World Cup sponsors to make. They had already gambled on soccer once and hit the jackpot with World Cup 94, why roll the dice again? For as much as American fans love big events, so too do American sponsors, and coming back to soccer in 1995 was like going back to the scene of a great party the day after: a little flat. For MLS and its two lead sponsorship executives Randy Bernstein and Kathy Carter it was an indication that the show was over and a new reality was about to set in.

In fairness to MLS it wasn't just the league that lacked appeal following World Cup 94, sponsors departed the sport en masse, citing many of the same reasons. (This is a lesson to any agency representing sports properties: try not to have all your sponsorships agreements end at the same time on the same day in the same year. The results can be catastrophic!) With sponsors baulking and investors yet to be convinced, Rothenberg made the not unexpected announcement that the league would delay its launch until 1996.

It wasn't all doom and gloom however, with both Nike and Budweiser stepping up to partner and ESPN agreeing to broadcast its games (for a price). Nike recognized it had been out of soccer too long and if it wanted to truly be a global brand had to get in, and Budweiser had been a long and loyal supporter of soccer in the USA dating back to the "dark days". ESPN agreeing to air games was a big step, even if the league did have to agree to pay for all of its own production costs. A television contract was critical to the league's credibility and now they had one.

The decision to push back the launch date to April 1996 gave the league a much needed chance to regroup, refine their investment pitch and find a fresh sponsorship pool to fish in. With the World Cup now over MLS moved offices to New York City, the home of the NFL, NBA, MLB and NHL, and the undoubted sports capital of America. They made it clear that they too wanted to be seen as "Major" and borrowed $5m from the Soccer Foundation to appear so!

Two tickets and a bit of food – that will be $300m please

MLS history (and hopefully this book) will show that the single most important event in US Soccer outside of the incredible success of World Cup 94 was the decision by Rothenberg to send two "free" tickets to the Italy versus Brazil final to Phil Anschutz. A nice seat, some great hospitality and tremendous crowds convinced him that Major League Soccer could work. What could not have been forecast at the time however was that it would be Anschutz's involvement as an investor and his decision in 2002/3 to carry the financial burden of owning six teams that would save the league from collapse and following the NASL into the annals of another failed attempt to launch soccer in the USA. I am sure the tickets and hospitality were the best the World Cup had to offer and that Anschutz had a great view of the game and a cool drink to quench his thirst, for over the next 10 years Rothenberg's hospitality would, as Anschutz jokingly relayed to him, cost him over $300m!

Who else is in?

As the league regrouped and repositioned it took the time to refine its investor pitch. First off the table was the requirement that the investors commit to building soccer-specific stadiums. It sounds a strange request considering the future of soccer now rests on building as many as possible. The league knew as early as 1992 the importance of teams having their own stadiums and even had World Cup 94 facilities designers scope out and design a turn-key "soccer stadium in a box" concept that investors could buy and have built. This was a great idea but ultimately was way too risky a venture for investors who feared that if the league failed they would be relegated to staging Sunday morning swap meets to recoup their money. Also off the table was the plan to acquire a broad array of additional soccer rights and properties including valuable television rights, again a risky and uncertain proposition that added millions to the initial investment. With these two demands eliminated, the pitch was stripped down to an understandable, controllable and, more importantly, affordable pitch. (It does of course raise the question of whether MLS should have forced investors to support the stadium plan or postponed the launch until it found a group of investors who would. Again business school logic would say yes, but had they done so chances are the league would never have got up and running. The best strategy sometimes is to just start!)

With a new more palatable "pitch", investors started to appear (or re-appear). Early on the horizon came John Kluge, head of Metromedia, a New York-based media conglomerate, together with the Kraft family, owners of the New England Patriots. The latter were enamored by the atmosphere and impressive crowds surrounding World Cup games hosted in Boston and the wonderful night for US Soccer when the USA humbled England (on field performances can sometimes have an unseen impact on business). Actually first to the table were Lamar Hunt and family, owners of the NFL Kansas City Chiefs and long-serving passionate soccer people. Lamar, seduced by soccer's allure after watching the 1966 World Cup Final, was to go on to own the Dallas Tornados in the old NASL and attend (with his family) every World Cup since 1966 (barring Argentina 1978 when kidnap threats kept them away). Hunt was also keen from day one to build a stadium and would have done so in 1996/7 had others followed. Clearly huge soccer fans, the incredible success of World Cup 94 banished to the background the huge personal losses incurred in the ill-fated NASL and once again reignited the belief and faith that professional soccer could "make it".

It was always going to be tough to get the first wave of investors on board with the common refrain "I am interested, but who else is in?". No one it seemed was keen to take on the task alone. Prospective investors knew this was a high-risk venture and wanted to make sure they had like-minded and financially capable investors in it with them. The Krafts were happy to invest knowing their respected business colleagues Kluge, Subotnik and Hunt were involved and vice versa, all early commitments seemingly contingent on the league delivering the other "investor names". By the spring of 1995, plenty of investor names "were in" including the man who would eventually go onto to save the league – Phil Anschutz – and the league looked like it might become a reality after all. It would take until October 1995 and a slew of meetings at the Kluge-owned Empire Radisson in New York before the contracts were papered and checks collected, but with the league now funded, it started in earnest with the planning. Which was just as well, because a fixed launch date of April 1996 left them just six months to plan everything.

The initial class-A partners, meaning those investors who agreed to pay $5m and in return were able to share in equal measure the profit and losses generated by the league, were: Phil Anschutz, a Denver-based multi-billionaire, who purchased the rights to a Denver Colorado team (and the rights to a second team in Chicago to be launched at a later date though he kindly paid $5m upfront for the privilege); The Kraft family through Kraft Soccer LP, owners of the New England Patriots who were granted rights to a team that would play in their NFL stadium in Boston; Lamar Hunt, owner of the Kansas City Chiefs NFL team, who was granted rights to operate teams in both Kansas City and Columbus; and John Kluge and Stuart Subotnik who, through their vehicle the Empire Soccer Club, secured the rights to run a team in New Jersey along with an option to buy a second team in New York City (at a fixed $5m). In addition, Los Angeles Soccer Partners, headed by Mark Rappaport, secured the rights to a Los Angeles and Washington Soccer LP headed by Kevin Payne and bankrolled and managed by API Soccer and related investors, including the famed investor George Soros, were given the Washington DC rights. In short, seven teams were assigned to investors with the hope that three new investors might be found before the season started, which however didn't happen.

How do we make money?

It had become very clear early in the search that the "single entity structure" was a strong motivating factor in convincing investors to sign up. Now on board, it was important to clarify just exactly how they would make money. Ultimately, the new owners had two responsibilities: (1) to run and operate their own local teams and (2) to provide the necessary funding for the league to function at the central level. The understanding was that everyone would share in the central costs (and profits) while individual owners would cover the costs and enjoy any profits surrounding operating their local team. In the early years it was estimated that the league would require $2m a year from each owner until it reached profitability and most local teams would need $5m–$8m in operating expenses to run efficiently. It was never going to be an easy balance to strike deciding which revenue streams should go where: for example who kept ticketing revenue? How was sponsorship money to be split? Who paid players? Who covered team travel? – along with twenty other similar decisions. It was all very well poring over spreadsheet scenarios but in truth the league was new, the single-entity structure was new and, to most owners, soccer was new. In the end, best guesses were made and compromises reached. A plan was put in place that would hopefully allow the league to grow and prosper and the local teams to make money, neither, however, would happen.

From the outset, it was always intended that player salaries would be paid centrally by the league. As a result, one team could not outspend another on the field, leaving the winner being the team that could hire the best coach, sell the most tickets, draw the most fans and run their operations most efficiently.

The following revenue share was put in place as the league began play (Table 4.1):

Table 4.1 Revenue and costs splits between league and clubs as at 1996

Who gets what

Major League Soccer	%	Local Operating Clubs	%
Revenues		**Revenues**	
Local Ticket Revenue	30	Local Ticket Revenue	70
National Sponsorships	100	Local TV Broadcast	100
National Television Revenue	100	Local Sponsorships	100
Licensing Sales	100	Stadium Revenue	100
Player Sales and Loans	100	Overseas Tours	100
Costs		**Costs**	
Player Salaries and Transfer Fees	100	General Admin Costs	100
Game Official Costs	100	Local Marketing Costs/TV/Promo	100
League Office Expenses	100	Stadium Operating Costs	100
League Marketing Costs	100	General Manager and Coaching	100
MLS Insurance	100	Team Travel Costs	100

Source: Compiled from interviews.

We will evaluate the impact of these decisions later and the wisdom of the choices made. Suffice to say the individual teams would find it very hard in the early years to make money, as indeed would the league.

The marketers step in

With a structure and revenue-share model in place it was now time for the league to decide on the elements of the game that really mattered to the fans: the names of its teams, the design of its uniforms, the quality of the players it would sign, and the nature of the stadiums it would play in – the fun and exciting side of the sport. The lawyers and accountants could put their pens down, hand over to the marketers and let the work of establishing the brand and identity of the league and its teams begin. Team presidents, general managers and marketing executives huddled around white boards, lunch tables and in meeting rooms, wrestling with names that would resonate and excite the legions of fans they all hoped to attract. The major apparel brands Nike, Puma, Adidas and Reebok set their design teams to work to create uniforms that would reflect the heart and soul of a club, its message and rallying call and its identity and values – uniforms that would establish an emotional bond between the fans and the team that would last for decades. A bond that would be passed down from father to son in the time-honored way: their first game together, their first shared Cup Final and the unbreakable promise that the season ticket *will* be left to him in the will.

On 17 October 1995, all was unveiled at a gala MLS team uniform launch in New York, which was meant to set the soccer world alight. Unfortunately, after months of planning and arguing, most teams would get it wrong, unleashing on America, and sadly the world, a set of names and uniforms that would in some cases embarrass the sport and in others leave fans wondering if the people who came up with them had ever kicked a ball. Ultimately, it was a lesson in what can happen if you let "creative" minds run amok.

What's in a name?

Essentially, the teams had two alternatives: to go for the Anaheim Ducks, Colorado Avalanche and Charlotte Bobcats theory of naming or look towards the more traditional European style of naming as in United, City or Real. Seemingly a matter of preference, it ended up however being much more than that, setting the tone and, in some cases undermining the credibility, of many of the teams (and as such the league) for years to come. As was expected, most teams chose the former and unleashed on the world names such as, the New York "Metrostars" (yes with associated yellow taxi cabs in their logos – not some of Nike's most glorious work) and the Kansas City Wiz (unbelievable really) as well as Columbus "Crew", complete with men dressed in hard hats (a throw-back to the Village People). Others chose less "out there" names but clearly were looking to Americanize the sport: Los Angeles Galaxy (cosmic), San Jose Clash (bland), Tampa Bay Mutiny (piratey!) and the Dallas Burn (never got hot), as can be seen in Figure 4.1. American sports are of course littered with engaging names created to sell merchandise, and very successfully too, with the American professional leagues selling billions

Figure 4.1 Major League soccer logos at launch

in licensed merchandise every year. These leagues however are mature businesses with established names, solid fan bases and massive television exposure. America knows what the Yankees, Cubs, Cowboys, Lakers and Packers stand for and the decades of sporting history they represent. My sense is that MLS tried to become a marketing brand before it became a soccer brand, which was a big mistake.

It's easy to be a "back seat driver" when analyzing business start-ups, criticizing decisions made and offering sage advice on "what they should have done". Experience has taught me that paths taken are often the result of compromises made, for financial or a myriad of other reasons. Lessons however should be learned and there were a few to be gleaned from MLS.

First, it is very tough to get a new league launched and certainly very hard to attract the level and quality of sponsors required to support it. MLS had signed multimillion dollar licensing contracts with the major soccer apparel brands and this income was critical to the league's future finances and stability. The price of admission however appeared to be to let the brands do whatever they wished and take the league and its teams in whatever direction they chose. Following World Cup 94, there was a great buzz surrounding soccer in the USA and MLS became the battle ground for brands looking to capture the market and establish their position.

Nike were making their first moves into soccer and looked at the sport as being the new edgy, fashion-led street-wear brand of a new America, replicating what the "hip" California brands Massimo and Hurley were doing for "surf dudes". Who could argue with the company that gave the world "air Jordan" and "just do it" and were possibly the smartest marketers in the world? The answer was that someone should have, because even the best get it wrong sometimes.

Nike completely misread the US soccer market at the time, delivering to the New York Metrostars uniforms and logos that were a circus-like joke: taxi cabs and shooting stars hardly evoked the emotion and passion a father would want to pass down to his son, or something that fans would rally around when times were tough (and they were to be). Built on the quicksand of trite New York stereotypes the team was always going to struggle for credibility. If the Columbus Crew and Adidas had their time again, would they really put men in hard hats on their badge? And what of their female fans? And as for the Kansas City "Wiz", well that defies belief and doesn't need any comment (and in fairness was swiftly rectified). The league therefore launched with a series of team names that alienated many core American soccer fans, especially those that grew up supporting teams in Europe and Central and South America. Seeing these names and the marketing approach as just another attempt to "Americanize" soccer, they questioned whether the league would treat the sport they loved seriously. Some would say that to be successful in the USA, soccer had to be "Americanized" but they would be wrong, and history would prove them so.

Changes were of course made in later years and now in 2009 most have adopted a traditional and conservative approach, one that respects the game's global heritage and America's position in it. In 1996, Nike was new to soccer and it showed. Take a look at the clean, slick and traditional uniforms the US National Teams wear today and it is clear that the approach in 1996 was wrong (Figure 4.2).

Unfortunately however, it was hard to undo. Blame must also be apportioned to the league officials and indeed some of the club officials that went along with it. It's tough to resist some young "cool" design genius from Nike, Reebok or Adidas who is

Figure 4.2 Authentic and soccer-focused sample logos MLS 2010 season

telling you "this" is the next great color or soccer represents a new frontier in American sports. It's equally tough to resist the cash when you need it most, but resist you must.

Why? Because 200 miles down the road D.C. United did resist and four MLS Cup wins later they were thrilled they did. D.C. United! – the name says it all, simple, clear, and traditional. Its mission statement: to serve the community and win trophies. That's it. Announced in 1996, it is still the mission statement today honoring the international game and respecting the knowledge and sensitivity of true soccer fans living in the DC area. No gimmicks, no catchy phrases, no pictures of the White House or the Presidential seal and definitely no shooting stars. Everything the New York Metrostars was, D.C. United was not. The ownership group steadfastly refused to follow the lead the league and its sponsor were espousing.

D.C. United were not trying to change the game or reinvent soccer anew in America, it was not trying to launch the next "hip street soccer brand" – it wanted to launch a soccer club that would last a hundred years. It wanted to respect the international game and take its place within it. They chose simple uniforms that represented the traditions of Adidas, the decades-old German brand that at the time dominated soccer both in the USA and around the world: uniforms that were a simple black and red with a traditional logo. While maybe suffering a trip to the "Tower" for saying so (if the USA had one) the stars and stripes uniforms that Adidas unleashed at World Cup 94 let it be known that it too could conjure up its share of garish fare. In fairness it was either loved or hated and I would guess loved by the bandwagon fans, hated by the core fans, but it's just a guess!

So what's in a name? Well D.C. United went on to be one of the most successful teams in MLS history, winning four MLS Cups including the first two and being regarded as a model for all future clubs to follow, with one of the most passionate and loyal fan bases in the league. New York has stumbled from season to season with little on or off field success and a fan base that is at best tepid: in an area that is a soccer hotbed and as multicultural as any city in America. The uniform and logo design (again quickly changed) was only a small part of the reason for its demise and something that probably a winning team and consistent management group would have overcome, but the approach was symptomatic of the direction MLS took in the early years – a direction that was to lead them to the brink of collapse.

In 2005, the New York Metrostars were acquired by Dietrich Mateschitz, owner of the RedBull energy drink company, and who renamed the team the New York RedBulls. Acquired for an estimated $100m ($40m for the team and $60m for a half share in a planned new stadium complex) the purchase represented great new investment in the league while allowing Phil Anschutz to divest himself of one of the four teams he still owned. Having a vibrant wealthy new owner in the league and clearly one with a tremendous acumen for brand building looked like a great coup. If they could harness even one-tenth of the brand strength they had built for RedBull and bring it to bear on the underperforming New York team, then the league would be thrilled. Allowing it to name the team NY RedBulls however was a mistake and one the league should not have made. There was nothing wrong with the brand, consumers seem to drink gallons of it. And there was nothing wrong with naming the ground the RedBull Arena, it sounds cool and exciting. But naming a team after an energy drink, now that's a tough one. Teams need to be more than coat hangers for corporate messaging and if they are not, then they have no future. New York has reeled from yellow cabs and shooting stars to sugar-filled drinks and marketing hype, suffering a major identity crisis along the way and alienating an entire soccer community. New York should be the strongest soccer market in America and the New York team the most profitable and well supported team in the league. After all this is where the Cosmos ruled supreme. Maybe this was the issue with fans expecting, but not receiving, the return of the Cosmos. There is no doubt it is a tough sports market with competition from nine other major professional sports teams, but New York is a soccer city and they come out in their thousands to watch top class authentic and meaningful games. With a great new stadium coming, New York needs to rethink its marketing and branding, hold a contest to rename the team as quickly as possible, re-engage with the community and start afresh with a new 10-year plan for winning over fans. If they do, it could become one of the storied teams of the league. It starts however with a name. New York needs a soccer club not a marketing campaign!

What the hell is a Cyber Bat?

What about some of the other teams, the Kansas City "Wiz" for example? Well firstly what fan wants to be known as a "wizzer?" What actually does a "wizzer" fan pass down from father to son or daughter? The team never really got off to a great start with an average attendance in 1996 of just 12,878, falling to 10,686 (17 percent decline) by 2008. Fortunately they changed their name after just one year to the more respectable Kansas City Wizards. You have to wonder if they had their time again would they go with the "pointed hat and magic wand" approach? Probably not. The Tampa Bay "Mutiny" at least had a rebellious anti-establishment ring about it, but somehow managed to have a high-tech "Cyber Bat" as its logo, and yes it was called a "Cyber Bat". The corporate design "speak" for this goes something like this: "it represents the juxtaposition between the rise of techno-logy, youth culture, comic book heroes and the future of soccer". In plain soccer speak " inane nonsense", but through to Tampa's eventual closure in 2002 the Cyber Bat remained (a real shame its echo-location features could not find a stadium or investor for the team).

The Columbus "Crew", Dallas "Burn" and the San Jose "Clash" all suffered harshly in the second season slump, along with NY and Kansas, each averaging anywhere from 20–40 percent fall in attendance, only D.C. United, New England Revolution and Colorado Rapids (who in truth started from a low 10,213 and rose to 11,825) baulking the trend and gaining fans in 1997.

With the luxury of hindsight, it is clear that the league and many of its teams wholly underestimated the soccer education level and lacked understanding of its core fan base and their sensitivities to wanting to support teams that represented the international game as they knew and loved it. They attempted to take professional soccer to the general market and young kids before cementing it with their core audience. In doing so, they alienated those most likely to want to establish a long-standing bond with the team and who were not impressed with "hard hats", "shooting stars" and the "wiz". They came to look in the first year, were not overly impressed and did not return for the second.

Over the course of the next 15 years, MLS and US Soccer in general started to grasp the importance of staying true to the international authenticity of the sport. There is nothing wrong in adding an American "touch" but true fans, the ones the sport needs to grow, want to feel they are part of the global game they watch, consume and look up to. Many of the newer franchises have chosen names that reflect the history of their cities or the wishes of their fans – always a good idea. Toronto FC supported by a fanatical multicultural fan base resonates with authenticity of the city and the international understanding of its Canadian fans. The Seattle Sounders name was voted on by the very fans that now support the team in their thousands. Although originally not even on the voting sheet, the fans demanded the team be called "Sounders" as a nod to the semi-professional (USL) soccer team that the fans loved. Thirty-two thousand of them now turn up every game to support the MLS Seattle Sounders, fans that feel they have equity in the name and the club. A similar process took place in Philadelphia where a new club will start playing in 2010. Involving fans in every key step of preparation, the fans voted in the name "Union" and a snake with the motto "join or die" as their logo. It is pretty clear what the Philadelphia Union fans will be like! All of these new teams are setting a new direction for the league and increasing levels of fan inclusion.

There are many factors that lead to the development of a loyal and passionate fan base. In the early years of the league one has the right to ask just what strategic thought was given to the brand identity of the league and its teams. New teams and franchises might want to take heed and give some very clear thought to this important task. Think as a fan, not as a merchandiser or clever brand manager. Fortunately, it appears that over the years the league and teams have adjusted and accepted that their fan bases appreciate authenticity and relevance in their names. It is important not to be intimidated by some "hip" young brand guy or powerful brand looking to stake out a market position as the chances are neither knows as much about the sport and the direction it needs to go than you. Designers might convince you of the "hot" color for next summer, but will it be in 30 years? And in 50 years, will grown men weep tears over a lavender scarf, with a hint of blue.

Finding players: anybody want a game?

With a legal structure in place, investors on board, and for better or worse, team names and logos presented, the league now turned to ensuring it actually had some players. With final contracts not being completed until October 1995 and a firm April 1996 start date announced, the league had less than six months to find 250 players for 10 teams. It was actually more like four months as it was hoped the teams might get chance to train together before kickoff.

A league with "Major" in the title needed players that lived up to the name: players that would excite fans, score goals, make miraculous saves and deliver bone-crunching tackles, hopefully making believers of millions. For many, World Cup 94 was their first exposure to top-flight soccer and they were now coming back to see more. Therefore much rested on populating the league with players that could deliver a similar experience, but with just $25m in the transfer "kitty" and $22m to spend on total player salaries for the entire league, it was pretty evident they would be hard pressed. So what could the league buy with their limited funds? The answer was, of course, 250 players – it had to, unless they planned on playing five-a-side. The process itself was to end up being an incredible logistical as well as financial challenge, and while you would like to think it was all part of a well-orchestrated master plan, Ivan Gazidis openly admits it was more a mad panic and scramble to fill rosters than anything else, but a scramble that if they got wrong could sink the league.

First, and most importantly, they wanted to bring back the US players that had enthralled fans in 1994. These were to be the stars around which the league wanted to launch and the stars who it hoped would draw suburban soccer families to stadiums in their multitudes. Unlike the old NASL which was clearly populated with international players, the new MLS was about developing and promoting American players and all stops were pulled out to bring back those that mattered most: Lalas, Harkes, Ramos, Wynalda, Balboa, Meola and more. The league however could not survive on American talent alone and needed a Hispanic flavor that would appease the huge Latino community that it hoped to attract. Choosing the right Hispanic players was critical, as those chosen had to resonate with the community, be names that were recognized and revered and above all else, had to still be able to play, for token "has beens" would not sit well with the critical and soccer-knowledgeable Latino fan.

Into the league came Campos and Hurtado, placed in Los Angeles, home to over 10 million of their fellow Mexican countrymen. Carlos Valderama, the mercurial Colombian and true world star, headed to Tampa, Donnadoni from Italy headed not surprisingly to New York alongside New Jersey natives Ramos and Meola. The remaining American players were easier to assign, being more interchangeable in the minds of most US fans. Balboa apparently became a condition of the Anschutz investment in Colorado (having been thrilled and excited over his incredible overhead kick against Colombia in 1994). John Harkes returned from West Ham United to play for his old college coach Bruce Arena at D.C. United. Lalas, the most expensive of all American acquisitions, headed to Boston because he "liked the vibe". Roy Wegerle moved from Coventry City to Colorado Rapids and Eric Wynalda from VFL Bochum to the San Jose Clash. The strategy was clear, bring back the best Americans at all costs and then the best foreign players it could afford with what was left. There still however remained the challenge of filling out the rest of the spots. For this the league cast its net far and wide.

Prior to the end of 1994, over 400 players were placed under some form of preliminary contract to be offered the opportunity to play in the league. There wasn't a soccer player kicking a ball straight in the USA that seemingly wasn't looked at or a form of the game not trawled. Indoor, outdoor, college, semi-professional and local club players were signed in the hope that a pool of credible and watchable players could be assembled. Ultimately, 250 of these players were invited into a 10-day player combine in Irvine, California, in January 1996, where new MLS coaches could evaluate and assess their skills, the best of which were then invited to a player draft hosted in New York City just three weeks later. For those unfamiliar with the concept of a "draft", it is a quintessential American phenomenon of choosing players across teams: simply put all players in a line-up and the coaches take turns picking their first choice. The players line up again and the coaches proceed to pick their second choice and so on until all players are allocated. There's a lot more hoopla and media-generated tension, but ostensibly it is no different to how teams are selected in school yards and playing fields throughout the world. Everyone who plays knows the pride of being picked first and the abject terror of being the last to be selected, knowing that you would be stuffed in goal and blamed for everything that flies past you. The MLS draft was significantly more important and selective of course and I highly doubt the last one selected ended up in goal, but the principle remains the same. It would be fair to say some good and some not so good players attended a combine and made it through to the draft. Not ending up in goal was the number one pick, Brian McBride, who went on to lead the USA to a quarter-final place in the 2002 World Cup and later captain of Fulham, and Raul Diaz Arce, the number ten pick who signed for D.C. United and became part of the famous United "triangle" of Moreno, Etcheverry and Arce that dominated the first two seasons of the league and led D.C. to claim the first two MLS Cups.

With the final stage of player selection complete, the league and teams announced their rosters to the world and as kickoff approached the league included: two-thirds of the current USA National Team, a great accomplishment for the league and a promise kept to fans; a spattering of "named" internationals, including Carlos Valderama and Roberto Donadoni; Mexican icons Jorge Campos and Eduardo Hurtado; and a number of not quite so known but still good internationals. The league was then rounded out with college and semi-professional players because the rules say you need eleven players on the field and by March 1996, the $22m budget was running on fumes.

Transfer fees: the Americans still lag

While many players were free agents, some required transfer fees to be paid. The most expensive acquisition, the Bolivian Marco Etcheverry, cost $1.2m – the highest fee paid for any player in the league (see Table 4.2). If done correctly you usually get what

Table 4.2 Foreign versus American transfer fees 1996

30% more for a foreigner

Foreign	Transfer	American	Transfer fee
Etcheverry	$1.2m	Lalas	$500–$700,000
Campos	$1.0m +	Harkes	$500–$700,000
Valderama	$1.0m +	Ramos	$500–$700,000

Source: Compiled from interviews.

you pay for and in Etcheverry's case the league certainly did as he went on to be one of the league's all-time great players. D.C. United's Hispanic player strategy, whether by luck or informed scouting, resonated with Latino and Anglo fans alike and formed the foundation on which its passionate fan base was built. Get it right and it was clear the Hispanic fans would follow you everywhere; get it wrong and they will vanish, probably never to return. D.C. United got it right: good players, known in their community who could still play and play with passion. This strategy was undermined by meddling league officials who decided to move one of their most beloved and revered players, the El Salvadoran Raul Diaz Arce, to New England in an effort to create some form of league parity while diminishing the dominance of D.C. United. The move backfired. Apart from undermining the credibility of the league, it removed 4,000 El Salvadoran fans from the D.C. United fan base, fans that were to never return. It also gave rise to the opinion that the league was some central "puppet master" manipulating teams and interfering in things it should not, a dangerous and potentially devastating accusation to the very sophisticated and sensitive Hispanic fan base. (The El Salvadorans did actually return to RFK Stadium, home of D.C. United – four thousand turning up once to see Arce play for his new team, New England Revolution in the following season.)

Transfer policy: make them an offer they can't refuse, literally

Imagine the scenario: Manchester United offer $150m for Lionel Messi, Barcelona say no but the Spanish league decides it could do with the cash to offset some operating losses suffered last season. The owners get together and have a vote, 70 percent of them decide it's a great idea. Under MLS rules, Messi would be packing his bags and heading for rainy Manchester before the Catalan fans could hit the streets and block the airport. As compensation the league would give Barcelona a replacement at some stage in the future and life would go on. This of course could never happen in Europe where clubs own their own players, but for MLS in 1996 and indeed today, it's the way it works. Probably the most controversial, politically sensitive and contentious decision MLS made in establishing the single-entity structure was that all players would be employed directly by the league and not by the teams. The reasons were pretty straightforward:

1 MLS were very aware of the fact that most professional sports leagues in the USA were wrestling with spiraling salary demands that were either threatening to bankrupt their leagues or exposing them to debilitating player strikes.
2 Centrally controlled players and salaries meant maverick owners could not drive up wage bills as a way to "buy" success, a move made by the New York Cosmos that many claim brought down the NASL. The only way to do this was to take the control of such decisions out of the hands of individual owners, who might be tempted, by ego or belief, to set wage standards that were unsustainable for the rest of the league.
3 With players' salaries under control a huge "unknown" was removed from the risk equation for investors deciding whether or not to "take the plunge". Investors hate unknowns!
4 If the league was going to fail it would almost certainly do so in the first five years (or sooner). As such, if you do have the benefit of starting with a clean sheet of paper, why open yourself up to the one thing that could be the biggest contributor to that collapse?

It all made sense really, except if you're a player that is. If you were a top "must have" player the landscape was not too bad, but if you were not, playing in the MLS was more like an expensive hobby. Once the "big boys" had taken their share of the $1.1m salary cap it was very much packed lunches and coupon clipping for the rest. But at least they woke up in the morning and played soccer for a "living" with many having to admit that if it wasn't MLS it would more than likely be a nine-to-five job.

As all players were owned and paid by the league there was no competitive inter-MLS team transfer market and as such the only way coaches could change their player rosters (and hopefully fortunes) was to orchestrate player trades (swaps) – I will give you Rooney for Torres or Messi for your entire team, type of deals. This was not ideal for players and certainly not a way to get rich. Leverage is often everything in business and in 1996 the players had none. This is still true in 2010, unless of course they are the next Ronaldo!

Stadium strategy: "Is anyone out there?"

A big-time league with big-time aspirations and big-time plans to compete with the traditional American icons of sport of course needed big-time venues. The original business plan fully understood the importance of having stadiums that could capture the excitement and atmosphere of the sport as it was played around the world. Unfortunately such stadiums did not exist in the USA in 1996 and no one was particularly interested in taking on the financial risk of building one.

The owners were equally not interested in launching the league in small secondary stadiums fearing, correctly, that it would send the wrong message to sponsors and fans alike. Go big or go home permeates the American psyche and MLS were no different, particularly coming off a World Cup where fans poured into stadiums in record numbers. It was to be major media markets and major stadiums or nothing at all. This was further endorsed by two of its key owners, the Hunt and Kraft families, who both owned NFL stadiums that would directly benefit from having 20 or so extra games per season each. The decision therefore to go "big" was made and the gamble taken and in hindsight it is hard to see what other choice they had. On Saturday nights and Sunday afternoons these stadiums had to be transformed into the Nou Camps, Anfields, Old Traffords and La Bamboneras of their day. They had to capture the atmosphere and excitement that separates soccer from every sport in the world. They had to convince fans

sponsors return

Turned down by just about every World Cup and US Soccer sponsor in 1994 the MLS folks did what every good sales group would do, they went to their competitors! Battered and bruised by the poor response to the initial launch, MLS officials spent the majority of 1995 looking for a new set of sponsors that would see the merits of joining the soccer explosion that was taking place in the USA. For everyone involved in selling soccer in the USA (including yours truly) it was like starting anew. MLS's pitch was much as before, soccer being a way to reach the large suburban, youth-family audience that represented a wealthy and educated and therefore attractive demographic. But they weren't alone. I was heading up API Sponsorship and our team was out-selling the USA National Team program and the three million member United States Youth Soccer Association, and groups such as the American Youth Soccer Association (600,000 plus members) were out-selling their programs. The marketplace was fragmented and competitive as the individual properties fought for their dollars and without a World Cup to "cap off" a four-year sponsorship cycle, it was a tough sales landscape. Usually it amounted to whoever got there first, to present their side of the story as to the best way to reach the soccer market, won and through perseverance and making what seemed a "million" sales calls, the money started to flow back in. MLS's counter-selling strategy was paying off. With World Cup sponsor Sprint not interested, they went to AT&T, who were. When General Motors said no, Honda said yes. When Coke passed, Pepsi stepped up. Classic counterselling and done well. They further added Pepsi's Allsport sports drink, MasterCard, Bandai, and Fuji, which, when added to the soccer shoe and apparel brands gave them a healthy stable of prestigious sponsors for their launch. Sponsorships varied in value from $750,000 to $2.5m per year over a four-year cycle resulting in revenues close to $13m per year in 96 rising to $20m through 2000. The sponsorship story for MLS in the early years was a good one and as the league launched, it was looking every bit the major property it wanted to be.

MLS on TV, at a price

The brutal reality of soccer in the USA during this time was the fact that, despite the tremendous success of World Cup 94 and the impressive ratings on both ABC and ESPN, neither was prepared to gamble on buying the rights to air Major League Soccer (or indeed US Soccer). The parties did sign a three-year agreement in March 1994 to air 10 games on ESPN, 25 on ESPN2 and the Championship game on ABC, but the networks were not going to pay for the privilege of doing so. In a not untypical scenario for a new property, the league was forced to purchase all of its own airtime, pay for production and then recoup the costs by including them in their sponsorship packages. The good news was that the games would be broadcast; the bad news was that it would cost them a fortune. (MLS did actually receive a small rights fee in the early years with ESPN International paying them $200,000 rising to $450,000 to air the games overseas. So at least someone had faith.) The league faired a little better with the Spanish language network Univision; the signing of Hispanic icons Campos, Hurtado, Valderama, and Cienfuegos convinced them their audiences would tune in. They paid just $225,000 in 1996 rising to a $1m in 1998 but importantly they covered their own production costs, which was valuable. The relationship with the league would not be a good one and at times acrimonious and, by 2000 they would be gone.

It all kicks off: the season begins (6 April 1996)

So all was set! Investors were on board, teams allocated, players signed, stadiums rented, sponsor checks cashed and television time purchased. Major League Soccer, the next great attempt to launch professional soccer in the USA, was about to blast onto the American sports landscape. Excited fans lined up, new owners bristled with optimism, and an air of excitement and anticipation once again swept through the American soccer landscape.

MLS could not have wished for much more as the opening day numbers came in. Over 31,000 packed into Spartan Stadium to watch San Jose beat D.C. United with a good, late Wynalda goal: 69,000 showed up at the Rose Bowl to see LA Galaxy and its Mexican stars beat New York's Metrostars and its taxi cabs. In Dallas, 27,000 lucky fans were treated to an exciting 0–0 tie (could no one have had a quiet word with the coaches?) Valderama drew 26,000 Cyber Bats in Tampa while 21,000 bought a ticket to see the "Wiz" click their heels and beat Colorado. The final team to open their home season was the Columbus Crew who drew a very impressive 25,000 to witness their 4–0 hammering of D.C. United all in the very cozy confines of the 110,000 seat University of Ohio "football" stadium.

The season came to a close eight months later with the first ever Major League Soccer Cup Final, a game between Western Conference Champions LA Galaxy and Eastern Champions D.C. United, played in front of 34,643 at a rain soaked Foxboro stadium in Boston. Fans were treated to a game and a spectacle that would have graced the final for any league in any country in the world.

It rained like I have never seen before in Boston that day, more like a Malaysian monsoon than New England, but on a water filled pitch D.C. United came back from two goals down to win 3–2 on a headed goal by Eddie Pope that still lives inside the fabric of MLS history. The hazy TV images (straining to focus through torrential rain) beamed around the USA and the world showed a flashing header from a corner that, through the golden goal rule, would win the Cup for D.C. United. Benches emptied and elated coaches and players celebrated in the mud. It was the stuff of highlight reels and sports shows. It was the goal that launched a soccer dynasty in the USA and cemented the passion and loyalty of MLS's most fervent fans. Every D.C. United fan can remember the "Pope" goal and the glory it delivered, their love affair with the club which began at RFK Stadium was consummated that rainy day in Boston and that flashing near-post Pope header.

The opening MLS season was nothing more than an overwhelming success exceeding everyone's expectations both on and off the field. Over three million fans had turned out to games, with the league overall averaging 17,000. The MLS Cup Final was deemed an instant classic and attracted a healthy 1.4 rating on ABC and the winning goal was the stuff of highlight reels for years to come. International stars, Valderama, Cienfuegos, Etcheverry, Donadoni and Campos had strut their stuff alongside most of the US National team heroes from 1994. Sponsors were ecstatic, with Black Tie Gala Awards Dinners hosted, League Officials and owners feted, all basking in the glory of delivering their first full season, and what a season it was. Amidst all the hoopla and backslapping however something was wrong, something no one had spotted or predicted, something that convinced 550,000 fans not to return for season two.

1997–1998: where did they all go?

The wheels started to come off MLS as early as 1997 and worsen through 1999. The opening day attendance dropped by 30 percent in season two and would have been much worse had LA Galaxy not drawn 53,000 and New England 57,000 for their matches. Overall, average attendance for the season dropped a worrying 16 percent (to 14,619) and ominous signs were looming that certain teams were not resonating within their communities. More worryingly the average playoff attendance, games you would think would excite fans, plummeted 24 percent to 12,563. The customary second season slump that hits every professional league was in full swing inside MLS but there was nothing on the horizon to suggest that it would not escalate into a third season catastrophe and ultimately fourth season collapse. The season was "rescued" by a spectacular 57,431 crowd at RFK to see D.C. United repeat as Champions in a 2–0 win over Colorado (the heavens once again opening up).

The 1998 season would see the league stagnate (never a good word) holding its average attendance at around 14,000. The playoffs however with newly launched Chicago Fire storming to the final saw a sizeable 21 percent increase (to 15,280) with the final again drawing a spectacular 51,350 as Chicago handed D.C. United their first MLS Cup Final defeat in LA. The interesting point (and an insight into US Soccer), is that neither team were obviously Los Angeles based. While both teams brought some "away" fans, the majority in the stadium were general soccer fans or those with incurable "big eventism". With MLS in a slump it was hoped that the US National Team (full of MLS players) might rescue the season with a motivating performance at the France 98 World Cup – wishful thinking as it turns out. The team was a disaster both on and off the field, slaughtered by the press and regaled by fans. (More on this later but not one of US Soccer's finest moments.)

Overall, it was a terrible time for professional soccer in the United States with a general malaise descending over the sport. It would get worse.

If not D.C. United, then who?

At the end of the 1999 season, D.C. United lifted its third MLS Cup in four years; the next day they were promptly put up for sale! Unwilling to continue to meet the onerous financial responsibilities of operating their team, Octagon and its partners wanted out, sending shock waves around the league; for "if D.C. United could not make it then who could?"

The league was left reflecting that since 1996, opening day attendances had dropped 45 percent, average attendances were down 18 percent and playoff crowds down 6 percent (see Table 4.3). If that was not bad enough, TV ratings were in freefall, two of its key sponsors wanted out and total losses were being reported at a staggering $250m, with seemingly no end in sight. Now, three times MLS Cup winners D.C. United, the most respected and storied team in the League, the flagship and beacon for all things good, were in deep trouble and so was the league. Following its explosive start in 1996, just four years later it was looking tired, worn and rudderless and unless some serious changes were made it was "curtains". So, what was going wrong?

There were lots of reasons why the league was faltering, some self induced, some out of their control and others forced on them by financial reality.

Table 4.3 Average Major League Soccer attendances 1996–99

A steady decline

Team	1996	1997	1998	1999	% + /–
LA Galaxy	28,916	20,626	21,784	17,632	−39
DC United	15,262	16,678	16,008	17,419	+14.1
Columbus	18,950	15,043	12,275	17,696	−6.6
Kansas	12,878	9,058	8,073	8,183	−36.5
NY Metrostars	23,898	16,899	16,520	14,706	−38.5
Dallas Burn	16,011	9,678	10,984	12,211	−23.7
New England	19,025	21,423	19,188	16,735	−12.0
San Jose	17,232	13,597	13,653	14,959	−36.3
Colorado Rapids	10,213	11,835	14,812	14,029	+37.4
Tampa Bay	11,679	11,333	10,312	13,106	+27.1
Miami Fusion			10,284	8,689	−15.5
Chicago Fire			17,877	16,016	−10.5
Summary					
Regular Season Avg	17,406	14,619	14,312	14,282	−18.1
Playoff Avg	16,611	12,563	15,280	13,871	−16
MLS Cup Final	34,643	57,431	51,350	44,910	+30
Winner	DC United	DC United	Chicago	DC United	

Source: Compiled from MLS Net and Media Guides.

Stadiums: the Achilles heel

They knew their Achilles heel from the beginning! They even designed stadiums for investors to buy and had they shown the slightest level of interest, would have built them for them. For without soccer-specific stadiums, the league had little chance of making it. You could ask that if they knew this, then why even start? The answer was, of course, what option did they have – pack up their bags, tell FIFA sorry, give us the World Cup again and we'll have another go? Not if they wanted to keep their reputation intact, they wouldn't, and another World Cup? There was little chance of that.

First season average attendances were actually better than the league had predicted, but in vacuous NFL Stadiums, not even 17,000 of the most fanatical fans in the world would generate the atmosphere required to convert spectators to fans. The heartbeat and oxygen for every true fan in the world is the sense of pride and passion gene-rated in their home stadium and by the fellow believers they worship with. Defeat at your home stadium is unthinkable, being out-sung and out-supported, unforgivable. The songs, the culture, where you stand in the stadium, who you abuse, what to sing and when, are all passed down from generation to generation, fan to fan, father to son. Fanaticism and passion for every fan begins at the spiritual home and could not be replicated in a cavernous and rented, American football or college stadium. Hard-core fans were never going to accept it as a replica and new fans were never to get the opportunity to taste a "real soccer experience". (On another practical matter, these stadiums were expensive to rent, looked lousy on television with their football lines, forced teams to accept poor game times and gave little revenue share for concessions and parking.)

Table 4.4 highlights the dilemma faced by Major League Soccer in 1996. On an average day most stadiums were barely one-third full.

Table 4.4 Stadiums capacity figures for opening season MLS 1996

Cavernous stadiums barely 30 percent full						
Team	Stadium	Capacity	Opening Day	% Capacity	Season Average	% Capacity
LA Galaxy	Rosebowl	100,000	69,255	69	28,916	29
D.C. United	RFK	55,672	35,032	62	15,262	27
Columbus	Ohio Uni.	66,120	25,266	40	18,950	28
Kansas	Arrowhead	79,409	21,141	26	12,878	16
NY Metrostars	Giants	79,469	46,826	58	23,898	30
Dallas Burn	Cotton Bowl	88,125	27,779	31	16,011	18
New England	Foxboro	60,000	26,473	44	19,025	31
San Jose	Spartan	32,000	31,683	43	17,232	23
Colorado Rapids	Mile High	80,000	23,711	29	10,213	12
Tampa Bay	Tampa	65,657	26,473	40	11,679	17

Source: Compiled from MLS sources and online stadium sites.

Fans were not connecting

By 1999, many fans had just stopped coming. The games not exciting enough, the atmosphere not absorbing enough and the players not "star quality" enough to make it compelling. There was however more at play than just MLS and its stadiums.

Kids would rather play

In 1996, and still true today, the US Youth Soccer family and in particular the kids were really driven by organizing and playing the game rather than watching. For these families everything centered on their practice, their match or their tournament. Watching professional soccer, while a fun night out, was not a "must do" event on their cluttered family calendar. The league and many of its teams were to spend millions convincing them it should be, but were up against tough odds. They might come to a game with their team, have a hot dog and pepsi, jump up and down for a while, but when they go home, it's onto the couch with dad to watch his sports. Those soccer moms, already swamped with running a home, organizing teams, ironing jerseys, handling snack bars, running tournaments and managing a calendar for three other kids, all while holding down a job, were always going to be a tough group to convince. And particularly if dad wanted to go the Hockey game, a movie or watch College Football.

Why should we cancel practice?

There existed, and still does, a strong sense of entitlement, some justified some not, within many involved in US Youth Soccer living by the mantra "we were here first, and we will be here when you're gone". It would appear a pretty cynical and negative approach to helping the game in the USA. It is however possible to see where the mistrust comes from. Many leagues both indoor and outdoor have exploded onto the scene, having made big promises, only to subsequently implode, so why as such should MLS be any different? The only constant in most soccer communities in America was the fact that thousands of kids played and it was the local youth soccer clubs that organized how and when they did.

There was and is however a more ego and "protectionism" driven reason. Local youth clubs and leagues wield a lot of power and sway in the local market and control the actions of thousands of players. If a club coach says "we are going to a MLS game next month" the chances are the parents and kids will go. If the coach schedules a game or tournament then they do not. Every MLS team has to some degree to dance to the tune of youth soccer and dance well. Those that did sold tickets, those that failed did not. I emphasize here "sold tickets", for selling to youth soccer is a game by game "special event" exercise with kids and their coaches coming once, and if the team is lucky, twice a season. They are a critical and important demographic to attract and for many teams account for 40–50 percent of all sales. However, in 10 years' time, if this number is not closer to 10 percent the league will have not progressed.

A worrying story and one that has hopefully now passed by, centers on the results that came out of a US Soccer Annual General Meeting in 1998 in Hawaii and relayed to me by Hank Steinbrecher, the then General Secretary. For the first time the election for President and a variety of other posts was held online and it was decided to use the opportunity to poll the members on their preferences within the sport. What came back was shocking: less than 2 percent of the members had ever been to a MLS game, less than 5 percent to a US National Team game and less than 35 percent had ever watched the US Team on TV, and these were the guys running the sport. It would be a good poll to run again … with harsh penalties for failing to improve!

Losing Hispanics, where's Raul?

It was clear that the youth soccer market was proving very difficult to coral with key soccer "influencers", coaches and administrators in many markets hostile or apathetic. The saving grace would surely be the Hispanic fans who love their soccer. Unfortunately the league was also failing to deliver a product that met the challenging demands of this very critical group. Unlike the youth groups this fan base had very clear ideas of what they wanted from Major League Soccer; ideas that would be almost impossible to deliver and sustain. Hispanics wanted MLS to replicate what they left behind when they entered the USA, full stadiums, thronging masses, top-class players and games that resounded with meaning and tension. This group, more than any other, wanted to see culturally relevant players on "their" teams (which by delivering Campos for example, they initially did). They wanted a team that played exciting and attacking soccer and won, and that was just on the field. They also wanted to be courted with special promotions, concerts and double-header games. Soccer matches to them were day-long parties to be lived and experienced. Small crowds in large stadiums regaled with football lines was just not going to cut it. Equally, whether it was or wasn't, the quality of play was never going to be seen to be as good as "back home", and they voted with their feet when they thought it was not. Finally, this was a community who were most suspicious and cynical about the whole essence of the single-entity league structure. They often had a favorite player on their team and were unimpressed when the league meddled to meet, in their mind, non-soccer demands of salary cap issues. It reeked of corporate America rather than soccer and left fans of course asking "where's Raul?"

The ex-pats – back down the pub

Man United versus Liverpool, or New England versus San Jose – you choose. Unfair really as one was a decades old bitter rivalry and the other, well, was not. This is a problem that MLS faced then and still does today. The English Premier League, formed in 1992, was to begin its rise to economic prosperity and world television domination throughout the 1990s, while at the same time the MLS was trying to establish a foothold in the USA. Fueled by incredible television contracts the teams got stronger, the players "bigger" and the television exposure wider, forcing itself into bars and onto TV sets throughout America. At the same time the Champions League blossomed and suddenly there was an explosion of international soccer coverage for ex-pats to get their soccer fix. Not necessarily good at the time for MLS. Always going to be judgmental and cynical, this group would need a lot of convincing: empty stadiums and "inferior" quality would not do it. This "lot" was generally back down the pub before the game ended.

If you sit in the middle of the road

The league, through its decision to market to soccer families and young kids, failed to realize it would be better to have 20,000 fans that come to 20 games each a season than 400,000 fans that come once. The former because (a) they will gradually turn into 25,000, (b) they will be there when times are tough and (c) they will consume media and merchandise. The 400,000 will be gone with the first cold wind, losing streak, re-arranged soccer practice or latest movie launch. By targeting the latter, it made decisions and initiated programs, such as the infamous "shoot-out" along with nicknames such as "cyber bats", that alienated the hard-core fans it really needed. (In their defense, the league had sold sponsorships to leading corporations who were looking to reach the youth soccer family demographic and as such expected to see them at games. Sponsorship money was critical to the league's survival and investor confidence.) The league was always cognizant of the fact they had huge cavernous stadiums to fill and were looking to cast their net far and wide and as such looked to appeal to everyone, fearing alienating anyone. At the end of the day the expression "if you sit in the middle of the road you get hit by cars coming both ways" seemed to fit. MLS hedged their bets and lost, failing to understand just how soccer-educated, authentic and sensitive their core potential fan base was.

Not another museum

Around the world, summer months for soccer fans represent empty days, family vacations, feigned interest in museums, camping trips and over-mown lawns, all just mental diversions to the only thing that really matters: the start of the new soccer season. However bad last season was, the promise of the new exceeds any rational logic. Everyone starts on "0" points and as the first game approaches every team is "unbeaten", and dreams of championships and cups flood the stands. A good measure of the fan support and loyalty might be to measure this anticipation (however unscientific): just how much had the fans missed their team during the winter months? Unfortunately for most MLS teams the answer was not a lot. By 1999, as can be seen in Table 4.5, most MLS teams had suffered precipitous falls in their opening-day attendance with only D.C. United seeing a gain. New York posted a 56 percent drop and LA Galaxy a stomach churning 75 percent drop. In a startling statistic the overall home opening attendance of the original 10 teams fell an astonishing 45 percent from the 1996 season. It is not a perfect way and of course the early 1996 crowds were almost "special events" but it would be fair to say fans were not pacing the house waiting for the start of the season.

The numbers were telling a story and opening a window to the psyche of the American soccer players and fans. As soon as last ball was kicked, 75 percent of the youth soccer players and their families switched off from the sport entirely, never to give it a second thought. NFL was in full swing, the SuperBowl just around the corner, College football on screens everywhere, the

Table 4.5 Comparison of opening-day attendance, 1996–99

Opening day woes			
Team	Opening day 1996	Opening day 1999	% + /−
LA Galaxy	69,255	17,343	−75
D.C. United	35,032	35,167	+0.4
Columbus	25,266	24,741	−2
Kansas	21,141	15,509	−27
NY Metrostars	46,826	20,307	−57
Dallas Burn	27,779	17,112	−38
New England	26,473	18,373	−31
San Jose	31,683	15,238	−52
Colorado Rapids	23,711	15,592	−34
Tampa Bay	26,473	n/a	n/a

Source: Compiled from MLSnet.com and MLS Media Guides.

NBA coming down the home stretch and pre-season baseball in their fathers' thoughts. Soccer was done and dusted and Major League Soccer forgotten. You could blame teams for not building the intense loyalty required to sustain an off season, but we need to recognize that in the USA, unlike almost every other country in the world, the options available to sports participants and fans are immense (see Table 4.6), many with decades of history and tradition behind them. As a result, each year, when April comes around, Major League Soccer teams have to re-awaken their fan base and re-engage the youth soccer family ticket base. With 40 percent of the season's turnout dependent on getting these clubs and teams to return, MLS lives and dies by how aggressive, smart and skilled their ticketing departments are. For unlike the NFL and many other leagues, the phones in MLS do not ring off the hook, 90 percent of all calls are outbound.

Television: is anyone watching?

If attendances at games were to struggle after the first year then the television numbers were to be even more disappointing and were to haunt both the league and its sponsors. Apart from the finals which were aired on ABC, people were just not tuning in to watch the MLS games. Soccer has always had difficulty translating to watchable television for US audiences (more on this later), with even the best games struggling. MLS however had a particular set of challenges that were at times to make it even more unwatchable. Once again it is back to the issue of stadiums and atmosphere.

It did not matter how many super digital, wide angle, narrow angle, tight shot tactical decisions TV directors made in showing MLS Games, the fact that most stadiums looked two-thirds empty could not be disguised. Add to this that most fields still had American football lines on them and that the camera men charged with capturing the game would not know "off side" from "off Broadway" and the picture becomes clear (or not as it turned out). As a vehicle for selling the dream of MLS it was woefully lacking. The core fans tuned in, and then out, bemoaning the fact the TV experience bore no resemblance to

Table 4.6 Sporting calendar for major pro-sports in the USA and soccer seasons

A crowded sporting landscape

	Jan	Feb	March	April	May	June	July	Aug	Sept	Oct	Nov	Dec
NFL	SuperBowl											
MLB										World Series		
NHL				Stanley Cup								
NBA				Playoffs	Final							
College Football	Bowl											Bowl
College Soccer												Finals
Youth Soccer			Spring Season						Main Youth Soccer Season			
MLS										MLS Cup		

Key: ▢ indicates playing season.
Source: Compiled online review of Pro-league sites.

Table 4.7 Television viewers: Major League Soccer 1996–99

Viewers vanish

Network	1996	1997	1998	1999	%
ABC Final	1,300,000	1,300,000	1,000,000	700,000	−46
ABC Regular			880,000	868,000	
ESPN	423,000	377,000	320,000	254,000	−40
ESPN 2	332,500	266,000	209,000	256,000	−23
Univision	382,000	345,000	270,000	277,000	−27

Source: Compiled from ESPN and Univision and MLS.

the English, Spanish and Italian soccer they were consuming elsewhere. Even the "uneducated" youth and parent audience brought up on diet of NFL and NBA with two-hour warm-up shows and three hours post-game shows, knew they were being asked to consume an inferior experience and so they didn't. To anyone else skipping through channels, it just reinforced everything they thought. In many ways MLS may have been better off severely restricting their television offering, but you don't get $2m per year sponsorship deals by doing that. (MLS had packaged sponsor commercials into their deals and were therefore committed to airing games, however empty the stadium or "lined" the field.)

The television numbers were not lying (see Table 4.7). Even the showpiece of the year, the MLS Cup Final, was suffering with the 1999 final between D.C. United and Galaxy having the dubious honor of being the lowest rated televised sports broadcast of the year on network television. In a further blow, Univision, the league's main Hispanic partner and the country's largest and most important network, decided not to renew its agreement to air the league. Falling ratings and an audience more interested in Mexican League soccer than MLS proved the death knell for their continued interest. The league put a brave face on it claiming Univision failed to promote the games and aired them at unpopular times, but the reality was this was just another blow to the league's morale and marketability. Telemundo, a much smaller competitor, was quickly brought in to replace them, but the damage was done and most Hispanics gone.

Hemorrhaging cash: "the patient is dying"

The first critical four years of the League were coming to a close and the scorecard was being reviewed. Teams were clearly struggling to cement their fan bases and TV numbers were plummeting. The vultures and cynics were circling with whetted appetites ready to write another epitaph for a failed professional league. There was no doubt that while the public face of the league and PR spin doctors was that all was well, behind the scenes it did not take a Warwick MBA to realize that the losses being sustained at team and league level were unsustainable for all but the richest and most committed owners. So how bad was it? Well, by the end of 1999 the combined losses were estimated to be close to $250m.

The league's key revenue streams were all under pressure and costs were way above those budgeted. MLS was still not receiving any major TV rights fees, which for most other leagues represented a significant portion of their income. To make matters worse in 1996 and 1997, the league was paying the production costs for all of its games, an onerous expense. The television landscape did get better in 1998 when ESPN, impressed by the sponsor roster for MLS, agreed a revenue-sharing agreement which reduced the league's exposure. Contracted sponsorship revenue, while not as high as had been hoped, was still significant rising from $13m to $20m by 2000, the only upward trend in a bleak picture. Not unsurprisingly, license-goods sales were less than impressive as soccer failed to become the "hot" new urban street-wear brand they were promised, earning just $1m for the league in 1996 rising to $3m in 1999. Overall, total commercial income for the four years rose from $14m in 1996 to $27m in 2000, a reasonable increase but nowhere near enough to offset escalating costs or hide the fact that it had no major television deal. It became very clear that in 1999 the owners were staring down the barrel of losses that were not only onerous but, more importantly, seemingly unending.

So if the league itself was bleeding cash, how were the local teams doing? Unfortunately, the answer was much worse. Key revenue sources for these teams included 70 pecent of all local ticket sales, 100 percent of local sponsorships (excluding national categories) and 100 percent of the local television revenue. It varied, of course, team by team but most teams were suffering with falling crowds from the opening season, no team had secured any significant rights payment from local broadcast partners (indeed many were themselves paying to have games aired) and they received nothing from licensed merchandise sales (all of this went to the league). From inception, it always looked challenging to see how local teams could make money and it was proving to be true, from 1996 to 1999 teams were losing approximately $1m–$3m per season locally. Some were losing a lot more with New York reported to be closer to $8m and the newly launched Miami Fusion about the same. In addition to absorbing their own losses $2–$3m had to be paid in cash calls to the league to ensure the lights stayed on in New York.

In 1996, the $5m entry fee to join the league looked like a steal: a hot new sport coming off an incredible World Cup, an exploding player base of millions of kids and a new influx of Hispanics who would surely embrace it and come out to watch. Four years later, the reality was much different and that $5m was not looking such a good deal after all; worse still there was seemingly no end in sight to the financial pain. To pour salt on their wounds and make matters potentially infinitely worse, the league found itself in a "fight to the death" battle with its players looking to cash in and share the riches.

The players' revolt with help from the NFL

While the owners and league officials thought the new and clever single-entity structure was all about investors partnering together for the "common good" to ensure the controlled and effective launch of a new risky sports league, the players were convinced it was nothing more than a clever legal maneuver to prevent them from earning more money in the transfer market, by being able to negotiate freely with any team in the league. The players argued that because the teams all "competed" against each other independently the idea that they were all "one company" was just some clever legal maneuver to hold down wages and restrict movement and as such in breach of US anti-trust labor laws. With the "spin" surrounding the league that it was riches all around and a resounding first season success, the players, supported by the National Football League Players Association Union (NFLPA) filed suit in a Boston Court to pierce the veil of the single-entity structure and win their "freedom". (1998: Fraser versus MLS). Had they won, the league was over. At the time however, there was a tougher question: just why was the NFL Players Union stepping in to help impoverished American soccer players? Why indeed?

One of the key components of the single-entity structure was the league's promise to its investors that no one would be allowed to outspend another team by paying inflated wages to attract the best players and as such driving others to compete, i.e. repeating the failure of the NASL. From a league standpoint, the only way to stop this was to have everyone singing from the same "hymn sheet" and to do so, they put in place a strict $1.1m per team salary cap, which rose to $1.7m by 1999. They did however allow teams to pay up to four of its marque players $175,000 each plus of course any lucrative endorsement deals they might be able to secure for them. As a result, players such as Ramos, Lalas, Harkes, Etcheverry and Campos all earned reasonable salaries, but absorbed much of the salary cap, leaving the rest of the players to share the balance, which obviously was not a lot. For most players, it meant salaries that ranged anywhere from $12,000 to $50,000 a year and a second job in the local soccer store or insurance company. This was not the fault of the "star" players who themselves were not really getting rich and not necessarily the fault of the league, more the fiscal realities of launching a new league in a very tough sports market. Players ultimately had three choices: (1) accept the offer, (2) move abroad or (3) get a real job. As for agents, well the two masters they answer to, money and leverage, were nowhere to be seen.

All players should have the right to fight for better conditions should they feel aggrieved and MLS players were no different. Those earning less than $24,000 certainly had reason to look for more and may have been better off in the Russian Third Division, but as with everything in life, there is a time and a place and a smart way to go about it. Unfortunately the players were to fail on all three. At the time, league spin doctors were talking a great game, proudly announcing two new teams in Chicago and

Miami, and a plethora of new sponsors and corporate support: the world of MLS appeared prosperous and growing. The players of course wanted in. It was after all they who the fans paid (or eventually didn't) to see. Every professional player will say they play for the love of the game but realistically it's always about getting that big "pay day", or hopefully many big "pay days" and why not, it's a short career and chances are when they finish they will have knees like wet spaghetti and arthritic hips. Around the world the ability of a player to leverage their skills and sell them to the highest bidder is at the core of the business equation and orchestrating an extra $5m because both "United" and "Real" want you is an agent's dream. For MLS players however (unless Real and United did want you) there was no domestic transfer market, the league decided how much you were paid and generally which club you played for. There was no point having your agent set up clandestine meetings as there was no one to be clandestine with, the league owned everyone. Unhappy with the system, the players filed suit. (Or some of them did claiming to speak for everyone and even today it's unclear how many were truly behind it.) However many were, or weren't, it was to challenge the very existence of the league. The players though, from beginning to end, were to get it wrong and were left feeling Shakespeare may have been right after all, and the lawyers should have been killed.

First, they challenged the legality of the single-entity structure itself claiming it violated anti-trust laws and restricted competition. You can be sure that Rothenberg, Gazidis and Abbott had done their homework on this fundamental tenet, which of course they had, resulting in the judge dismissing the claim out of hand, before it went to trial. Second, they claimed single-entity restricted the ability of the players to earn a living in soccer. With MLS being the only Division One Professional League in the country, they claimed that if they couldn't freely negotiate with the likes of Columbus, San Jose or Miami then they were being restricted in the right to work. At trial, MLS quickly destroyed the credibility of this premise detailing what everyone in soccer already knew, that the labor market for soccer players was not just restricted to the USA and that if a player is good enough they could play anywhere in the world. To prove it they produced, at trial, a 10 foot chart that listed in intricate detail the foreign teams that many of the MLS players had already played for. A tough bit of evidence but hardly Sherlock Holmes! With the basic thrust of their case undermined, the jury "found" for the league and dismissed all claims and the players, represented by one of the biggest and best player unions in America, were left wondering what the hell went wrong. The "players" did appeal the decision but once again lost and after six long years and $10m in legal fees (for MLS) the battle came to an end.

The importance of the league winning this case should not be underestimated. Had it lost the league would have folded, and the victorious NFLPA given the privilege of putting the 250 MLS players out of work. Of course there is always bluff and counter bluff in these situations but from all I have interviewed it is clear that with losses of $50m per year the owners could not and would not have tolerated escalating player costs. If the single-entity structure was to be dissolved then so too would the league.

So just why did the National Football League Players Union take up the cause of the down-trodden American soccer player? It certainly couldn't have been for the money. Weren't the MLS players just a little bit curious to find out why a Union, whose members spent more on jewelry a month than they earned in a year, were coming to their rescue? After all since when had American football players really cared about soccer and why indeed should they? The NFLPA were at the time apparently looking to expand and diversify, but fighting the cause of $20,000-a-year soccer players does not, to me, seem like the path to riches. So what was it? I could be doing them a huge disservice here but if you were in their shoes, wouldn't this "single-entity structure" sort of bother you? What if the idea gained traction? What might happen to their highly paid members if the NFL team owners decided to join together and do something similar or at least threatened the possibility of doing so in labor negotiations? Again I could be wrong and it was the camaraderie and kindness of one fellow players group giving back to another but I somehow doubt it, although you never know. Maybe the MLS players weren't just a pawn in a bigger game.

MLS claim that while they would never have compromised on the issue of the single-entity structure they had been prepared to negotiate on player salaries, and indeed expected to be doing so in the first few years of the league anyway. Gazidis explained that MLS offered to settle the case rather than "waste" close to $10m on lawyers, money that could have found its way into players' pay packets. This offer was refused by the NFLPA in a "storm out the room, see you in court" moment. Clearly they were only interested in the big prize, bringing down the "single-entity structure", though along with it would have come Armageddon. It's a shame they never settled as $10m would have gone a long way. As it was, while the sides were in "legal dispute" MLS could not, or it made no sense to, discuss normal annual player salary and benefit increases and the process was frozen until a resolution was achieved or a "day in court" delivered. A day that eventually came in 2001 and destroyed every position or claim the players had.

The lesson to be learned here is that although players should have every right to improve their "lot" in life, they should choose the right battle at the right time and fight it with the right partners. Attacking the league after just one season was foolish. Attacking a legal structure developed by serious attorneys who had spent years researching it was foolish. Not understanding that MLS would claim with all justification that the labor market for soccer players was global, was foolish. Being swayed to follow the advice of a competing sports union was foolish. With losses now publicly recognized at $250m, it was clear the owners were not running off with all the money and were in fact dipping into their own pockets again and again to keep the league afloat. It was the wrong time to make such an aggressive attack on the league and then to attack and try and break the core tenet of operation, the "single entity". As such it became a fight to the death for the owners who were never going to give it up and suicide for the players if they won. But at least they had the comfort of knowing the NFLPA were right behind them! (By the way $10m could have given each player in the league a $40,000 Christmas bonus. MLS were not Santa Claus of course and it would not have happened but you get the point.)

Soon after the case was finished, the players regrouped, ended their relationship with the NFLPA and formed their own union, the Major League Soccer Players Union (MLSPU). They sat down with the league and negotiated a new collective bargaining agreement (CBA) which covered all players. As this book goes to press the players and league are locked in negotiations for a new agreement that will come into effect when the old one ends on 31 Jan 2010. The league is in a much different place to where it was from 1996 to 2002 and it will be interesting to see how the new agreement reflects this. One thing is certain; the legality of the single-entity structure is not on the table. The players' main beef: guaranteed contracts and freedom of movement. Yes, they want more money of course – but it seems to be about more than this. My sense is the leverage between players and the league is evening out and some interesting times are ahead!

First leg: battered and bruised

At the end of the 1999 season, the first leg of the great game to get professional soccer launched in the United States was over. MLS was coming off the field (one with "football" lines of course) and into the dressing room battered and bruised, conceding goals from all over the pitch and scrambling to get out of its own penalty area. Its teams were jaded, its players restless, its fans deserting, its viewers tuning out and its owners looking to bail out. It did not take a José Mourinho to realize that if the league did not take some drastic measures there wouldn't be a second leg. There would be no chance to change tactics and surprise the opposition, no chance to bring in some new players and revitalize the team, no chance to undo mistakes and no chance at redemption.

Well there was a second leg, and an eventful one at that. MLS came out with a new boss, a new game plan, some new players and a whole new approach to its tactical formation. The old boss (Commissioner) Doug Logan paid the price for a run of poor results, as they always do, and his replacement was a 15-year National Football League veteran who had spent the past three years trying to sell "American Football" to the world. The irony was palpable.

CHAPTER 5

Back from the Brink

Don Garber could never have imagined as he drove past Giants Stadium, windows down listening to the roar of 70,000 Cosmos fans, on his way home from the NFL offices in New York, that one day he would be called upon to rescue and rebuild the future of professional soccer in the United States. Approached by the Kraft family, owners of the NFL New England Patriots and MLS New England Revolution, the offer was attractive enough to convince Garber to jump sports and take on the task of marketing real "football". Feeling "Commissioner Garber" represented a great career move and recognizing from his NFL travels just how enormous the sport was everywhere he went, he saw no reason why, in a shrinking world, soccer could not make it in America. He had no idea, however, as to the minefield that was MLS he was walking into. Probably for the best really

Garber inherited a league that was looking tired and failing to live up to expectations both on and off the field. Average crowds had settled at a less than impressive 14,282, TV ratings were at best tepid, and most teams were locked into stadium deals that were expensive and unworkable. Two of its leading sponsors Fuji and Bandai were pulling out, its players were fighting them in the courts, losses were piling up and the shining example of all things that were right with the league, three-times MLS Cup Champion D.C. United, was up for sale, its owners unconvinced of the league's future.

When the reality of the size of the challenge hit home, there must have been a passing thought given to how nice it had been to fly to Spain to discuss the support NFL was going to give the Barcelona Dragons over a nice lunch and maybe take in a game, then off to Edinburgh to see how the Scottish Claymores were doing. MLS however was a different beast and his thoughts quickly settled on the challenges of San Jose, Dallas and Miami.

It was clear that changes were needed. The patient was bleeding to death and "two aspirins and early night" was not going to save it: radical surgery and a new lifestyle was required. Garber commissioned Octagon, one of the world's leading Sports Marketing agencies, to talk with coaches, fans, players, general managers and to report back. This task fell to myself (Managing Director of its Properties Division at the time) and a colleague John Guppy, who would go on to be President of the Chicago Fire, and the message that came back was loud and clear. The league lacked authenticity, gave a lousy stadium experience, was of dubious quality, had teams that had alienated the soccer community, was not connecting with Hispanics, was laughed at by ex-pats and was at times unwatchable on television (apart from that it was OK!) The obvious question for Garber, apart from "why on earth did I take the job?" was "where do I start first?"

Smartly he addressed the things fans would most notice and that would give him some early kudos with the fans. Away went the much hated "shoot-out" replaced by two five-minute overtimes. Ultimately these too were removed when he realized that, while general American sports fans hate a tie, hard-core soccer fans (the one's the league needed) had no problem with it. The changes sent two messages: (1) the sport was turning authentic and (2) the "commish" was listening. While important, this was the easy stuff; much more pressing, and potentially league threatening, issues were piling up on his desk, issues that if not resolved, would put the lights out on MLS forever.

The patient is getting worse

Garber and his team spent the 2000 season working on a new plan and direction for the league and a model that would change its fortunes. While it did this, the patient took a turn for the worse.

Average attendances continued to slide with regular season crowds dropping (4 percent) to 13,756 and playoffs down (28 percent) to 10,257. The patient was clearly getting worse and in fact bordering on terminal! D.C. United's owners, failing to close a deal with the investment group Warburg Pincus, "handed back the keys" with Phil Anschutz stepping in to underwrite operations and assume control and with the 2001 recession biting hard and finances strained, other owners were making ominous sounds that they too had had enough of the pain and wanted out. Then on 11 September 2001 the world changed forever and what was thought important, suddenly was not. Garber immediately suspended league play but completed a shortened season with the LA Galaxy defeating San Jose in the MLS Cup Final. If he had thought it could not get any worse than 1999, it just had and for everyone involved in Major League Soccer it was clear that a day of reckoning was coming, and coming soon.

Sometimes in business, moments and events take on almost mythical status and for soccer the "Meeting at the Ranch" (Phil Anschutz's ranch to be precise) certainly did this. Taking place in late 2001 the agenda was simple: Item One: "Should we continue with Major League Soccer?" Item Two: there was no item two! The most nervous man in the room was Don Garber, for it was his plan, and the acceptance or rejection of its recommendations would be the deciding factor.

Unfortunately for owners losing millions every season, his plan was the last thing they wanted to hear. Garber had concluded that to have any chance of surviving, the league had to take on far more risk and invest far more money than it ever had. (I wonder how that went down over early morning bacon and eggs?) His rationale was that the league alone, at this stage in its development, could not organically generate enough money to make itself profitable and that the only way to do so was to take a "gamble" on launching a sister company that would invest in acquiring rights to other soccer properties that if successful would generate a profit – a profit that could be used to underpin the losses in MLS. His conclusions and recommendations for the future were based on the following assumptions:

1   It was Major League Soccer's business model that was wrong and not the fact that the soccer market itself was struggling. In fact the market was growing and profits were there to be had if approached correctly.
2   The soccer industry was highly fragmented with too many groups vying for the same dollar, confusing the corporate marketplace.

If MLS was to succeed it had to eliminate this competition or control it. As these competitors included: US Soccer, US Youth Soccer, Concacaf, the Mexican Soccer Federation and a multitude of promoters representing Manchester United, Barcelona and a myriad of other clubs looking to play in the USA, it was clear they had little chance of eliminating them, so they needed to invest the necessary money to acquire their rights, and control them.

3 A rising tide lifts all ships and up from the bottom would float MLS. By acquiring these "rights" MLS would ultimately be able to control the commercial landscape for soccer in America and as such shape their own destiny. The bigger and more professional the "soccer pie", the more likely fans and corporations are to get behind the league.

4 By controlling rights to televised soccer and promoting games for the world's best teams on American soil, the league can both educate the fan base and cross promote MLS teams. An educated fan base leads to a more involved and passionate fan base and hopefully therefore fans that would gravitate to MLS. (It of course had the danger of highlighting the teams' inadequacies compared to the best but this could not be hidden anyway.)

The plan was big picture and sent a clear unequivocal message to the owners. We cannot fix the league by just trying to fix the league problems in isolation. The problems are too deep and any turnaround is going to take years of patience and substantial continued financial losses. We need to use the powerful and potentially economically compelling forces of soccer in all its forms to support and lift the league to a position where it can survive long enough to be "fixed" and ultimately succeed. In essence, spend more and gamble on making money in other areas of soccer, then use these to save the league. Or as Tim Leiweke expressed "sometimes you have to make the problem bigger in order to solve it"… well it was going to get big very quickly.

Garber's first recommendation was to spend $40m on buying the English Language Television Rights to the 2002 and 2006 Men's World Cup, and spend another $30m on production and studio shows. The league will then license the rights to ABC and ESPN for free, sell the commercial time themselves and pocket a sizeable profit. He would either be thought "nuts" or a "genius" but it certainly wasn't lacking in boldness and reeked of what the NFL might do in a similar situation. Offering some solace to owners (as they picked themselves up off the floor) he did recommend closing down or selling the three cash-sapping league-owned teams in San Jose, Tampa and Dallas as well as significantly reducing the overhead and league office expenses in New York.

So there it was, the plan for saving Major League Soccer. Spend more, gamble more, and in essence "double down" on what had already been a losing bet. It would take nerve, it would take belief and it would take very deep pockets.

Meetings and side meetings, arguments and counter arguments, alternatives and other options, the discussions went on over the course of the day. Ultimately it came to decision time. "Let he who is in stand up and be counted", and not all got up. Kluge and Subotnik, owners of the New York Metrostars, had taken a severe battering during the 2001 recession and wanted out. Ken Horowitz, owner of the Miami Fusion, who had invested $30–$40m in the team but gained little traction, wanted out. The D.C. United ownership were already out. Legend has it that at this stage, Anschutz asked all those that were not on board to depart leaving just the Hunts, owners of the Kansas City Wizards and Columbus Crew, and the Krafts, owners of the New England Revolution in the room. The question was simple: "are you with me?" making it clear that Anschutz was prepared to continue investing if the other two would do the same. If they blinked or hesitated he was out and the league was done. Fortunately for everyone in soccer they did neither. The Hunts and Krafts were equally "soccer guys" with both deep pockets and great patience. In spite of the recession, in spite of mounting losses, they did what probably made them rich in the first place, they took a calculated risk and rather than chucking in their cards they "doubled down" betting on both the league and on American soccer. Anschutz, already operating the Los Angeles Galaxy, Chicago Fire and recently D.C. United, agreed to take over the New York Metrostars; the Hunts agreed to take over the Dallas Burn and the Krafts stepped up to operate the San Jose Earthquakes, while for the Cyber Bats (Tampa Bay) the game was up. It was equally over for the

Miami Fusion whose owner Ken Horowitz had lost the stomach, and the money, for the fight. As such MLS would kick off the 2002 season with just 10 teams, all owned by one of three owners with Anschutz himself controlling five.

"In for a penny in for a pound" as the saying goes, but they also didn't think Garber was "nuts" and backed him to the tune of $70m to acquire the World Cup rights. This was just as well because none of the major networks had "bid" for the rights and it was highly likely Anglo-American soccer fans would be back to the "old" days of tuning into Univision with Spanish phrase book in hand and only really recognizing the words "futbol", Andres Cantor's commentary and his infamous signature "gooooaaaaal, gooooaal, goala goala gaola"!!! (Trust me it went on longer than I have time to write.) All soccer fans whether they supported an MLS Team or not had much to thank the league and owners for in both 2002 and 2006 (the average attendance jumped by 1,000 in 2002).

Without being too dramatic, the commercial future of soccer in the USA rested on a knife edge during the weeks leading up to and surrounding these meetings. Those intimately involved and present reflecting that the league came perilously close to collapsing. Tim Leiweke, President of AEG and owners of the LA Galaxy were convinced it was hanging by a thread and contemplated pulling the plug on the Home Depot Center; Jonathan Kraft was quietly making contingency plans for winding down the New England Revolution. Had they lost the legal battle with the "players" it almost certainly would have been the final straw and the impact on the commercial development of the sport immeasurable and disastrous. Without MLS and its owners' commitment there would be no new soccer stadiums, no career path for US players, no English language World Cup coverage, no 2018/2022 World Cup bid, no corporate dollars supporting soccer programs, no Beckham, fewer jobs for American coaches, no industry for soccer executives along with many more missed opportunities. The collapse of MLS and the departure of its wealthy owners from the sport would have forever doomed professional soccer in the USA and along with it, the respect of FIFA and the soccer world. In their minds the USA had been provided with a perfect platform for professional soccer to finally make it; the fact it had failed again was just testimony to the opinion that soccer was just not an American sport. MLS was, and is, not perfect: but picture a US Soccer landscape without it.

History will show the league survived, it might not however reflect how close a shave it was!

Anschutz versus Anschutz

The 2002 season kicked off with just 10 teams, five of which were owned by Phil Anschutz, not an ideal situation but the alternative was much worse. Tellingly, no new outside investors had come into the league since Horowitz in 1998 (Miami Fusion) and that wasn't exactly the poster child for how to make money in soccer! The league had certainly been aggressively looking for new investors, particularly for its league-owned teams, but had come up short, not surprising considering the turmoil the league was in. It was left to follow through on the plan and close Tampa.

Tampa Bay or Manchester United?

The Cyber Bats were unlucky from the start really. They spent their first season playing in the cavernous Tampa Bay Buccaneers stadium drawing an average of just 11,679 but led by Valderama, went on to top the Eastern Conference. The unfortunate bit was their ticketing manager who ran off with $200,000 of their fans' money. Nick Sakiewicz (now founder and part owner of the Philadelphia Union) was sent down to fix it and while its attendances peaked in 1999 at 13,000 they fell by 27 percent in 2000 with just 5,583 showing for its playoff game against the LA Galaxy. Gates improved the following season by some 20 percent but with no new investor in sight and no new soccer stadium in the near, or far, future, its fate was sealed. It could however have been so much different. The Glazer family, owners of the NFL Tampa Bay Buccaneers, were in serious discussions to buy the Tampa team but could not reach an amicable agreement. Not long after they were, of course, to buy Manchester United for $1b. If just a fraction of that billion could have found its way into MLS

Tampa, soccer fans might have been able to recapture the glory days of Rodney Marsh and the famed Tampa Bay Rowdies.

Miami Beach or the Miami Fusion?

Further down and across the Florida Coast, the Miami Fusion was about to close its doors for good, drowned by unsustainable $7m-a-year losses. The "Fusion" had always struggled to gain relevance in its market. Playing in an expensively renovated Lockhart Stadium in Fort Lauderdale, its average attendance of just 10,234 in its opening season in 1998 was not a good sign and when it dropped to just 7,460 in 2000 it was clear the league had a disaster on its hands. The club had managed to alienate about every powerful youth soccer club in the market, and so were made to pay. To show that sometimes it's all about treating your fans with respect, Doug Hamilton, an ex-director of soccer for Adidas, was brought in to fix the problem and fix it he did, increasing attendance by 61 percent and steering the team to the conference final. Unfortunately it was too little too late with the crippling losses sinking the team. (Doug was to go on to be the very successful General Manager of the LA Galaxy but unfortunately passed away in 2006, a great friend and sadly missed by all in US Soccer.)

On a side note, South Florida has often been a graveyard for professional soccer. Eager promoters and investors are always convinced that the huge Hispanic market is just waiting for soccer to arrive. What they fail to do is pick up a US Government Census report. Yes, South Florida has a huge Hispanic population but dominated by Cuban and Dominican Republic Hispanics, read "baseball not soccer" and even baseball struggles. Also think about the region itself: great beaches, incredible nightlife, a huge tourist and entertainment industry and any number of distractions to keep people away from soccer. Then add that in the summer (that is, the MLS season) when temperatures can rise to 99 degrees with 99 percent humidity and it's no wonder sports teams struggle. Who wants to stand in a baking hot concrete stadium when the gentle breeze of the beach is beckoning? On a second side note the $20m expansion fee charged to Horowitz for the team actually sealed its fate. Teams had not increased 400 percent in value since inception and in fact most were bleeding cash and clearly while Horowitz might be thinking differently, the league knew the truth. Of course it is naïve to think the league should turn down a $20m check, but had Horowitz paid $5m and been forced to put $15m into escrow for marketing and operations it may have given Hamilton enough time to fix it for good; we will of course never know. I still think the beach and baseball wins out in Florida!

Tough decisions had been made and life-saving "triage" completed, resulting in the MLS playing field being reduced to just 10 teams. It was a gutsy and risky move with the ever-present cynics sharpening their pencils ready to proclaim it was just the first familiar step in professional soccer's inevitable demise, a steady funeral procession to "eight" then "six" then over! In one respect the cynics were of course right, ten teams "did not a Major league make" and if MLS was to have any chance of surviving it had find new investors and add more teams, and do so pretty quickly. The problem was that it wasn't looking like an investment any sane rational man would want to make, certainly not anyone looking at the league's past history. The secret of course was to sell the future!

It was clear in 2002 that soccer in the US and MLS in particular needed some good news. It needed something that would take away the taste of the last few years: the soaring losses; the battle with its players and "survival at the ranch". It needed a spark of life that just might let everyone in soccer know there was light somewhere down the tunnel. Fortunately the spark arrived and ultimately from the only place it could: on the field.

Written about later in the book, the performance of the US Men's team at the 2002 World Cup lifted morale and the interest of soccer fans everywhere. Even non-soccer fans were intrigued and fascinated as to why thousands of people were waking up at two in the morning, or lining up in bars at 8AM to watch soccer. It once again, as in 1994, put soccer onto the front pages of leading magazines such as *Sports Illustrated* and *Vanity Fair* and the guest list for late-night talk shows, with David Letterman convincing the players to kick balls off a Manhattan rooftop. Whatever "hoops" the players went through, the exposure was great and at last soccer was back in the public eye and more importantly (as with World Cup 94) the investor's eye. This time however investors would buy into stadiums.

Bricks and mortar – back to basics.

Back as far as 1992 it was always envisaged that to be successful soccer needed its own stadiums. Abbott and Gazidis had included it in the original plan but the numbers scared off potential investors, afraid of committing bricks and mortar to such a high-risk venture. A decade later existing owners were all scrambling to build their own stadiums, understanding it was the only way forward and new investors were not allowed in the league without a plan to build or control one. It was not easy though and MLS had to prove that buying a team and building a stadium for them to play in represented a profitable enterprise. To do this the league needed proof points and examples, bricks and mortar and profit and loss statements. It needed its first soccer specific stadiums. Fortunately they were on their way.

Stadium 1: Columbus Crew

Sitting around a table with his leading advisors, Lamar Hunt asked for opinions as to whether he should build a new soccer stadium or not. To a man they responded negatively and advised strongly against it. Lamar (with eight World Cups under his belt) disagreed and America's first soccer-specific stadium came to be in 1999 – the 22,000-seat Crew Stadium at a cost of $25m. It's impact was immediate, with average attendances jumping 44 percent to over 17,000 in its first season. Owning all of the key revenue sources, the team was bordering on profitability in its first year with only the lack of a lucrative naming rights sponsor stopping it from realizing the full financial value. Importantly attendances held strong for the next six years through to 2005 when the lack of any real success started to erode interest. Attendances bounced back in 2008 as the team secured its first MLS Cup win proving that however good the stadium is, however tasty and cheap the hot dogs and drinks and however attractive the cheerleaders might be, ultimately it's about what takes place on the field: a nice cold beer served super quick cannot mask a poor team team and if you have one crowds will fall.

Stadium 2: LA Galaxy

In June 2003 AEG (Anschutz Entertainment Group) played its first match at LA Galaxy's new 27,000 seat state of the art, Home Depot Stadium, part of an 85-acre 10-soccer-field sports complex that would also become the new home and training center for the US National Team program. While Columbus was a good star, this was a quantum leap forward in developing a model that would be both a great home for the team but also a revenue-generating machine for the owners. Home Depot was quickly signed as a naming rights sponsor, paying an estimated $4.5m for the privilege along with a myriad of other founding partners and suit-box owners, revenues that "proved out" the concept and that, if needed, could be used to secure funding from banks for construction. Not every investor could afford to spend $150m but the message was clear that if you get it right the fans and profitability will be there. The Home Depot project was a turning point for investors in the league and over the next seven years, five new soccer-specific stadiums would be built with three more slated for construction. Investors were buoyed by the model and the feeling was that if Anschutz was prepared to invest $150m in soccer, something must be happening.

Garber equally made it clear that every new expansion team would have to have a soccer specific stadium plan in its arsenal.

Moving from the 90,000 seat Rose Bowl where staff operated in temporary PortaCabins parked in the stadium car park, the luxurious Home Depot center breathed life into the team, fans and front office alike. Opening in 2003, the stadium helped cement a solid 22,000–26,000 fan base that finally had a home to call their own and made the Galaxy the best-supported team in the league (prior to the 2009 arrival of the Seattle Sounders). The venue itself is used extensively for concerts and other sporting events and was the first US home for the David Beckham Soccer Schools and eventually, of course, Beckham himself. (Beckham Soccer Schools closed down in LA, proving no one is immune from the recession.)

Stadium 3: FC Dallas: where's the cattle?

In August 2005, FC Dallas (previously the Dallas Burn) opened the newly titled Pizza Hut Park a 21,000 seat $65m–$70m stadium complex. The facility not only had 24 full-sized soccer fields but also housed the headquarters of the 3.2 million-strong United States Youth Soccer Association. (Unfortunately for Dallas its members were scattered throughout the country.) The impact was immediate with attendances increasing 50 percent in its first full season (8,000 to 15,000) but unfortunately these were not sustained as seasons of on-field mediocrity took their toll. The stadium is also located in a Dallas suburb a good distance from downtown making it "easy" for many to not go. The new stadium did drag attendances back up from a gut wrenching 8,000 average in 2003 but a 13,000 average in 2008 still represents a disappointing crowd in one of the largest Hispanic markets in America. Once again soccer specific stadiums are the answer but the product on the field and connectivity to the fan has to be present. It's a great and popular saying in Texas when referring to a man who promises much but delivers little. "All hat and no cattle"... well, Pizza Hut Park is a big and impressive "hat" but it has yet to rustle up the right cattle. At least it has a hat though and that means it has a chance. Had the team remained at the cavernous Cotton Bowl it would surely have suffered the fate of Tampa.

Stadium 4: Chicago Fire

The Chicago Fire were to start play in their own purpose-built 20,000-seat stadium on 6 June 2006 with the opening of Toyota Park, a stadium whose entire $90m cost was funded by the city of Bridgewater. Seen as a catalyst to the redevelopment of the city with plans for retail, movies, indoor sports facilities and more, the stadium was also built with an internal stage for hosting outdoor concerts on those 12 nights a year when it is not freezing in Chicago. Toyota quickly stepped up as naming rights sponsor paying close to $1m per year. The challenge however for any team playing in a stadium funded entirely with public money is negotiating an agreement by which it can share in the all important concession and parking revenue. The Fire were ultimately not to benefit fully from these but could draw upon the fact that they now had greatly reduced operating costs compared to Soldier Field (their previous NFL home) and a perfectly sized intimate 20,000-seat stadium for their fans. Their reward for providing this great new stadium was an 18 percent decline in average attendance (17,238 to 14,111) over 2005, when they played in downtown Chicago. Bridgewater can be a tough place to get to and clearly 3,000 of its fans were sufficiently fickle enough to not make the journey. By 2008, the fans had returned (or new ones found) with the average once again reaching 17,000. Originally owned by Phil Anschutz since it launched in 1998, it was sold in 2007 to Andell Holdings, a Los Angeles based private investment fund. The challenge, of course, was to work out a way to generate a profit as a tenant rather than a landlord, not an easy task. For MLS however it's another soccer-specific stadium in their stable. In 2009 the Chicago Fire made the Eastern Conference final playing Real Salt Lake at Toyota Park. The game was electric, the fans remarkable, and the atmosphere was as good as most teams in Europe. A tight 21,000-seat stadium, packed to the rafters and covered with flags, scarves and smoke was a glimpse of what the league might become. Just one quick side note and something Hank Steinbrecher raised: does anyone not find it strange that the team is named after the greatest physical disaster in Chicago history, the great fire of 1871, not necessarily earth shattering but strange? It would be like calling Coventry City the Coventry Blitz (remembering when the Luftwaffe flattened the City), a new team in New Orleans the "Flood" or a new NFL Team the London "Plague". Just a thought.

Stadium 5: Colorado Rapids

In September 2003, Anschutz, happy to reduce his ownership level (which was neither good for him or the league), sold the Colorado Rapids to Kroenke Sports Enterprises, owners of the NBA Denver Nuggets, the NHL Colorado Avalanche and now over 29 percent of Arsenal FC in the English Premiership. In 2007, they opened "Dicks Sporting Goods Park", a $131m 18,000-seat stadium with 24 soccer fields and 900 acres of developable land around it. Seen as a catalyst for the development of Commerce City the project was funded with 75 percent public money. The first full season average attendance in the new stadium jumped 22 percent to 14,749 before falling 7 percent. Their final season game in 2009 against New England saw 16,000 plus fans show up and had they made the playoffs, they would most probably have "sold out". They however didn't and we keep coming back to same point: a stadium alone is not enough.

Stadium 6: "Real" Salt Lake, 2009 MLS Cup Winners

Investors were clearly buying into the team ownership and stadium model and next to come on board was David Checketts, former President of Madison Square Garden, looking to start a team in Salt Lake City, Utah. You knew the team was in good hands when it was named "Real" Salt Lake and a close tie-up with Real Madrid announced. His new 20,000-seat $110m stadium, funded with both private and public money opened in October 2008 in Sandy on the outskirts of Salt Lake City. With a solid 16,000–18,000 plus fan base the team is well on its way and the stadium is a first-class facility. Embarrassed when Chivas fans by the busload invaded their stadium, their fan groups and in particular their Hispanic ones have taken up residence behind the goal and begun to mark out their territory. Real went on to win the 2009 MLS Cup in Seattle, taking a strong support to the Pacific North West and to round off a good year sold 49 percent of the club to Dell Loy Hansen, a local Utah based real estate developer with daughters who love soccer!

Stadium 7: Redbulls Arena, opening 2010

For New York RedBulls, a new arena is at the very heart of its ability to reinvent itself. Estimated to be losing anywhere from $8m–$12m per season (depending on how many concerts they put on to attracts crowds), the realization that it's all about the team on the field, the fan experience in the stadium and the outreach and

respect given to soccer consumers in the market has no doubt
dawned. If ever a team needs a new home and a new lease on
life then it's the RedBulls. AEG had been working to develop a
stadium since it took over the team after the infamous "meeting at the ranch", eventually settling on a site in Harrison, New
Jersey across from the river from Manhattan. In 2006, AEG sold
the team to RedBull Limited along with 50 percent of the stadium project for a reported $100m, RedBull later assuming full
100 percent control of the stadium. With a 2010 opening date,
"RedBull Arena" promises to be one of the most soccer friendly
and soccer-conscious stadiums in the league. With 25,189 seats,
a roof and a first row just 21ft from the field, the spectacular stadium has the potential to create the most volatile and intimidating
soccer atmosphere in the league, if of course they re-engage with
the fans that is. The league needs New York to be a successful
team; it needs sellout games and fervent New York soccer fans.
If Redbull can pull it off, it will become one of the great soccer
experiences in the country, period! If they don't, there will not be
enough of their company's drink to get them through it.

(Redbull Arena has one other great attribute in that it sits
alongside the main commuter rail line into New York City's Penn
Station and Wall Street. Thousands of commuters coming into
the city each year will see "soccer" on their way into work and
"soccer" on their way home from work. It's got to help.)

Stadium 8: Philadelphia Union

In 2010, Major League Soccer will get its ninth new soccer stadium located in Chester just 20 minutes south of one of the most
enthusiastic sports cities in America, Philadelphia. The $156m
project funded with $81m of private capital and $75m of public funding will build an 18,500-seat stadium on the shores of
Delaware River, again as a catalyst to regenerate one of the most
impoverished neighborhoods in the state. The stadium has been
designed and built with its fans "the sons of Ben" (more later)
in mind and with the intent of making the Union home the most
intimidating and inhospitable place in the league for the opposition
to come and play. Just as it should be! Its vocal fans will stand

behind the goal, furnished with benches (they did not want to sit) and will be the first thing Union and the opposing players will see and hear as they come out of the player tunnel, positioned directly beneath them. Built for fans, in cooperation with fans, it will be their stadium, their home and protected to the death. All good soccer stuff!

A summary of the initiatives of the MLS teams is provided in Table 5.1 that follows.

And there are stadiums that are coming soon, hopefully:

Kansas City

Kansas City Wizards has perennially struggled at the gate from day one. Burdened with being called the "wizzers" and playing in one of the largest stadiums in the country, the Kansas City Chiefs Arrowhead stadium, it was clear that without a significant stadium plan it would take a very brave and wealthy man to continue throwing money at it. The Hunt family represented some of

Table 5.1 New stadium initiatives by MLS teams: 1999–2010

			Nine new stadia		
Team	Stadium	Cost	Naming Rights*	Capacity	% of Public Funds
Columbus	Crew Stadium	$25m	none	22,555	0
LA Galaxy	Home Depot	$150m	$3.5m	27,000	0
FC Dallas	Pizza Hut Park	$80m	$1.5m	21,193	69
Chicago	Toyota Park	$90m	$750,000	21,000	100
Colorado	Dicks Sporting Goods	$84m	$2m	18,000	75
Toronto	BMO Field	$62m	$2.3m	20,000	71
Real Salt Lake	Rio Tinto Stadium	$110m	$2m	20,000	40
New York	Red Bull Arena	$200m	$3m	25,189	0
Philadelphia	PPL Park	$110m	$2m	18,500	70

Note: Naming rights fees are per year.
Source: Compiled from MLS and interviews.

America's most passionate soccer believers but even their patience was wearing thin. Unable to find support or funding for a new stadium, the team was sold in August 2006 to On Goal LLC, a group of local businessmen keen to keep its soccer team in town. Quickly moving the team to a smaller more fan-friendly intermediate stadium, Community America Stadium (10,385), it offered a more cost effective and intimate setting within which to consolidate and grow its fan base. In January 2010 they announced the approval of a $400m project that will see OnGoal and Lane4 Property Group develop a new stadium and sports field complex – which, with a covered roof, seats 16 feet from the field and a tight 18,500 capacity stadium should provide the atmosphere crucial to every club's success. The deal, as with Philadelphia, was as much about economic impact and job creation as MLS but it took passionate soccer people in a tough soccer market to keep the dream alive. It is not a downtown stadium and falls more into the FC Dallas and Colorado mold than Toronto. In 2003 and 2004 they averaged 15,000–16,000 per game so, with a new stadium and a winning team, the 18,500 capacity could work out well and the cauldron where the Wizard fans reside should be bubbling!! The technical director and manager at Kansas: Peter Vermes – the man who so nearly snatched a dramatic equalizer in Rome 20 years earlier.

D.C. United

Now here's an ongoing soccer tragedy and soap opera if ever there was one. The best fans in the league (sorry Seattle and Toronto, impressive as you are you need a few more years under your belt and a few more seasons paying your "fan dues" before dislodging this lot. I have watched D.C. fans lose 4–0 to Chicago in the playoffs and still applaud their team off the field) and the worst stadium in the league. It all looked so good in 2008 when new owners Will Chang and Victor Macfarlane acquired the team and the promise of a new stadium just a few miles from the White House, on the horizon. But if a week is a long time in politics it's a lifetime in soccer stadium politics. In fairness, the sale of the team had everything to do with the potential rewards of using the team as an anchor tenant for a major $1b real-estate development at Poplar Point in Anacostia, one of DC's most under-served and under-privileged communities and an area screaming out for the sort of economic stimulus a new stadium and associated real-estate development could bring. Years of community outreach had convinced a population 95 percent African-American brought up on basketball and NFL that soccer could be good for their community, and it could. D.C. United had excelled not only in rhetoric but also on delivery, running after-school programs and organizing local teams. All looked well as the recently elected Mayor of DC sat on the dais with Garber, Macfarlane, Chang and Payne announcing the sale to the press. Promising to do everything his administration could to facilitate the project, the future looked good for the team, the fans and the owners. For the league, their flagship brand would at last have its own home in the nation's capital and the embarrassment of 1999 expunged forever. Less than six months later, United's stadium plans would be in tatters. Failing to come to agreeable terms, the excitement and promises made faded into a political and administrative vacuum. To many, the writing was on the wall when 53,000 fans turned up to RFK to see David Beckham make his first appearance for the Galaxy, the hottest ticket in town, the most exciting sports event of the summer, and thousands of the Mayor's important voter base, but alas no Mayor. He may, and probably did, have a more pressing and more important issue to attend to, but politicians normally gravitate to crowds, so who knows? The Mayor was never seemingly a soccer man and as such D.C. United still remains at RFK, still loses money and are still searching for a new home for its tremendous fans. It's unfair however to expect the owner Will Chang to continue to fund "inevitable" annual losses, and unless the city government acts to help, ultimately the team may have to move. It's not right for the league, it's not right for the team and it's devastating for their loyal fans. This however is a business book!

New England Revolution

New England Revolution is a tough, resilient, hardworking team, reflecting the attributes of the city of Boston and the working class ethics of its coach, the ex-Liverpool stalwart Steve Nichol. A strong franchise, the Krafts have been trying to secure the urban soccer-specific stadium that would strengthen their club for several years but have been unsuccessful. They remain instead at the NFL home of its owners, the New England Patriots. Though designed with soccer in mind, it is still a cavernous stadium that has in part been responsible for its attendance dropping from 21,423 in the early years to as low as 11,000 in 2006. It's a tough team in a great city and made the MLS Cup Final three years in a row from 2005 to 2007. There is a sense however that the crowds should be bigger. The fact still remains however that the games are often played in a stadium that is two-thirds empty and on fields with NFL football lines. Not good for fans, not good for television and ultimately, not good for the league. They did however help launch the league and help save the league. If they don't get a stadium however, the team will struggle, with only 7,500 turning up for their 2009 semi-final playoff with Chicago.

Houston Dynamo

You cannot do much more than win the MLS Cup twice in the first two years of your existence, draw 30,000 crowds to your playoff games and have ownership that includes AEG and the boxer Oscar De la Hoya. The team plays in a 32,000 capacity stadium and draws an average of 17,000 per game with a strong Hispanic flavor, not surprising considering Houston is the one of the largest Hispanic cities in America. It is in discussions for a downtown stadium that will become a passionate home for its fans.

San Jose Earthquakes: again and again and actually again

The San Jose Earthquakes (formerly the Clash) won the 2003 MLS Cup and then promptly left town in 2005 unable to find any viable stadium solution. The team moved to Texas and started play as the Houston Dynamos in 2006, looking to gain foothold in one of America's leading Hispanic markets. The name however remained on the west coast and a "new" San Jose Earthquakes began to play in 2008 (are you still with me?) With stadium plans in tow the team currently plays at the small 10,500-seat Buck Shaw stadium, awaiting planning and construction for a new stadium. By my reckoning since the old NASL days this will be the third iteration of the Earthquakes and hopefully in a positive way, the last.

I have purposely saved the two latest additions to Major League Soccer until last for it is Toronto and Seattle that may foreshadow the future of professional soccer in America.

Stadium Toronto FC: a boys night out!

Toronto FC, the league's first Canadian-based team, owned by Maple Leaf Sports and Entertainments, blasted onto the league's landscape in the 2007 season playing at the purpose-built BMO field just a 10-minute train ride from one the of the world's most cosmopolitan cities. While struggling to make an impact on the field it was an instant success off it. A vociferous, passionate and knowledgeable fan base arrived almost overnight and filled the $62m (71 percent public money) 20,000-seat stadium for every game. The crowd reflected the city, young (24–34), international and passionate about sports with about 80 percent male. Toronto quickly became the poster child for what MLS hoped to achieve in all future markets around the country. Why success so quickly? It is difficult to pick just one factor but in a city of diverse ethnicities and therefore a strong understanding and experience of international soccer, the atmosphere generated from day one in their home stadium was one that reflected what many felt soccer should be-loud, passionate, intimate, intimidating and somewhat rowdy. BMO field is a true "home" stadium for Toronto FC and a daunting experience for away teams and fans. Just as soccer should be! The stadium is pretty basic with little in the way of luxury boxes and comfy seats, but it is close to downtown, has a direct commuter rail link and has in just two short seasons become the spiritual home for Toronto fans. These fans are also not afraid to travel away as the "crew" in Columbus were to discover.

Seattle: "the march of the sounders"

If the future of the league is Seattle then the sport is in great shape and the future of MLS secure. With an average attend-ance 2009 of 31,203 (of which 23,000 are season tickets holders) expected to rise to 38,000 in 2010, the Sounders bedeck the Seahawks stadium in a sea of green creating an atmosphere only the best in Europe replicate. Regarded as one of the most successful launches of *any* professional sports team in recent history they have the support of the city, the media, the soccer community, one of the founders of Microsoft, Paul Allen, movie mogul Joe Roth and television star (and huge soccer fan) Drew Carey. They blasted onto the scene in 2009 and although playing at the home of the NFL Seattle Seahawks, have created an atmosphere that shrinks the stadium and delivers to fans and television. At some stage it is hoped they will get their own stadium, particularly if MLS ever move to the European season, but with 2,000 fans traveling to a recent "away" game and thousands marching to every home game from the city center (or city center pubs to be correct) the team and its fans are along with Toronto changing the face and future of Major League Soccer. Sure, they have captured lightning in a bottle but that's what you plan to do when you start. Smart management, tight focus, and a constant dialog with its fans ensure the Seattle Sounders have a sense of identity hard to imagine after just one year. How much did Seattle listen? Well when choosing a name they balloted fans but failed to put the old "sounders" name on the list. The fans responded loudly that a "sounder" is what they wanted to be. How much are the fans involved? Well, impressed by the club membership philosophy of Barcelona, they insisted their fans have the ability to direct key decisions. Every four years the fans vote to either keep or fire the General Manager! The future looks great for Seattle and their passionate fans if the success continues, and it is reasonable to believe that at some stage they will invest in their own soccer-specific stadium, as eventually all teams should. Until then let the *"March of the Sounders"* continue.

Owning not renting

As the 2002 season kicked off, there were 10 teams, three own-ers and one soccer-specific stadium, but by the start of the 2010 season MLS will have 16 teams, 11 new investor groups and an additional 8 new soccer stadiums. People may criticize the on-field game but off the field these were world-class results. Particularly considering Vancouver and Portland are waiting in the wings to join in 2011. Driving this growth was the success of the Home Depot Center; the incredible success at the gate of both Toronto and Seattle, the gravity and quality of the ownership group and the belief that with real hard-core assets in the ground, in the form of stadiums, the worst days of the league were behind them and the future worth buying. At the core of it all were soccer-specific sta-diums and the transformation of MLS teams from being renters to landlords, the difference was immense on every level. By owning or controlling their own stadiums and revenue streams, teams are becoming operationally profitable and by controlling the calendar they can schedule games at times and dates that work for them-selves and their fans. How important is this? Well the Chicago Fire once spent 102 days on the road because of lack of stadium availa-bility, which is hardly conducive to building loyalty. It's not rocket science to understand that owning (or controlling) your own sta-dium is critical; it is however, quantum physics to work out how to get investors involved, stadiums built and public money to support it – part financial, part politics and part alchemy. But for MLS, the results speak for themselves, the challenge was now to create enough meaningful games to excite fans and fill the stadiums.

Off the field, the business story is clearly resonating strongly. On the field, it is still a struggle. The average attendance in 2002 was 15,821, the average in 2009 was 16,120, so after 8 seasons of remarkable stadium growth and $1b later there were just 299 fans per game extra to show for it. But this does not tell the whole story. Play-off attendance jumped 95 percent (highlighting maybe that the interest and intensity of fans was improving) and finally with 5 new teams, the number of American fans being exposed to Major League Soccer each season rose by 1.3m (61 percent) from 2.2 million to 3.5 million, a key number in the strategy to turn America into a soccer nation (see Table 5.2).

Table 5.2 MLS fan attendance 1996–2009

More teams, more fans

	1996	1999	2002	2008	2009
Total teams	10	12	10	14	15
Total fans	2,785,000	2,742,000	2,214,000	3,456,000	3,562,000
Season average	17,406	14,282	15,821	16,460	16,120
Playoff average	16,611	14,165	10,907	15,438	21,313

Source: MLS.

While many struggle, certain MLS teams are making money, and if they are making money, their value is increasing. Let's look at the winners and losers and why. The following information, in Table 5.3, was compiled by Forbes Magazine for a 2008 article on Major League Soccer Team Values and I have added attendance numbers and the price paid for each team.

The numbers do not include the contribution each team has to make to league operations, which as noted previously can be anywhere from $2m–$3m per year, with an offsetting $1m from SUM. In 2008 and 2009, the league adopted a very aggressive expansion program selling new teams to Seattle, Philadelphia, Portland and Vancouver, each selling for between $30m and $40m, more than offsetting league losses for the year. From 2008 onwards, it is highly likely that capital calls to the league are not necessary and may not be through to 2011, when the last two teams come on board. With operating losses of $25m per year it might be in the minds of league officials that an "expansion team a year keeps the doctor away" – certainly the banker anyhow.

No new numbers have appeared for revenue and income for Major League Soccer since 2007 and the league make a point of not releasing information (and have never confirmed or denied the Forbes 08 article.) In truth it's way too early in the League's development cycle to assess the true value of the clubs and anyone buying in now still needs to be looking at a 5–10 year maturation process. While the 2009 season saw regular season attendances climb 10 percent this was in the main due to Seattle exploding onto the scene as the best supported team in the league (30,897

Table 5.3 MLS team revenue and estimated values (2007 season)

A long way to go

Team	Revenue $(m)	Income $(m)	Crowd	Stadium	Price Paid $(m)	Value $(m)
LA Galaxy	36	4.0	24,252	Yes	26	100
Toronto	17	2.1	20,130	Yes	12	44
Chicago	16	(3.1)	16,490	Yes	30	41
FC Dallas	15	(0.5)	15,145	Yes	0*	39
NY RedBull	10	(4.5)	16,530	2010	30	36
DC United	13	(3.0)	20,967	No	32	35
Houston	10	(1.8)	15,883	No	22	33
Colorado	11	(2.2)	14,749	No	7.5	31
RSL**	7	(2.1)	15,960	Yes	10	30
New England	10	(1.5)	16,530	No	5	27
Chivas	10	(1.0)	14,305	No	10	24
Columbus	6	(4.5)	15,230	Yes	5	23
Kansas	5	(2.9)	11,586	No	20	22

Notes:
*Dallas was transferred from the League to the Hunt Group for no fee but assumption of operating costs.
**RSL new stadium did not open until 2008.
San Jose and Seattle were not in the League in 2007.
Sources: Compiled from *Forbes Magazine 2008* (operating income prior to interest and tax) Attendances, MLS. Excludes capital calls or distributions from Soccer United Marketing.

average) and adding 463,000 new fans. Without Seattle and in part San Jose (211,000) the overall attendance for the league would have dropped 10 percent, from 2007, with teams like D.C. United falling 23 per cent and New York 24 per cent (both missed the playoffs). Playoff attendance however increased 20 percent and television ratings for the playoffs and final were substantially higher. So the economy aside, it's tough at this stage to say clubs have either increased or decreased in value, it's just too early. What value has been added to the league by the staggering success of Seattle, the new stadium and launch at Philadelphia, the signing of two new clubs Vancouver and Portland in the soccer hotbed of the Pacific Northwest, who each paid a reported $35m? MLS is still in my mind a work in progress whose final plan is yet to be written. There are internal forces at play in the

USA and external factors in global soccer that will come into play over the next 10 years that will change the dynamic of American soccer and the value proposition for MLS. But let's ask a simple question as an investor (not a fan): would you rather buy West Ham United, reported $180m in debt and have a mature fan base of 30,000, or Seattle, which next year will average 38,000 and are profitable today? Sure, the glamour of the Premiership is compelling, but relegation to the Championship and financial ruin is not. Over the next 10 years as MLS develops the penny will drop in the global soccer market. (For the purposes of this book we will use the Forbes.com number as a way to compare MLS to other American sports and will assume the value and ranges they use apply in 2009.)

The model for MLS teams to be profitable appears to be a mixture of the following:

1 Own your own stadium (or low rent and strong revenue-share partnership).
2 Own the naming-rights sponsorship $$ for the stadium.
3 A strong jersey sponsor.
4 Strong and committed fan base (20,000 plus).
5 Good corporate sales and suite sales.
6 Player costs matched to revenue of club. No superstar that can't pay his way.
7 Be close to town and urban if possible drawing 16–35 males with disposable income.

Toronto and the newly formed Seattle are the models that highlight two of the ways to profitability. The former has a hard core and loyal 20,000 fan base that turn up for every game, mainly 25–34 males (80 percent) who, as Forbes details, spend an average of $4.00 on concessions per game. The stadium is not necessarily "plush", it has very few luxury suites but it's compact and atmospheric, close to downtown and is a "cash generating machine" on game day. Newly opened Seattle (2009) is a downtown team with 32,000 fans and major sponsors and although they do not own their stadium (its owned by the NFL Seattle Seahawks) I presume they have a very strong revenue-share agreement as according to their owner Joe Roth, they will be profitable in their first year. (If not they actually may have a problem for its hard to see it getting any better than it already is.) Real Salt Lake started their first season in 2008 and with both a jersey sponsor and a naming-rights partner should be profitable. Colorado own their stadium and have both a naming and shirt sponsor but the fan base needs building before they will make it. If the NY RedBulls can reconnect, they could explode – great stadium, great location. Chicago will struggle to turn a profit as although they have a shirt sponsor at $2m per year with Best Buy the stadium is 100 percent publicly funded and the team receive very little of the important concession income and nothing from the $750,000 per year naming-rights agreement with Toyota. No more than a tenant, Chicago will struggle unless new agreements are reached. Columbus struggles from being in a small media market that has made it tough to generate the all important naming rights and corporate revenue that would see them to profitability. All other teams need workable stadium deals and until they achieve this, it's a long road to profitability.

The new boys

Philadelphia Union, who begin playing in 2010, negotiated a very strong agreement for a new stadium and are confident of being profitable in the second year. The new franchises in Vancouver and Portland who begin in 2011 equally look like they have every chance of turning profitable. Both will be downtown stadiums, both should draw a strong urban 18–35 male audience, both should, if they are smart, have negotiated a reasonable rent and revenue-share agreement (both teams are playing in renovated stadiums being retro-fitted for soccer), and both are in the Seattle "sphere" for rivalry and competition that will drive fan rivalry and media attention. If these three teams can capture the Toronto and Seattle experience the league could have six or more clubs generating positive cash flow, a critical ingredient to increasing club value – though let's face it, since when has normal business rationale applied to sports?

Is it a good investment compared to other sports?

The truth of the matter is, soccer does not and should not worry about where it currently stacks up against other potential sports leagues and investment opportunities. It needs to stick to, and focus on, its own game plan, trying to chase other more entrenched sports is a recipe for financial ruin. Around for decades, they are all at a stage of maturity MLS is not. It is too early to compare and judge with any relevance, although, however, it is interesting to look.

With all other leagues having higher ticket prices, higher average attendances, and except the NFL, more games, it is hardly surprising their revenues blow MLS away. The average ticket price for a NFL game is $88.00, for the NBA $66.00 but for MLS it is $25.00 (for some of its teams, a lot less). Only the LA Galaxy come close with $36m in revenues, excluding the 300,000 Beckham Galaxy shirts at $70 a "pop" that Adidas sold (licensing revenues residing with the league). (See Table 5.4.)

It is television however where the most startling disparity can be seen. MLS has only just secured its first paid TV contract which while an evolutionary step for the league, would hardly keep the NFL in plasma sets for its locker room. Only one thing "moves" TV rights income and that's ratings. MLS doesn't have them yet. We will look at television ratings for soccer in the USA later in the book, suffice to say, there's a lot of upside left.

Not good enough

The overriding complaint from any soccer fan not engaging with an MLS team is that the quality of both players and play is not good enough and definitely not as good as they can see on television seven days a week. They are of course right. It is clear to every soccer fan in America and Canada that watching Chelsea versus Real Madrid in a Champions League match on Fox is of an infinitely higher quality and more exciting than Chicago versus FC Dallas on any day of the week and three times on Sunday.

Table 5.4 MLS financial performance and valuations compared to major professional sports leagues in the USA

Plenty of upside!

League	Top Revenue ($m)	Bottom Revenue ($m)	Avg Gates	Home Games	Av Ticket Price ($)	Team Salaries ($m)	Player Player ($m)	TV Income	Team Value High	Team Value Low
NFL	345	208	66,629	8	88	142	1.1	$4b	$1.65b	$797m
NBA	209	91	17,141	41	66	78	5.4	$1.2b	$667m	$254m
MLB	375	139	32,528	81	36	36	3	$640m	$1.5b	$48m
NHL	168	66	17,147	41	40	53	1.4	$232m**	$470m	$138m
MLS (2007)	36	5	16,460	15	25	3	3	$22m*	$100m	$22m

Sources: Pro-league numbers extracted from Forbes.com 2009 business of sports. MLS Salary average from MLSPU public report (excludes Beckham's $6.5m salary).
* Includes fees for US Soccer games.
** Additional revenue received for games aired on network television.

The combined wealth and salaries of Chelsea and Real Madrid could buy both of the MLS teams outright, including their stadiums, their players, the players' houses and for good measure put all their kids through college. The MLS players know it and so too do most of the fans, owners and league executives. While we are at it, let's put to bed one other issue, just because a MLS team might tie or "just lose" to Chelsea, Real Madrid, AC Milan, Juventus or Barcelona when they come to the USA to play a friendly, it does not mean that they are maybe "close to being as good as them" or could at least compete in the top half of the Premiership or La Liga from which they came. It is a great experience and a good chance for players to grow and learn, but on a cold Tuesday night in November, with a "Champions League" place on the line, they would be chasing shadows. This is not to disparage MLS players, just to emphasize a point, that when Ronaldo is sold for $140m and earns $250,000 a week we have no right to expect to compare our teams on the field or on television to them and trying to do so is both unfair and results only in disappointment. Reality is important in moving forward and the reality is that if soccer people wait until MLS teams are as good as the "foreign" teams or until MLS teams can afford to buy the best players, before engaging, they are going to be "wheeled" in wearing a hearing aid and incontinence pants before they see a game! Everyone knows the quality needs to improve but it's a matter of doing so without sinking the league or driving its teams to bankruptcy. Pele was brilliant, but the NASL and its teams however went bust.

We would all love to see the world's best playing in MLS but their absence should not be used as an excuse for stagnation. The future of Major League Soccer lies with the "club", not the player; it lies with the passion and loyalty of fans, not the "hired" skills of a transient star and it lives in ideals and beliefs ingrained in the badge rather than the size of the paycheck written. Yes, teams will ultimately need to spend more to attract better players, but they should also spend to attract more fans. For real fans it's never about the player, it's about the club. (The examples are legions of fans worshipping him when he plays for you, and hating him once transferred.) MLS teams need to wake up each morning not wondering where their next player is coming from but rather their next "fan", and I don't mean spectators, most teams have had 15 years of knowing where they are.

It's make your mind up time

MLS still has many challenges ahead of it but here in my opinion are five important ones:

1 Replicating what is happening in markets such as Toronto and Seattle and Los Angeles and ensuring that all new expansion clubs learn from these best practices.
2 Working with existing teams to increase fan "identity" and "loyalty" while switching or expanding their fans bases into the 18–49 male/female market.
3 Ensure every team has a stadium "solution" that enables them to move into sustainable profitability.
4 Decide which clubs and markets are not going to make the above happen and move them to markets that can. (As a soccer fan myself this hurts but if the losses are unsustainable and perpetual, the club will eventually fold.)
5 Ensuring new stadiums are located where the fans are.

The last point is a tough one as it is difficult to turn away from a good land deal and supportive local city willing to spend millions. The question becomes: do you build a perfect stadium with playing fields and amenities (targeting youth soccer) on the outskirts of cities or a simpler, less complex stadium close to town and your new target audience? The league and owners must decide but I know which way I would lean, as near to the urban 21–35 year olds and the bars and communities they inhabit, as possible.

Morning Joe

There is a great news show on American TV every morning called, appropriately, "Morning Joe" hosted by Joe Scarborough (a big soccer man by the way). At the end of each show he has each of his co-host and panelists summarize, usually humorously, just what they have learned today.

Here are fifteen things I have learned about MLS:

1 It survived … it nearly didn't though!
2 There must be a viable Division One Professional League in the USA and MLS must be it. This is the last chance and it must succeed. It's important for the sport on **every** level.
3 MLS might not provide riches today but in the next 10–15 years it easily could.
4 American soccer kids need to be instilled with the dream of becoming a professional player whether with MLS or as a stopping point or thru-way to Barcelona. Either works.
5 The current ownership is as good as soccer has ever had and likely ever will investing over $1b in stadiums. This is professional soccer's last shot and we need them to prosper. If they go away we are done!
6 The future of MLS fans are 16–45 year old, urban, with disposable income and time.
7 20–30,000 seat stadiums preferably in or close to downtown areas.
8 It's okay to support another team. Nothing wrong in being a Real Salt Lake and Arsenal fan or LA Galaxy and Barcelona fan. Different teams, different countries. Soccer Americans should pick and support a MLS team however.
9 MLS cannot break the bank on players that it cannot afford. Teams that can afford it should within reason be allowed to spend more on quality if they wish. Parity is not necessarily the right path. There will always be big and small clubs. The league however needs cautious growth until fan bases, stadiums and profits are in place.
10 20,000 fans, 20 games per season, rather than 400,000 spectators once a season. The future lies in deeper interaction with the fan, build out from there.
11 There should never be another MLS game "ever" shown on television that has American football lines showing. It damages the team, the league and the sport.
12 Any team without a soccer-specific stadium solution that creates the right atmosphere for fans and profitability for its team needs to seriously look at moving.

13 The argument over quality is one that will never go away. Toronto are no Real Madrid, but have great fans and a 16,000 waiting list for tickets. First become the best league in the region, better than Mexico's Futbol Liga. Buy their players, scout the best talent, then build.

14 Cynics and soccer snobs need to see the bigger picture. Europe and South America will probably always have better leagues and players, and the games on television are superior. However you are living in America, these are your cities and teams and you should get behind them. For soccer to be seen as a true success in America it needs a strong professional league. *Everyone* in American soccer will benefit from it.

15 It's been a tough road, but the worst is behind it.

On a special note, I am always a believer that individuals change the course of events and that American soccer in particular has needed such committed "friends" to guide it through very turbulent times. In Lamar Hunt MLS was fortunate to have a man who loved soccer, had taken his family to every world cup since 1966 (except when the Argentineans were threatening to kidnap Americans), sent his son Clark to train with West Ham in his summers, lost money in the NASL yet still backed MLS, built a stadium in Columbus when everyone said "don't" and backed Anschutz at the "ranch" when the wheels were coming off the league. A soccer man through and through who though diagnosed with cancer after France 98, made it to Korea and Japan, visited every stadium and as Clark told the story, lived to witness his proudest moment in soccer as the USA Team nearly, and probably should have, beat Germany to make the World Cup Semi Final. He passed away in December 2006 – a good soccer man lost.

Here are ten things I am sure MLS know:

1 There is still a "disconnect" between the young kids playing the game and professional soccer. It's been 15 years and many kids still don't get MLS.

2 Television ratings are still small and until these rise MLS will never command a major television deal. Production quality has improved dramatically as has the overall presentation;

digital playbacks improve everything. Playoff television games for 2009 had excellent atmosphere and ratings increase.

3 Quality of play is an issue for many and will keep fans away. Assuming the top five players will always go to Europe, MLS needs to keep the rest and work out a reasonable cap to do so. Will need better players over the next decade to succeed.

4 The American soccer fan is getting more educated and can see high quality soccer from all over the world both on TV and now live through Soccer United Marketing efforts. Is it good for MLS; are they creating a monster?

5 The older MLS Teams were truly the pioneers, but many are now looking tired and weary and struggling to re-energize their fan bases. Tough choices ahead.

6 Many teams are still losing money; as is the league. Profitable teams are emerging and they need to learn from them.

7 MLS's role is to put the best teams on the field, not to build a USA National Team. When the league improves US players will improve.

8 There is a need to further engage Hispanics. Population shifts demand it. Step one is to become better than the Mexican league, merge with them, buy their players and win Concacaf tournaments.

9 It is important for the MLS that its coaches are as highly qualified as their international counterparts.

10 Millions of soccer Americans are still not engaged with MLS.

It is still a difficult road ahead for MLS and while it is on solid ground with deep-pocketed owners, new stadiums and vibrant teams, there is still much to do and challenges to face. Many of MLS's greatest successes are off the field, namely: staying alive; building stadiums and amassing a great ownership group. Not the glamorous front of house stuff that fans get excited by and I have yet to hear fans sing in unison "there is only one Phil Anschutz" or "Garber Garber give us a wave", nor should they, but if they knew how close it all was to collapsing they might have.

More on the future of MLS later in the book but if the first 15 years has been about survival and balance sheets the next needs will be about fans and players, in that order.

Beckham (or "goldenballs" as Posh quaintly refers to him)

Probably deserving of a whole chapter, and indeed a book has already been written on the saga, for my money, Beckham has been phenomenal for US Soccer, elevating it in the media beyond anything the sport could have dreamed in 2007. He is gracious to every kid, parent and fan, signing autographs, posing for pictures and personable to a fault, his move to AC Milan necessary and his return eventually to help soccer, in the States inevitable. To the fans that booed him, fair play that's their prerogative, it's what fans do. The Beckham saga is a daily ritual in Europe and cannon fodder for the newspapers and media. Has it damaged soccer in the USA? Not a bit, as the real fans know why he has to go back on loan and do not begrudge it. As for the others, he will probably be back before they do.

By the way, despite what the media might say Beckham is not the savior or future of soccer in America and I am sure he would agree. Stadiums are more important, fans are more important, committed owners are more important, television is more important, and a league of talented players – not just one – is more important. My sense is Beckham might play a bigger role off the field than he does on it and, if his public commitment to help build soccer in America is as genuine as it seems, then his contribution could be immense. He has single-handily rescued England's faltering 2018 bid and, if he can bring the same enthusiasm to promoting US soccer, we are in great shape. One of his kids is named Brooklyn so it's a start.

Chapter 6

Soccer United Marketing

It's "soccer" on the phone

In 2002, if you were the Chief Marketing Officer for a major American corporation trying to understand the soccer market your assistant might be putting through the following calls:

- it's US Soccer on the phone, they would like to talk about sponsoring their teams
- it's MLS on the phone, they would like you to sponsor their league
- it's US Youth Soccer on the phone, they have 3.2 million kids you can sponsor
- it's Concacaf on the phone, do you want to sponsor the Gold Cup?
- hola, its the Mexican Federation, their team is playing next week ... would you like ...?
- it's Manchester United on the phone, do you want to sponsor their tour?

You get the picture. The marketplace was fragmented, competitive and confusing to just about everyone in corporate America. Companies may have thought they wanted to buy "soccer" but had very little idea as to what that really meant. Other sports were simpler, if corporate America wanted baseball they could buy the "MLB", football the "NFL", basketball the "NBA", but soccer, well, that just confused them and as such the "boss" was most likely off to the SuperBowl again! Garber recognized four things about the landscape he viewed, each one reflective of the turnaround plan presented "at the ranch".

1 Every dollar that went into a soccer property other than MLS was a dollar lost.

155

2 The intense competition was confusing the market and pushing dollars away that might otherwise come into the sport.

3 If they could gain control of these properties they could probably generate revenues that could offset losses in MLS.

4 They could use the properties to build awareness and fan support for MLS.

It was clear that soccer would never succeed commercially if it could not be understood and purchased in a simple, deliverable and professional manner. Sponsorship spending is usually a zero sum game and the "big guns" had no intention of letting soccer steal their share. To be successful soccer had to be unified, build gravitas and as usual punch above its weight! Garber set about rolling out his plan.

First, as proposed, MLS went ahead and acquired the TV rights to the 2002 and 2006 World Cups, gambling they could turn a profit by selling the advertising. With $70m to recover they needed to sell a lot. To accomplish this they formed a new company Soccer United Media (SUM) in partnership with Dentsu. You would like to think that fortune favors the brave in business and fortunately for MLS, in this case it did. The USA team was to have its best World Cup ever in 2002: stunning Portugal 3–2 in the opening game, beating its fiercest rivals, Mexico, in round of 16 and losing (some would say unluckily) to Germany 1–0 in the quarter-finals. The late rounds games brought advertisers scurrying to the table. Throughout America, soccer fans awoke in the middle of the night and early morning to congregate in bars and at special screenings, to watch live games. Over 3.5 million viewers tuning in at 7.30AM on the East Coast (4.30AM Los Angeles) to watch the USA's quarter-final match with Germany, making it the most watched soccer broadcast in ESPN television history. Financially, 2002 represented a small return but on the back of the team's great performance and in the hope of a repeat, corporate America pre-bought much of the World Cup 06 Germany coverage before the first ball was kicked, which was just as well really as the USA team crashed out in the early rounds. While lamenting the loss, the league could gain comfort in counting their $10m return on the $70m investment, coincidentally just about enough to cover the battle they had fought with their players.

Rolling up rights

World Cup rights were just the first phase of an ambitious plan to control the commercial destiny for soccer in the USA and with the formation of Soccer United Marketing (SUM) the MLS owners had a vehicle and structure with which to launch their attack. The process of rolling up the rights however would take a serious commitment of both time and dollars. Acquiring the rights to sell MLS was probably not too tough given that the owners of Soccer United Marketing also owned the league, SUM agreeing to pay MLS (itself) $5m per year for the rights to sell national sponsorships. These rights gave SUM vital inventory, geographic scale and a solid and expansive set of deliverables to offer.

Next on the radar screen was acquiring the rights to the United States Men's and Women's National Teams and therefore, the power and importance of the Red, White and Blue, highlighted in an earlier chapter. Since 1998, the US Soccer marketing rights had been held by a partnership between Nike and IMG guaranteeing the Federation close to $15m a year, with Nike delivering $11m of this for the right to be the exclusive apparel sponsors and IMG's role being to find additional sponsors. With little success apart from an attractive $2m-plus-a-year deal with Philips, it was no surprise, with expensive guarantees to meet, that they happily agreed in 2004 to hand over the responsibility to Soccer United Marketing. The Federation of course did not lose out with SUM committing to pay them $3.5 to $4.5m per year, a number which I am sure mirrored their previous agreement. They were equally thrilled that 16 of their games would be aired on ABC, ESPN and Univision each year without them having to pay for the privilege.

Mexico: the best supported team in America

It had not escaped the notice of SUM that the best supported team in America was Mexico and that they accounted for 67 percent of the 35 million Hispanics that call the US home. AEG had actually been the first to act, which being based in LA, home to 10 million Mexicans, was no surprise, securing the rights to act as sole marketing agent and promoter for the team in the USA. With the creation of SUM, these rights were transferred to the new marketing entity for all to share and of course pay. Initially guaranteeing the Mexican Federation $1m per year rising to $2m in 2005, fees then rose dramatically in 2006 when it had become eminently clear that marketing Mexico was a very lucrative venture, with a new four-year deal giving Mexico $18–$20m for playing a total of 22 games over the period. The partnership poured millions of dollars into the Mexican Federation's coffers, which depending on your viewpoint is a good or bad thing for the progress of the US National Team. Its strongest benefit for SUM however was its ability to open doors to US Soccer corporations that were searching for ways to reach the Hispanic audience.

The Concacaf Gold Cup: help thy neighbor

Continuing to round up properties that would appeal to the US Hispanic community, the next step was to acquire the rights to the Concacaf Gold Cup (a European Championships-style event) that pitted the region's top national teams. The prize was not a lot of money but a lucrative invitation to the FIFA Confederations Cup, which in 2009 saw the USA beat Spain to make the final. The event, held every two years, still has a way to go to become a must-win trophy on the US Soccer calendar, as witnessed by the "reserve" team it sent out in the 2009 event – a reserve team hammered and humiliated by Mexico 5–0 in front of 79,000 fans in New York with millions watching live on television. This was not one of US Soccer's greatest days, or decisions, with most Americans not understanding it was a "reserve" team and simply seeing "Mexico humiliate USA" spread across the sports pages.

Increasing their offering of Hispanic properties, Soccer United Marketing acquired the rights to Interleague, the qualification tournament that Mexican Club teams have to go through to qualify for the prestigious South American Copa Libertadores. Interestingly, the qualification process only involves Mexican teams yet they stage it in the USA, usually LA, Houston and Dallas, cities with huge Mexican populations, the dollar proving just too much of an allure. For SUM it was increased inventory and worth the $1.5m a year they paid. In what might be a future trend, SUM decided to expand its offering by creating a new Superliga – $1m "winner takes all" prize for the top four Mexican and top four MLS teams. In a final nod to the burgeoning US Hispanic market SUM also acquired the marketing rights to Chivas de Guadalajara, Mexico's second best supported team in America. (This is a little like owning the marketing rights to Manchester United in Asia except Chivas can play 10 times a year in the market.) With most of the competitive Hispanic and Anglo properties now locked in there was only one further area of weakness in Garber's plan for total domination of the commercial landscape for US Soccer and that was the attack that came every year from overseas.

Every kid a fan

For years rumors have swirled around the world as to the huge new soccer market opening up in America and the potential riches to be gained from it. With 18 millions kids playing the game, most without a fixed allegiance to any soccer team, the big clubs set sail like Columbus centuries before, to conquer unexplored territories and open up the "new soccer world" for themselves and the great game. Their hopes, of course, were for a Barcelona, Real Madrid, Manchester United or Chelsea shirt on every kid in America, a lifelong fan, an unexpected player they could sign and of course a few dollars in their back pocket. Ten years ago they had no hope, five years ago there was some light but today, as we enter the 2010 season, the battle for the minds and attire of American fans and players is on and worth fighting for. Why? Because the convergence of soccer on television, access on the internet, EA Sports and the appearance of the world's greatest teams and players on US soil has created for the first time in American soccer a universe of American soccer fans and players that are highly interested in and educated to the international game and the teams and players that dominate it. English Premiership, Champions League La Liga, UEFA Cup, Bundesleague and Italian league soccer can all be seen every day on some television channel in America somewhere along with news of Ronaldo's $140m transfer, Chelsea outspending the world and then getting outspent by Manchester City, Messi tormenting for Barcelona, and Manchester United's theater of dreams. Seeing this, they switch on the computer, fire up FIFA 2010 and live it for themselves. They buy Rooney, decide tactics for AC Milan, sack Mourinho, transfer Fabregas and win the Champions League. While just a computer game it's also soccer osmosis, educating a nation of young kids. Ask a young American soccer player who his favorite soccer player is and the chances are it will be a Messi, Rooney, Ronaldo, Henry or Torres, rather than Dempsey, Altidore or Donovan. This of course needs to change but at least they have a favorite player whereas five years ago most did not.

It's no wonder that Europe's best come knocking every year. It's also the reason why Soccer United Marketing wanted a piece of the game promotion pie and why not? The teams were going to come and play anyway so why not become a promoter, share in any spoils and cross-promote with MLS, while at the same time generating even more inventory and sponsorship opportunities for its corporate partners.

Man United get booed

Manchester United had made the first real push to "crack" the US market, first entering into a landmark "joint marketing" deal with the New York Yankees, phenomenal on paper and in the papers, but delivering little as the YankeesNet Company, charged with executing the deal, dissolved. The reality was that Giggs, Scholes, Neville and everyone else in the United team, bar Beckham (when he played for them) could all have tap danced in the middle of Time Square wearing cowboy hats and pink tutus and 99.9 percent – make that 99.99 percent – of New Yorkers would not have recognized them. Hard core soccer fans around the country would however and they embarked on a summer tour in 2003 that took them to Seattle, Los Angeles, New York and Philadelphia playing against the likes of Club America, Barcelona and Celtic along the way, averaging 68,000 per match for their first appearance in the US for over 20 years. They returned the following year to play three matches that saw them draw 62,000 – still impressive, but not as. By putting out a "c" team in Chicago, they were booed by the crowd (more educated than they thought) and quickly flew out a few more stars for their next match in New York. Ferguson was getting a quick and sharp lesson that American soccer fans will pay to see the best, but the best had better show up. It's a very precarious business promoting games in the USA and many companies have gone "under" trying, as Champions World, Manchester United's promoter did, not because United didn't draw but because other teams brought in to expand the tour did not. The reality was that only the very best teams "draw" in the States and that probably shortens the list to United, Barcelona and Real Madrid, with maybe Chelsea a close fourth. The remainder, while attractive, are not must-sees and over-paying them a sure fire way to losses – SUM signing a long-term marketing agreement with Barcelona while promoting Real Madrid in 2009 emphasizes the point.

While staging some of the biggest games of the summer SUM does not have a monopoly and independent promoters still bring teams into play. Creative Artists (CAA), one of America's largest talent agencies (Tom Cruise among others), have ventured into the game promotion business bringing in Chelsea, AC Milan, Inter Milan and Club America, averaging a very respectable, if not blockbuster, 56,102 fans per game. In total over the course of 51 days in the summer of 2009, including exhibition tours, over 100 professional soccer matches were played in the USA with 2m fans pouring through the gates in 27 different cities and stadiums. (See Table 6.1 for example.) That's a lot of soccer and some big crowds for a country still developing as a soccer nation.

Multiple touch points

Clearly by 2010 the strategy of creating a company that would control all of the key commercial rights for soccer in the USA was working and resonating strongly with sponsors. Sometimes it was the classic "if you want Mexico, you must buy US Soccer or if you want US Soccer, you must buy MLS or if you want MLS, you must buy Concacaf", but whatever the approach, it was working. As much as soccer is a tactical game so too is selling soccer, just with different players and uniforms. Having a variety of properties was the key to delivering any soccer demographic

Table 6.1 Major attendances: summer of soccer 2009

Big games in any country

Game	Attendance	City
Barcelona v. LA Galaxy	94,194	LA
Barcelona v. Seattle	66,848	Seattle
Barcelona v. Chivas	61,572	San Francisco
Real Madrid v. D.C.United	72,368	Landover md
Mexico v. Haiti	82,252	Dallas
Mexico v. Venezuela	51,115	Atlanta
Mexico v. Panama	47,713	Houston
USA v. Honduras	55,173	Chicago
USA v. Mexico	79,156	New York

Source: MLSnet.com.

a sponsor demanded, whether that be 25–34 year-old males, soccer moms and their kids, or fervent soccer-mad Hispanics, the chances are Soccer United Marketing had a property that could fit (and maybe even two). Doug Quinn, President of SUM and a 15-year veteran of the NFL, calls it "multiple corporate touch points". I call it "covering all bases", the former of course sounds a lot smarter (see Table 6.2).

With success however comes responsibility and with major corporate sponsors comes scrutiny. There was little point in amassing a portfolio of properties if they could not all be delivered to the same professional standard. The adage that you're only as good as your weakest link certainly applied to Soccer United Marketing and exacting sponsors would listen to few excuses. For the strategy to work, all properties have to deliver and, once in the portfolio, SUM spent a tremendous amount of time and resources marketing, positioning and where necessary, professionalizing the property. This was particularly true for the Mexican national team program, once ad hoc and random (notorious for just showing up and playing), was now organized, systematic and programmed to meet the increasing demands of fans and sponsors alike. Mexican national team games are now day-long events with fiestas, soccer festivals, music and of course

Table 6.2 Sample of sponsors highlighting strategy of bringing multiple brands into soccer

	Selling the sport					
Category	USA Team	MLS	Mexico	Gold Cup	Concacaf CL	WPS
Apparel	Nike	adidas	adidas	Puma	Nike	Puma
Beer	Budweiser	Budweiser	Budweiser	Miller Lite		
Insurance/ Banking			Allstate	State Farm	State Farm	Citi
Credit Card	Visa	Visa	Visa		Master-Card	
Telecoms		AT&T	AT&T	Sprint	T-Mobile	
Soft Drink	Pepsi	Pepsi	Coca Cola			
Auto	Volkswagen	Volkswagen		GMC		
Home Improvement			Home Depot	Lowes		

Source: Compiled from Soccer United Marketing.

sponsor activations, planned months in advance and executed professionally. This was equally true of the Concacaf Gold Cup, which was started in 1991 as a one-city event with no television, but as a SUM property, in 2009 the tournament was hosted in 13 cities and broadcast nationally.

The overall strategy, while hard to execute, was clear, to present a unified professionally organized suite of high quality soccer properties for corporate America to purchase. It allowed SUM to ask sponsors for a bigger "buy", delivering larger programs with more deliverables, wider reach and depth, which were critical if soccer was to compete with the scale and size of programs being offered by their competitors, the NHL, NBA, MLB and NFL.

Rolling up television rights: soccer gets paid

FIFA had much to be grateful for to SUM and its broadcast partners ABC and ESPN in ensuring that both the 2002 and 2006

World Cups were aired on English-language television in the US and for also proving it could be a profitable exercise. This was to matter little however when NBC made a pre-emptive $350m strike to acquire the rights for the South Africa 2010 and Brazil 2014 World Cups, a strike that left everyone in US Soccer scrambling, but FIFA accepting was a tremendous blow to Garber's strategy of unifying and dominating the commercial US Soccer market. His approach to soccer was always "big picture" with World Cup the biggest picture of all. The thought of these rights not being in friendly, and by friendly I mean ABC and ESPN, hands, was enough for him to go on the offensive, to form an alliance of the willing and battle to fight off the threat. Not that NBC weren't a great network, they indeed had a long history of delivering tear-jerking Olympic "moments" and patriotic flag-waving vignettes, it was just that they had nothing invested in soccer in the USA and had never been part of the soccer landscape. In fact, it was even felt that when NBC did have the opportunity to air soccer (the 1996 US Women's Team Gold Medal match for example) they invariably decided against it. While giving NBC the World Cup would benefit NBC, it would likely do little for soccer in the USA and it was this message that winged its way to Zurich. Garber rallied Chuck Blazer, General Secretary of Concacaf, to "request" that a stay of execution be placed on ratifying the NBC deal, recognizing that while it had been accepted there was still this final procedural hurdle to clear, a request that after a few thumps of the table was granted. With breathing room secured, Garber rallied John Skipper from ABC/EPSN, David Downs, at the time President of Univision, his MLS owners including Phil Anschutz and anyone else who could bring pressure to bear on influencing the decision. Two weeks of back and forth meetings and presentations and it became clear that FIFA was wilting, coming to understand the role that World Cup coverage played in promoting the growth at all levels of the sport in the USA. It also helped of course that the new ABC/Univision proposal of $425m for both Cups was $75m more than NBC had offered. In the end and despite the fact that NBC were convinced the deal was "theirs to lose", they lost, with FIFA changing their minds and assigning the rights to ABC, ESPN and Univision, who, relieved to get back in the game and, indeed controlling the game, were now ready to pay the quid pro quo for MLS efforts in fighting off the usurper.

The quid pro quo

First, ABC agreed an eight-year deal to air three MLS games per season and a game of the week on ESPN/ESPN 2. They equally agreed to air 16 USA National Team games in the same package – paying $8m per year and covering all production costs. The deal also allowed MLS to sell those games not covered in the ESPN agreement to other English-language channels with Fox Soccer Channel paying $2m a year for a Saturday night "game of the week", a game that would also feature on Fox Sports Espanol. To emphasize the strength of the strategy, SUM also gave Fox the rights to air two US National Team men's games, two women's games along with giving them annual rights to exhibition matches, which over the next four years would include Barcelona, Real Madrid and Chelsea.

Univision! the other beneficiary of the last minute smash and grab on NBC World Cup ambitions, returned to MLS, a league they had left with some acrimony in 1999. They too signed an eight-year deal paying $10m per year for the Spanish language rights to all US Soccer and Soccer United Marketing games. The deal gave them ten US National Team games, fourteen Interleague games (more later), five other major international and first rights to a "muted" new SuperLiga competition that would pit the top eight club teams in Mexico and MLS against each other, for a potential $1m prize. Univision agreed to air its MLS games on Sunday or Wednesday nights but of course insisted that its slate of games were top heavy with Hispanic fan bases and LA Galaxy, Houston, Chivas were top of their list, as a diet of Kansas versus Columbus would not cut it. It was not all perfect and SUM would have to pay all production costs surrounding the games (which as they were already producing the games really just meant providing a "clean feed") and equally the games would also not be aired on its main Univision network (the BBC of the Spanish TV world in terms of reach) but instead the US Team games would air on Galavision and MLS on Telefutura, their smaller sister networks. It was not perfect, but a substantial rights fee and MLS were back in with Univision.

An English viewpoint

It's a pretty unique situation to have one company control so much of the commercial landscape of a sport. To put it in perspective, it is like Richard Branson and his buddies owning and operating the English Premier League, marketing and selling the England National Team, broadcasting all games on Sky Television and BBC, and for good measure staging international matches on behalf of Scotland in grounds around England. Not possible of course and maybe even illegal in European law, but in the US without this unified approach it is highly doubtful that soccer would be as commercially successful as it is today. (The worst part of the above for an Englishman of course would be doing anything to help Scotland get better, we like them just the way they are, and by the way we do want our Wembley turf and cross-bar back some day!)

Is it helping MLS?

Buying World Cup "rights", marketing Mexico, hosting Barcelona, expanding Concacaf and developing Mexico's leading club, Chivas, is all very well and clearly profitable but is it achieving what it was originally created to do, namely:

1 offset losses by building sustainable new profit streams;
2 increase fan awareness and attendance for Major League Soccer; and
3 expand and develop the US Soccer market?

The first it actually achieved and although owners had to initially put capital into SUM to get it started (about $1m each per owner over the first four years) this money was recouped in 2006 when on the back of $46m in World Cup advertising sales and a $16m profit for the year, it made its first ever "distribution" sending $1.3m per team back to their owners.

Offset losses?

Distributions back to owners are of course most welcome and a consistent $1m to $1.5m a year certainly helps. It's a little like "robbing Peter to pay Paul" as the same owners receiving the "windfall" need to then contribute monies back to MLS league operations to cover costs. It does however represent money that league operations themselves would not generate, and as such "found". It cannot however mask the fact that the league and the teams themselves need to stand on their own two feet and generate organically the profits they need to survive and thrive. With MLS losing anywhere from $25–30m a year (through 2006), requiring $2.5m to $3m in capital calls, and most teams locally losing an additional $1m–$3m, a million-dollar distribution is not going to solve the big picture financial woes. SUM are now out of the World Cup Rights business and therefore will not have the potential windfall (or risk), needing to maximize their existing properties and create new ones to continue "feeding" their owners.

Bigger gates for MLS?

This has been achieved. One of the key foundations of the 2002 turnaround plan was that a rising tide would raise all ships and the more people that were involved, attending and watching soccer in the USA, then the more would come out to watch MLS. The numbers reflect that this actually did pan out. From the league's darkest days in 2002, the overall number of fans attending MLS games in 2009 increased by over 1.3 million (albeit on the back of five new expansion teams). The overall MLS league average rose from 15,821 to 16,120 per game, a 2 percent increase.

There are two schools of thought here, the cynical one that goes 16,120 is still a poor crowd for a professional sports team in America and the 2 percent rise comes from a depressing low in 2002; and the optimistic one that says hey 16,120 is better than the alternative, which was closing the league and by its very survival MLS has at least given itself a chance to "kick on" to the next level. Many leagues that started either at the same time or during MLS's rise have collapsed including the much vaunted XFL

Football League, with its NBC millions, Arena Football (Bon Jovi owned a team), and unfortunately the Women's Professional League (WUSA). The two schools of thought are both true but the latter at least gives MLS a chance to fix the former. The longer the league survives, the longer it puts down stadium roots and the longer it stimulates the US Soccer market, the more is the likelihood that the converging forces of increased attendances, control of revenue streams, corporate involvement and broadcaster competition will drive it to profitability. The signs are however that this might not be that far away, with LA, Toronto and Seattle leading the way.

Major League Soccer and Soccer United Marketing are inextricably joined at the hip. A different corporate structure but the same owners and the same intertwined goals. Without launching SUM and successfully executing its strategy the league would have collapsed. It was started to save MLS and while it has grown to have a life and identity of its own it's achieved its original purpose: the league survived.

It is interesting to note however that the concept for rolling up marketing rights appeared in the first business plans for league soccer way back in 1993, along of course with soccer-specific stadiums, both yanked from the plan. The first because it was feared a land grab for marketing rights would scare off the Board of Directors of US Soccer whose vote they needed to form the league, the second because of cost and risk. It doesn't mean they were bad ideas – just that it was the wrong time. Polished up and enhanced, they are now the building blocks for the future.

CHAPTER 7

The Agents Arrive: There Must be Money Somewhere ... Or Is There?

In the era of $350,000 per week contracts, orchestrated by avaricious agents for their pampered stars to parade their wares in Spain, Italy and England, it's interesting and at times disheartening to look at just how the USA domestic players have fared over the past 20 years. While in 2009 Clint Dempsey, the Fulham striker and Texan native, signed a reported $75,000 per week five-year contract and Tim Howard at Everton and Brad Friedel at Aston Villa both "pull down" serious salaries, what of those however not driving Bentley convertibles down the Kings Road in London? What of those toiling in Kansas, taking second jobs in D.C. and freezing in Chicago? What of the plight of US-born professional soccer players?

I am sure there are days when an American soccer player waking up to make morning practice secretly wishes that their sporting gifts blessed them with 6 feet and 10 inches in height, muscles the size of bowling balls or an arm like a catapult, as opposed to dexterous feet, a hard head and the ability to run all day. For any one of the first three attributes would likely open the door to the riches of the NBA, NFL or MLB, while the ones they inherited destined them to a life of connecting flights, mid-level hotels, per diem expenses, second jobs and financial struggles. It's a good job that most American players love the sport and are willing to sacrifice financially to play it every day as a profession, but the harsh reality is that the sport will never succeed professionally until money is the driving force. Only then will it get the six foot, ten inch 12-year-old to direct his attention to nurturing dexterous feet and a hard head in the hope that one day he can play professional soccer, make a fortune and lead the USA to World Cup glory. For when the money arrives, as sure as night follows day, so will the best US athletes and of course their agents. There are of course some great "athletes" in American soccer, as there are players who earn a very respectable living – players such as Landon Donavon, earning close to a million dollars a year with the Galaxy and blessed with multiple endorsements. Equally players such as Altidore (Hull City loan), Onyewu (AC Milan), Guzan (Aston Villa), and Spector (West Ham) are all earning exceptional livings from the sport, though they need to go abroad to secure it.

If you are a professional player in America you need to make sure you are on the US National Team coach's Christmas card list, because without his call up and validation the chances of making a decent living are slim. It is only the US National Team player that earns coveted World Cup bonuses and gains the international exposure that might secure a big money move to Europe. Want a better salary in Major League Soccer? Then you need to play for the national team. Want a lucrative move to the Premiership? Then you must have played 75 percent plus of your country's national team games over a given period. This applies to those wishing to play in England – the PFA fought for it to protect their members. It is of course obvious to say that being an international player will improve your value as it does for players all over the world, but in the USA it is infinitely more critical. In the Premiership a player can be a great midfielder but not play for England because Gerrard and Lampard are keeping him out; he can however still command £40,000 a week from a host of teams all bidding for his signature. In the USA the soccer world will not consider you a great "anything" unless you are a member of the USA Team, period. With no National Team recognition there is no leverage and with no leverage there is no money – it's that simple, according to both Mark Levinstein, the long-term legal counsel for the US National Team Players Association and Richard Motzkin, one of the first true soccer agents in the USA representing among many others Lalas, Donovan and Freddie Adu.

With the above in mind let's look at just how far the USA players have come in labor negotiations with both the United States Soccer Federation (US Soccer) and Major League Soccer and whether there is realistic hope that the money needed to entice America's best young athletes to take up soccer will ever appear.

It would be fair to say that the relationship between players and the United States Soccer Federation has been a roller coaster of brinksmanship, strike threats, bluff and counter bluff, ultimatums and at times bitter confrontations. Which is exactly the same as every other professional sport in America, the difference being that the owners of the other professional sports teams are businesses and corporations, not a "not-for-profit" governing body of a sport. The distinction is huge, with the former having a very dispassionate and hardnosed appreciation of the business proposition they are selling and a clear focus on the bottom line. Players and owners understand the symbiotic nature of the relationship and while often fractious, they recognize everyone "must feed at the trough". Some may want to eat more than their share and it gets ugly but ultimately it's resolved. The player and the owner are equal in understanding the real game, to keep the show going and the cash flowing. There has always been, and still to a degree is, an imbalance in the player–management relationship born of the fact that for the past 20 years, the US Soccer player has had little or no leverage and when at that rare moment leverage came along they were either afraid or just too disorganized to use it. The underlying message from US Soccer, however subtly delivered, was a simple one, you either accept what we are offering or you do not play on the US National Team, the consequence of which is that you will not play in the World Cup – the threat alone a searing dagger to the heart of any American player. There are many forms of leverage but this was a particularly cruel one, as it played on the hopes and dreams of players and threatened their very future. With no National Team there is no leverage, with no leverage there is no money, no World Cup, no exposure, and no alternative: therefore accept the deal offered, which invariably they did. The tactic was more prevalent in the early 1990s, used at Italia 90 to bring players in line over wearing Adidas shoes, again in 1994 when players would have accepted just about anything to play on the team, but became less overt and aggressive later in the 1990s with the arrival of Nike as a major sponsor and bene-factor of the Federation, allowing them to act more generously. In defense of the Federation it may have been rightfully using the only leverage and weapon it had. Because what may have not been commonly known was that despite the fanfare of the World Cup and the signing of the marketing agreement with SUSAP, the Federation was financially very weak and teetering on the edge of financial collapse for most of the early and mid-nineties. It was only rescued, and ultimately made prosperous, by the influx of Nike money in 1998 who agreed an $11m per year sponsorship package.

With this undertone always present and the leverage used like a well oiled "Smith and Wesson" the players were hopelessly outmatched and never as a group or individually committed to risking their chances of being selected. There was of course a value exchange, US Soccer got players for the price they wanted and the players got a platform for personal exposure, with airfare, hotels and food supplied.

There is the old courtroom saying "only a fool represents themselves", well in that case during this period the USA team had close to twenty of them. Few had agents and with most acting individually rather than as a collective, they were picked off like trailing zebras, separated from the pack, and while not devoured by a pride of hungry lions, were brought in line and with pen provided, they duly signed on the dotted line.

World Cup 1994 changed much of this and while the two key components, money and leverage, were missing, the promise of such was enough to incubate a nascent soccer-agency industry. Motzkin left US Soccer, took over the spare bedroom in his apartment and with the only true American cross cultural star, Alexi Lalas, in tow opened his doors for business. Five years later he would still be there.

Across the country in the nation's capital, the powerful law firm of Williams and Connelly, attorneys to the political elite, who according to their website enjoy representing clients in "mortal danger" (which included President Clinton's first impeachment), decided for some inexplicable reason to take on the challenge of representing the US National Team who had eventually come to the startling conclusion that they were stronger together than apart. (I am sure the core of every team talk every coach had ever given them.) A chance encounter on a flight between a senior attorney at the firm and Shelley Azoff, agent to a number of US players and wife of multi-millionaire music entrepreneur Irvin Azoff, founder of Giant records, was enough to convince them there could be money in soccer or at least money if they could get inside Azoff's music empire. Whatever the true motivation,

Mark Levinstein was given the task and over the next 15 years could never quite have imagined the journey he would take and the battles he would fight to get acceptable rights for his clients, the Men's USA National Team, ultimately improving their lot significantly.

How bad was it for players in the early 1990s? Well with no major professional league to underpin their income (though some played in the American Soccer League with minimal salaries) players relied solely on the goodwill of the payments they received from the Federation, and I have described already how forthcoming they were. Some that played abroad obviously earned more but these were few. Players were paid $500 if they started the game and $200 if they came on as a substitute (not a lot, but worth jogging up and down the touchline to catch the boss's attention). The team as a whole would receive a win bonus that varied from $10,000 to $20,000 depending on the competition; $5,000–$10,000 for a tie and should they lose, which they often did, they would receive nothing. The win over Switzerland in a rain-soaked Orange Bowl in January 1991 earned those that played $750 and the subs that came on $400. Players that made the starting line-up for all 18 games that season would have earned around $15,000 before tax. Things got better in 1992 with SUSAP bringing in sponsors and revenue and the Federation coffers improving. With a hint of leverage appearing, it became clear that World Cup 1994 and US Soccer needed the team to perform and so a $20,000 per point team bonus was initiated for US Cup games with another $75,000 thrown into the pot if they finished first. They were not, I am sure, expecting to pay out, but Bora was working his magic and the team duly beat Ireland 3–1, Portugal 1–0 and tied with Italy 1–1 to be crowned champions, earning $275,000 in bonuses along the way. Interestingly players were paid $500 appearance fee to start against Italy and Ireland but only $400 to play against Portugal, how times have changed. In 1992 players starting all 21 games would have earned $24,000. With the World Cup fast approaching, the big event of the summer was the US Cup 93, an event that Brazil, England and Germany used to prepare and acclimatize for World Cup 94 (a wasted journey for England of course). The players were again heavily incentivized at $20,000 per point with a $75,000 "kicker" should they finish first. Faced with much tougher competition they only secured one win and it wasn't against Germany or Brazil. Beating a hapless England, they secured a $60,000 single game bonus, nothing compared to the memory of the win. They say goals change games and Lalas's soaring header to put the game beyond the reach of the English certainly finished this one off. As he ran to the touch-line, his crazy hair billowing in the wind, I wonder if it was to hug his fellow players or ask the accountant if his $250 ($150 after tax) substitute appearance fee would be a check or cash. Either way it was not enough to pay for a restring for one of his precious guitars. But hey, as MasterCard would say, "beating England: $150, scoring a goal that made headline news around the world: priceless." The team earned around $100,000 for its appearance in the US Cup 1993, the Federation made close to $2m. It might have been nice to have slipped a couple of extra bucks in their pockets.

Surely the World Cup arriving in 1994 would be a financial bonanza for the players and set them on their way to greater riches. Everyone knew it was critical that the team performed well, for on their shoulders rested the success of the event and the launch of Major League Soccer. Appreciating this, the Federation first paid every player that made the squad $10,000 and quadru-pled their team win bonus from $7,000 to $27,000. Starting play-ers would get $5,000 per game (up from $500) and substitutes $2,500 up from $250. (This time worth flailing your arms and setting off fireworks to get noticed.) Each point gained would earn a $50,000 team bonus and qualification for the second round would earn a whopping $1,000,000 super bonus.

In a stunning performance the USA beat Colombia which along with a tie with Switzerland sent them qualifying out of their group and on to play Brazil in the round of 16. Although they were to lose this game the team had done enough to earn $1.67 million in bonuses, which, when divided, sent each player on their way with $75,000. The full rewards for competing in a World Cup cannot of course be measured in dollars and cents, but the money earned represented a substantial uplift in income for the year for players typically earning between $20,000 and $50,000.

World Cup 94 went on to generate a $60m legacy for soccer in the USA, revenue many thought went into the Federation coffers, which it did not (it went to the United States Soccer Foundation).

The highs of 1994 were soon to be replaced by the miserable lows of 1995 as the stark realization that the "show" was over hit home. To make matters worse the new professional league scheduled to start in spring 1995 was pushed back a year as sponsors left the sport and investors prevaricated. Players that once had hoped to drop straight into the new league now had to rethink their careers and plan once again to travel abroad. For US Soccer it was just as bleak. It had already decided to take game promotions in-house and reworked its deal with SUSAP to reflect this. It meant however there was no longer a $2m guarantee payment but US Soccer would now have to take the risk associated with staging games. On the plus side, Nike had decided to make a move into soccer, a sport they had ignored longer than they should have. With law suits threatened and acrimony all round, Nike ousted long term US Team apparel sponsor Adidas. With an offer apparently 10 times more than Adidas, the Federation secured a deal giving them $1.5m in cash and close to $2.5m in merchandise. The merchandise was important particularly as in the early 1990s the Federation, lacking in funds, had to stop the players exchanging shirts at full time, unable to afford a replacement. Maybe Adidas paid the price for not providing enough shirts or for delivering to the world the infamous "stars and stripes" ones they wore at World Cup 94 (either loved or loathed) – either way Adidas was out and Nike in!

The Federation for the first time found itself the possessor of those masterful partners: leverage and money. Nike had the money, Adidas wanted to stay, out came the "Smith and Wesson" again and a very lucrative deal was completed.

With the players feeling, justifiably so, that they had done their part to ensure the World Cup was a resounding success, they were looking forward to being rewarded with a new four-year agreement for their services, hopefully on much improved terms. It would sound reasonable and right but since when had these been guiding principles in sport? The realities of the new landscape would hit home as Lalas, Harkes and Balboa, none of them shrinking violets, led the campaign for a new deal.

With players scattered around the world, consensus was tough to orchestrate. Lalas was pushing for all players to get the same but others wanted a seniority scale, and although they talked a good game and threatened to strike and not attend the 1995 Copa America, the players were never united and once more they were picked off, agreeing to travel and play for new temporary coach Steve Sampson. It actually worked out very well for them financially with shock wins over Argentina and Mexico, making the semi-finals and earning an unexpected and much appreciated $20,000 per player and overall annual salary of $40,000. Still unable to reach agreement, the players continued on a game to game basis, with both sides meeting usually around national team games. Breakthroughs came only to be quashed, with an offer of 20 percent profit share proposed and accepted only to be withdrawn later, leaving players both frustrated and understandably annoyed. In late 1996 the stakes were raised even higher, with the Federation sending a "take it or leave it agreement" to over 83 players that they considered might at some stage over the next four years be considered for the USA national teams. With Major League soccer in full flow and most of the National Team players home, the 83 players listed represented a good proportion of the starting players for the league. Players were sent a letter stating that they either agree to the terms laid out and consequently sign and return, or they would no longer be considered for World Cup qualification matches. A recurring theme, as said before. The Federation were of course bluffing and had the players stuck together they would surely have defeated it, but they either knew or made a calculated gamble that the players were not united and were as usual "individually" desperate to play in the World Cup. They were of course right on both fronts. The players filed lawsuits claiming unfair labor practices and threatened to join up with the MLS union representatives, the NFLPA, in a combined attack. A match in Peru brought things to a head with many senior players refusing to sign the agreement and hence not play. Six fringe players however broke rank and signed, players that would never make the team in normal times but seizing the chance to earn a "cap". Still with only six on the roster and the law stating you need eleven it looked likely that Rothenberg, Gulati and Steinbrecher might appear on the team sheet if things did not improve.

Ultimately and predictably the players relented and agreed to play. The six players that broke ranks were "rewarded" with the trip, supported by ten others, all being paid the usual $2,500 per game match fee. The disunited team were hammered 4–1 but it surely would have been a lot worse with Gulati in goal, Rothenberg at center half and Steinbrecher as an overlapping full back.

Eventually a new agreement with the Federation was reached and one that would see their appearance fees treble to $1,500 per game for standard games and $2,500 for major games such as World Cup qualifiers and Concacaf Gold Cup events, with additional individual win bonuses at $500 to $1,000 per player based on opposition. The new agreement was to ensure that players earned an average of $40,000 to $45,000 per year for the next two years leading up to France 98. For World Cup qualification games the players earned the maximum $2,500 but were not paid a win bonus, the pride of competing in the World Cup and a $1m team bonus for qualification being deemed enough. Equally they were to receive a 100 percent increase in the amount received for making the World Cup roster going from $10,000 to $20,000 per man. With agreements reached, if not signed, the team set out for World Cup 98 in France with high hopes after an excellent pre-World Cup European tour.

To say France was a disaster would be an understatement. Internal bickering among the players (made all too public in the press) caused a fractious environment that resulted in three straight losses. Gone was the glory of 1994, gone were the plucky young Americans taking on the world and in its place was amateurish backbiting and petty squabbles. Finishing last, the team had come full circle and were left humiliated and defeated. Worse than the defeats was the lack of heart and passion displayed by the team. To most soccer aficionados it was not unexpected that they would lose to Germany and Yugoslavia, which they did with little fight. Losing to Iran however, with all it represented in American politics, was unforgivable. International soccer is always more than just a game. The loss resonated in the "news" section of the national press and damaged both the team and the players as well as soccer in general. Not that the USA necessarily had any natural right to beat Iran on the soccer field, but to mainstream America it just reinforced their belief that soccer was not an American sport, because if it was we would not lose to Iran. Michael Jordan would never let it happen, Dan Marino would never let it happen and Mike Tyson would just plain knock their lights out.

We should have read the omens really. The night before leaving for France, US Soccer hosted a "send-off party" for the team at the ESPN Zone in New York. Six of the team including Coach Steve Sampson and yours truly stepped into an elevator heading for the ground floor. The inevitable of course happened and the elevator broke down leaving Americas finest (and me) trapped for 90 minutes as the New York Fire Brigade ripped off the roof and had the team clamber to safety through a greasy torch-lit elevator shaft. Two things struck me: first, was figuring out I was the least crucial to what was going to happen on the field at France 98 as they elected me to go last (talk about Lord of the Flies) and second, that when we got out, there were no flashing light bulbs, no cameras and no hyper-ventilating news crews – a sure sign the sport still had a long, long way to go. Can you imagine if this happened in Italy or Brazil?

Financially for the players it was the most lucrative World Cup to date as each earned around $100,000, but to a man would probably have returned the cash to rewind time and handle the whole experience differently. Their agents of course would not have let them but even they realized that tremendous damage was done to their clients' images, the team and the sport of soccer. No one emerged from France 98 with their reputation intact.

With the $100,000 banked, most players were also heading back to MLS to resume the league season where they might be earning anywhere from $70,000 to $200,000 plus per season. MLS however was starting to make ominous sounds as news leaked of mounting losses. While France 98 did not negatively impact gates it did make sponsors jittery and owners a little less buoyant in their belief that soccer could make it.

It was also a seminal moment for relations between US Soccer and its players. If the players thought they lacked leverage before 1998 they were left in no doubt after it, a furious Federation made it very clear that they would not tolerate a repeat. There was however light at the end of the tunnel for the players and a hint of leverage that could work for them. Prior to the start of the World Cup 98, US Soccer entered into a reported $11m a year sponsorship agreement with Nike, who then brought IMG to the table for a further $3m–$5m a year to buy out the marketing rights once held by SUSAP. Flashed across the media it was portrayed as a historic $250m multi-faceted multi-media deal that would change the face of soccer and in fairness it did. For while probably not $250m, it poured tens of millions of dollars into the sport at a time when it most needed it and continues to do so. I wonder if on the flight home, after losing to Iran, Nike checked if there was a 30-day "get out of jail" cancellation clause in the contract. With Rothenberg involved however there clearly wasn't going to be one. Nike of course had no intention of bailing and had committed itself to a course of playing "catch up" and eventual global domination of soccer. Being an American company they wanted to own their "home" team and were prepared to pay a premium to do so, and did. (They also wanted I am sure the Nike swoosh on millions of 5-year-olds running around the field. The brand loyalty game starts early.)

While having little leverage, the players certainly knew there was money, and the belief maybe that with the ink still not dry on the contract, the last thing the Federation or Nike wanted was a long protracted battle with its most important asset, the players. They were of course right but US Soccer was not yet prepared to let go of the leverage the 1998 fiasco provided. Out came the old well-oiled Smith and Wesson and the ground rules were set. The Federation insisted they only wanted to pay for success and the players wanted to be paid whatever, and after much back and forward, a deal was struck. Accepting that the team in 1998 was poor, Levinstein negotiated a deal through 2002 that made the players exceptionally well paid if they performed. Four years, $10m and a World Cup quarter-final later, the team was flush.

The new contract meant the players would earn around $3,000 per game in appearance money plus bonuses allowing them to earn around $50,000 per year if they played most games. The real game changer however came with the creation of a set of World Cup performance bonuses that clearly let everyone know the true focus. From this day forward the Federation made it clear it was to be all about "Winning a World Cup". Project 2010, Rothenberg's now infamous statement that the USA wanted to win the World Cup by 2010, treated with universal cynicism around the world (and actually to soccer aficionados in the USA who knew the reality) was all about impressing Nike and why not, with $250m on the line who could blame them?! As I said, Nike were new to the game. (Equally though it goes against the grain of everything that's American to think the USA couldn't win it and Nike did not become one of the top brands in the world by thinking small.)

Offered $1.0m to qualify and $100,000 for each point gained in the first round, it was clear US Soccer were looking to make sure there was no repeat of the 1998 debacle. The big incentives however came if they actually moved on. Qualifying out of their group would earn them a $1.85m bonus, making the quarter-finals, a further $1.5m. After last place in France this was probably as much as anyone's mind could stretch. At their best when no one really gives them a chance (Rome 1990) the team shocked Portugal 3–2, tied with Korea, passed "go" and collected the $1.85m bonus. Not content they carried on to beat their arch rival Mexico 2–0 collecting a further $1.5m. Storming into the quarter-finals, the team met the power and might of the Germans in what, easily from a playing and credibility standpoint, was the most important game in US Men's soccer history with the impossible dream of a semi-final just 90 minutes away and the "to infinity and beyond" possibility of making the final maybe just a lucky last-minute penalty away after that. The truth is the USA could have beaten Germany that day: they played well and forced the game and, had the soccer gods wanted them to win, they would have. In the end they lost 2–0 and bowed out of the World Cup with the soccer world's respect ringing in their ears. Their pay for that day was $3,000. (Had they won they would have shared close to a $2m bonus or $87,000 per man for the game.) Overall the players did well in Korea 02; earning $203,000 each. Four years later in Germany 06 they were to earn just $65,000.

On a profitable side note, the agreement reached with US Soccer for 2002 included a small clause that stated they would get paid an extra $80,000 for every three months the team was placed in the top fifteen of the FIFA world rankings. Laughable following 1998 and probably "thrown in" with a wry smile. However, the quarter final run in 2002 vaulted them into the top ten and as high as eight by 2005. This "hopeful" clause added $1.2m into the players' pool as they went on to spend sixteen consecutive quarters in a "paying position". (Germany 2006 put paid to this as they slumped to 31 in the world, not to return until April 2009.) But it was good for the players while it lasted.

The performance in Korea was a watershed moment for soccer in the USA on almost every level. Fans poured into bars and pubs throughout the country at all hours of the day and night in a celebration of soccer, media lapping up the great stories and images. Soccer United Marketing who owned the broadcast rights ensured all 64 games were aired, with the clash of the regional giants USA/Mexico earning a 2.29 rating (2.9 million viewers) and delivering the highest 18–34 year male audience of the weekend for ABC. It was of course critical for fans and players but it also became an inspiration and reaffirmation to the owners of MLS, who, struggling through years of mounting and crippling losses, were having very serious doubts as to the future of the league. In an effort to increase revenues and underpin losses they had purchased the rights to both the 2002 and 2006 World Cups, without which the games would not have been broadcast on US television (except in Spanish). It was a huge risk and could have backfired, possibly sinking the league. Fortunately and much in part to how well the USA Team played, the advertising poured in for the late round of 16 and quarter-finals games ensuring the owners would see a profit. Not enough to offset the losses incurred in MLS but a profit none the less and one that led to a renewed belief that if they just get the model right there could be money to be made in the sport. It was a like a shot of "RedBull" (gratuitous) to the sport of soccer and investors kicked on.

Had the US lost all three games and viewers and advertisers deserted them, there might well have been a long line at the passport office and 300 MLS players brushing up on a foreign language.

The point is that "on field" performance can and does have a strong impact on the sport of soccer in the USA. Investors need to be given constant reassurance that the sport can be profitable, fans want to feel "this time it is here it stay" and "our players are getting better every year" and media need to be given a constant supply of reasons to write positive, not negative, stories.

It is impossible to write a negative story when the USA makes the quarter-final of a World Cup.

In England, Italy, Germany and Spain the professional century's-old clubs are in the most part immune from the performance of the national team, sure it might depress or enthrall their fans but it wouldn't stop a Real Madrid fan following his team or the owners of Arsenal throwing in the towel. It wouldn't even cause the owners of Lincoln City, a small second division club in England, to rethink their existence. The fact is the sport of soccer is so entrenched and embedded it matters little. This is not the case in the USA. The question always asked is "will soccer ever make it?" It is first necessary to sell investors the sport and then the program. Major League Soccer launched by convincing investors that the sport of soccer was a growth industry and owning a professional league in it could be a profitable venture. When in 2001 they realized that this might not be the case and having $300m–$400m of combined losses to prove their case, Don Garber convinced them that it was not the sport but the "business model" that was wrong. Soccer was great but MLS had it wrong – an important and critical distinction. Had the investors believed the sport had no future, it would have been all over, but if it was about a business model, well this they could understand, work on and change. None of them had amassed their fortunes by getting it right every time; they all had their share of business plans and launches that went wrong. Fixing them was what they did well. They just had to be convinced it was worth fixing. There had to be hope.

The USA National Team making the quarter-finals and the outpouring surrounding it convinced investors there was light at the end of the tunnel, and there was indeed hope: hope delivered by a team's performance and delivered when the sport needed it most.

The question then obviously becomes, "well how much should the players earn for representing the US National Team?". The flag-waving heart-pumping patriotic answer is of course, nothing. Players should be thrilled to even be asked to play and be honored to pull on the Red, White and Blue which is of course true. (I am sure there is not a single player that has ever worn the shirt that does not feel that way.) This is of course unrealistic and goes nowhere to solving the problem. If soccer does not get more money into the sport it will never win a World Cup.

To win a World Cup the USA "only" has to find the "right" 11 players that come through the system together (or around each other) so the coach can put them on the field at the same time in the same seven games at a World Cup (probably with a couple of subs). It is not enough to have just two or three, but they could get away with between seven and ten (the USA always produces great goalkeepers so that's a given). Manchester United's fortunes changed when Beckham, Giggs, Butt, Scholes and the Neville brothers all came through the system together and broke into the first team around the same time. Not easy to replicate but that is what the US needs.

To have any hope of finding this group, the sport has to become more financially attractive to the best raw athletes in the country and cast its net into new areas to find these. Soccer has to become a way forward for the African-American, the Hispanic and the economically displaced. It has to become a great "option" for the suburban kid that has the choice of a baseball or football career. There are soccer coaches with far more talent than I to discern what these ten will look like but the financial "dream" has to be present and the sport won't advance until that dream becomes an attainable reality.

There are only three ways that I can see of doing that currently: (1) bumping up players' salaries in MLS, (2) paying them more to play for the US National Team, and (3) pushing them abroad for someone else to develop and pay. Let's look at the pro and cons.

Asking for more from MLS

With losses of over $750m and counting, Major League Soccer is still a long way off being able to pay the sort of salaries that might attract the best young players. It does not have lucrative Premiership-level television contracts (£1.7b over three years domestically and a further £1.6b for international TV and other rights) that fuel the astronomic salaries that players demand, and does not yet have the huge and loyal fan bases that drive everything. MLS is focused on getting 20 LA Galaxy Home Depot style or similar purpose built soccer stadiums in place as soon as feasible. It has 10 complete or close to completion. These multimillion-dollar commitments and continuing losses for the teams are not conducive to blowing the gate open on player salaries. It's really a matter of holding the losses as low as possible, keeping the confidence of investors, expanding correctly and making sure "the league is around long enough to succeed". This will change over time. A well-run team, with a strong fan base and its own stadium can make money in the MLS. When the league has 18 such teams, the economics will change and the players will benefit. The old NASL again raising its head convincing MLS that unless all ships rise together the league could fail. There is also one other important point to remember here. The "raison d'etre" of Major League Soccer is not to produce a winning World Cup Team but to produce the best "clubs" it can. It would hope that these clubs have American players and that they develop American talent but ultimately it wants the best product for the club and its fans, whatever mix that is. Apart from Landon, Donovan who in 2009 was the highest paid US player ($900,000), others either on, or flirting with, the USA Team earn between $150,000 and $300,000 and if you are not a USA National Team player and just entering the league you need a second job! ($34,000–$100,000) (see Table 7.1).

Asking for more from US Soccer

History would show that this has been tough with every negotiation appearing fractious. I suppose the answer to how much, centers on the following:

1 What they can "force" them to play for (Smith and Wesson)?
2 What they can afford to pay (in the 1990s not much, since 2002 more)?
3 What the players want paying (always more than a federation will give)?

I will add another,

4 What will inspire young athletes to want to pursue the soccer dream?

Table 7.1 Top 5 earning players: USA and foreign in the MLS 2009

A foreign passport helps

American	Salary US$	Foreign	Salary US$
Donovan	900,000	Beckham	6,500,000
McBride	385,000	Blanco	2,943,700
Marshall	320,000	Angel	1,798,000
Keller	300,000	Ljunberg	1,314,000
Clark	248,000	Luciano	758,000

Note: In 2010 Donovan signed a new contract reported to be worth $2m per year.

Source: Compiled from Major League Soccer Players Union.

A new long-term "Collective Bargaining Agreement" (CBA) was put in place immediately after the 2002 World Cup and for the first time in a decade stability and peace prevailed, well at least through 2010 it does. The content and structure make it very clear that qualifying for, and progressing in, the World Cup was all that really mattered.

The agreement covered two World Cup periods, the first from 2003 to 2006 and the second from 2007 to 2010. The amount paid in the second was influenced and indexed based on how well they did in the previous. A 20 percent increase if they did not qualify for the World Cup, 22.5 percent if they did and 25 percent if they progressed out of the groups. (When a Columbia University professor and World Bank alumnus is negotiating the agreement it is never going to be simple. Makes you yearn for the days when the boss just slipped £20 into your boots if you won and made you walk home if you lost.)

For regular season games in the first quadrennial the players received $3,675 a game which rose to $10,000 if they played a team ranked in the FIFA top 10; $6,000 if they were in the top 25 and $5,800 if they were below 25. If the team qualified for the World Cup in 2006 they received $1.35m, plus $2.4m if they progressed out of the group and a variety of bonuses as they went on – it would be the same for South Africa 2010 but with a 22.5 percent increase. Take away all the complex calculations and scenarios and it came down to this: win the World Cup in 2006 and we will pay you $850,000 per man, fail to win a game and we will pay you around $60,000. (The USA went on to lose to the

Czechs and Ghana and get a point from Italy and left Germany with $70,000 each.) Win the 2010 World Cup and we will pay you $1m per player, a very impressive number. However should they draw Brazil, England and Spain in the first round and leave empty handed they would only earn $65,000 – a not so healthy number (see Tables 7.2, 7.3, 7.4 and 7.5).

If you have done the math, you may be asking where was US Soccer going to get the $20m to pay the players if they won Germany 2006 and where will they get $23m if they win in 2010. (It's actually impressive for them to be able to say they could write the check themselves and still have a few million in the bank, which is an amazing feat considering the struggles of the 1990s.) They, of course, would not be called on to empty their bank account for however much the players were paid in bonuses the Federation was paid more, in prize money from FIFA.

One of the things that need to be remembered is that players are typically on a four-year cycle with agreements that run from World Cup to World Cup. With bonuses top heavy based on the actual performance at the World Cup final itself the players' average earnings for the cycle vary dramatically. In 1994 the Federation placed most of the team under annual contract and put them into Mission Viejo training camp where they were guaranteed $25–45,000 each, irrespective of results. Since 1994 this has not

Table 7.2 World Cup prize money 2010 ($420m)

A rich tournament

Placed	Prize Money (m)
Preparation	$ 1.0
17–32	$ 8.0
9–16	$ 9.0
5–8	$18.0
4th	$20.0
3rd	$20.0
Runner Up	$24.0
Winner	$31.0

Note: If the USA wins the team will receive around $23m in bonuses.

Source: Compiled from FIFA press release.

Table 7.3 USA Men's National Team bonus scheme through World Cup 2010

It pays to play well in the Finals

Stage	Korea 02	Germany 06	SA 2010
Regular games			
Player appearance fees	3,000	3,675	4,410
Win bonus			
FIFA top 10 team		10,000	10,000
FIFA top 25 team		6,000	6,000
FIFA below 25		5,800	5,800
World Cup			
Team qualifying bonus	1,000,000	1,350,000	1,500,000
Making the roster*	3,000	3,750	4,500
Per point in group stage	100,000	150,000	180,000
Qualify from group	1,850,000	2,300,000	2,850,000
Win round 16	1,500,000	2,775,000	3,400,000
Win quarter-final		2,225,000	2,700,000
Win semi-final		2,625,000	3,215,000
Make final		3,000,000	3,675,000
Win final		3,750,000	4,593,000

Note: * per player.
Source: USA National Team Players Association.

been the case but with the launch of MLS, players do have a fixed salary to call upon. The big payoff is a great run in the World Cup itself. A losing run will get you neither noticed nor paid.

In real terms, players' earnings for the 2006 cycle went down, a rarity in any other professional sport. Of course they could climb 500 percent in the SA 2010 cycle if they win, but with only six teams in history ever winning a World Cup, it's unlikely.

All other events pale in comparison to the World Cup both in the importance US Soccer bestow on them and the bonuses they are prepared to pay players. Had the USA beaten Mexico in the 2009 Gold Cup Final, instead of losing 5–0, they would still have only received a $6,000 bonus per player. Their incredible performance at the Confederations Cup however did reap a richer reward, receiving a $10,000 bonus for any game won, $16,000 for

Table 7.4 USA team bonus for performing at World Cup finals

Boss "How much if we beat Brazil in the final?"

Bonus	Korea 02	Germany 06	SA 2010
Best case: win World Cup	14,550,000	19,387,500	23,650,000
Per player (if win)	632,000	842,000	1,060,000
Per player (if lose)	44,000	59,000	65,992
Actual bonus earned			
Team bonus	4,750,000	1,500,000	?
Player bonus	206,000	65,217	?

Source: USA National Team Players Association.

qualifying out of their group and $22,000 if they made the final. Their 3–2 semi-final victory over Spain, while it sent shockwaves around the world, also meant a lot financially. Had they lost, the players would have gained their customary game fee of $3,675 – the victory however put an extra $32,000 in each player's pocket!

Does the money matter? Well players were certainly calling long distance to their representatives in Washington DC to check.

It is pretty clear that the road to sporting riches does not as yet lie with soccer. In the early 1990s it was clearly more a passion than

Table 7.5 Average bonus earnings over a typical 4-year World Cup qualifying cycle

It pays to just show up for the finals

	USA 94	France 98	Korea 02	Germany 06
Games played	99	64	65	64
Total team bonus	3,176,000	4,538,000	10,400,000	6,700,000
Average team bonus	32,081	70,906	160,000	104,687
Average player bonus	1,604	3,545	8,000	5,234
Average player per year	39,700	56,725	130,000	83,750

Note: The figures assume that a player appeared in all 64 games over a four-year period and played in all World Cup Final games. (This is of course unlikely but the numbers indicate the $$ available.)

Source: USA National Soccer Team Players Association.

a profession, and the pre-World Cup years almost embarrassingly so. Although the players were paid a fixed salary in 1993 and brought into camp at Mission Viejo the $25–$50,000 salaries did not much more than continue the dream. Prior to this they were earning less than $25,000 per year, with only the bonus earned at World Cup 94 making it palatable. Many lived at home and many had second jobs coaching or playing. The Federation itself was also impoverished and it was still very unclear whether or not the World Cup would make money. These were indeed pioneering days for everyone.

Players now have second soccer careers in MLS or Europe with a few earning substantial salaries: the majority maybe $50,000 with the USA team and $150,000–$300,000 with their clubs and if they are lucky, with a 10-year career.

Of course national pride and patriotism are important motivators. However, if you are playing in Europe for your club team and are being asked to travel to potentially over 60 games, half of them in another foreign country and you receive $3,650 for the privilege ($2,000 after tax) you might well be tempted to stay in Europe as Brad Friedel did seven years ago. Get drawn in a group with Czechoslovakia, Brazil and Germany and your chances of securing the "super bonus", the one that makes or breaks your income for the four years, are slim. Of course it can happen as Korea showed but it's tough. The World Cup draw has a major impact both on and off the field for the players.

It was clear that following France 98 "pay for performance" was the only way US Soccer was going to move forward, a minimal risk strategy, particularly with Nike and FIFA underpinning finances. With $50m in the bank it is a strategy that has worked exceptionally well for an organization once teetering on the edge of financial collapse. They are absolutely right in making it clear to the players that the USA should always qualify out of the region, with four World Cup spots and a regional competition including smaller nations such as Costa Rica, Honduras, Guatemala, and Trinidad – the only real "strong" competitor being Mexico – the players should be ashamed of themselves if they do not qualify. There are two problems with this assumption. The first is that many of these teams are improving rapidly, particularly Honduras and Costa Rica. Mexico are on a rapid rise. Clubs around the world are scouring the fields of many Concacaf countries for players and taking them into their systems. Honduran Palacios moved to Tottenham for $25m, his team mate Figueroa to Wigan, so you can bet your life there will be more hungry and impoverished kids in the Concacaf region seeing a clear path out and more European scouts and avaricious agents willing to help them. Over the next decade this region is going to get a lot tougher. Second, the USA has to build a team that can go into a group with Czechoslovakia, Italy, Spain, England, Argentina, Brazil and come out of it. Germany 2006 proved it cannot. The favorable draw for South Africa 2010 will be a telling bell weather. Algeria and Slovenia are teams that by now the USA should beat, which worries me. The USA have always been better underdogs than favorites and the American public will "expect" them to qualify out of their group. Failure to do so will be a huge setback. The players of 1994 were under the same pressure and came through, the players of 2010 need to do the same. The Confederations Cup, while a great performance and morale booster, is not a significant tournament and while no victory over Spain and 2–0 lead over Brazil is to be diminished, the World Cup is a different animal.

Over the next 15 years the USA is going to have to improve the quality of its professional players if it wants to be more than just a perennial but limiting Concacaf power. To do this it will need the next generation of American soccer player, the player that can match the hungry kids from Italy and Spain and those of Mexico, Honduras and Costa Rica that are either here already or coming soon. For this, the sport in America has to cast its net wider in its search for the best athletic talent and to attract them, it will have change the economic perception of the sport. US Soccer – and ultimately and primarily MLS – has a role to play in this and while it is not about paying average players more than they are worth, it is about setting a groundwork that will entice the very best athletes to see the road to riches (Tables 7.6 and 7.7).

Of course we could always leave it to foreign clubs and send our best players abroad (which is what is happening now).

Table 7.6 Player salaries for Major League Soccer 2007–09

They are not all paid like Beckham

	2007	2008	2009
Number of teams	13	14	15
Players	367	399	342
Average per team	28	29	23
Total league salary	41,972,028	47,726,000	49,666,752
Average per team	3,228,618	2,962,618	3,311,117
Average per player	114,000	119,616	145,224
Mean average	53,378	58,000	88,125
Without Beckham's salary included			
Average	97,000	104,000	126,950

Source: Public records Major League Soccer Players Union.

It is important to delineate between the roles of Major League Soccer and US Soccer when it comes to the ability of each organization to pay players more, and ultimately why the onus lies with MLS. By its very existence US Soccer is responsible for the development of the game at all levels and is required to fund major youth initiatives and national teams at all levels (both male and female). Games and programs involving these teams (outside of World Cup qualifiers for the men) invariably lose money but still need to be supported. Major League Soccer on the other hand answers to no one but itself and can make decisions based on commercial forces. In short, if the American player is to get rich, in America, it will need to be through MLS!

Table 7.7 Average salaries for other professional sports in the USA 2009

Some catching up to do

	NFL	NBA	MLB	NHL
Salary	1,100,000	5,400,000	3,000,000	1,400,000

CHAPTER 8

Pony Tails and Dollars: "Anything a Man Can Do"

As the ball nestled firmly in the back of the Brazilian net in the sixth minute of overtime in the gold medal match of the 2008 Beijing Olympics, Cari Lloyd, the game-winning scorer, was mobbed by excited and jubilant team mates as the realization dawned that the ultimate prize was heading their way. The life-long dream of every sportsperson in America, to win an Olympic Gold Medal, was about to come true, forever lifting them to the highest echelons of sporting success. Because, wherever they would go for the rest of their lives they had joined that elite group of athletes that were "Olympic Gold". It may have also dawned on them, and made the hugs a little bit tighter, the understanding that the team had just secured a $1.2m team bonus that would be hitting their bank accounts as they landed back in the States to be followed soon after by a further $1.2m for the mandatory "Victory" tour across America. Making their day even brighter, they would be going home to compete in a new Professional Women's League that would be paying them $30,000 to $40,000 while at the same time continuing under contract as a National Team player pocketing a further $40,000–$70,000. And should they continue their winning streak, a nice $1,250 per game win bonus could add another $30,000 to their burgeoning wallets. For in 2010, the life of an American Women's National Team Soccer player is certainly a lucrative and enjoyable one. In a non-Olympic or World Cup year they will earn between $70,000 and $125,000 per season, while in the years these events are held (and assuming they win them), they could earn anywhere from $250,000–$300,000 per year and possibly more. No wonder the embraces were so heartfelt and the smiles so broad. (Of course they will all say Olympic glory was enough, but the money didn't hurt.) No Federation in the world invests more in Women's

Soccer than the United States and no one deserves the investment more than the women who compete and the millions of girls that play on fields across America every week. For make no mistake these have been as much a part of the success of soccer in the United States as anyone.

Of course it wasn't always this way and the impressive rewards the women have achieved have been built on the back of a group of pioneering, committed and tough women who did two things exceptionally well: first of all, they won and second, they battled for gender equity and improved rights for women's soccer. It wasn't always pretty and often acrimonious; there were equally many times they were unrealistic as to the economic realities of the "women's" game they played, but one thing was certain, these girls were not to be stopped.

As with everything in US Soccer in the late 1980s and early 1990s, money was tight and programs sparse. The same Federation that was struggling to work out how to build a program for its Men's Team with the World Cup approaching was having to also find dollars to support its fledgling Women's Team, a team traveling to matches in two mini-buses and sleeping four to a room in "economical" hotels, supported by a fan base you could count by adding up the number of family members in town that day. The "problem" was these girls were really good and would soon achieve a result that would mean they could not be ignored, patted on the head and sent on their way with a token gesture of support and a trip to a few tournaments. For on 30 November 1991 in Guangzhou, China they beat Norway 2–1 in front of 63,000 (bussed in) fans and were crowned winners of the first ever FIFA Women's World Cup and the world of soccer in the USA changed overnight: not in the awareness or publicity they received (my magazine Soccer International was the only American media outlet in attendance), nor in the financial rewards they reaped, for there were none.

But America now had a team of strong young girls with big personalities, a pressing desire to build the sport and the skills and competitive fire to force everyone to take notice. They were also what all Americans admire: winners. In fairness to the Federation this team had been funded as well as any other in the world at the time and in the year of their victory had played

24 games in eight countries. This was contentious at the time, as the feeling was that what limited resources they had should be focused on the Men's team, but the gamble paid off and America had its first FIFA World Cup. Despite arriving back in almost total anonymity, they were, as world champions, given the obligatory invite to meet the President. George Bush stated "Leave it to an American Women's team to win our first world soccer championship … for the sake of male ego I hope the men start catching up". Meant as light humor, it foretold a battle for parity and equity with the men that would play out over the next decade. Equally, in jovial spirits, he quipped "it's great to join you in honoring a group of women who reflect a favorite American pastime … its known as winning". He was right, as this team went on to conquer all before it. It was not however to yet make the players household names, this would come later in the decade, or generate the sponsor interest that would see them adorn cereal boxes, this would also come later in the decade. Michelle Akers said it right in late 1992: "We are not mobbed in the grocery stores by fans. We are not millionaires (yet). Despite being the first to win the world championships, our accomplishments have not led to fame and fortune. Our hope however is that future players will benefit in that way." Benefit they would, but just not yet.

The women's team were to only play at home twice during the 1992 season (both times interestingly against Norway, the team they beat in the 1991 final, and both times they lost). In 1993 they appeared nine times and only three times in 1994, the World Cup year. It was pretty clear that they were playing second fiddle to the all important men's program. The reality was that what limited resources existed had to be focused on the Men's Team, whose success was critical to the World Cup and the launch of the new Professional League. Equally women's soccer was just not a profitable venture at the time, with every game losing money, crowds small, costs high and no television demand. For the women, I would have thought the quicker the World Cup was out of the way the better. With the event complete, a $60m legacy and huge interest in soccer created, this might just be the time for the Women's Team to break out. Just when the timing looked right, they traveled to Sweden for the 1995 World Cup but disappointingly relinquished their crown by losing to their arch rivals Norway in the semi-final. For the first time in four years, just when they could have done with the title they were no longer the best team in the world. But as I said, these girls were tough and they soon bounced back in spectacular style.

API Soccer, formerly SUSAP, took on the financial burden of broadcasting and televising the games from Sweden: crowds were low, ratings poor and losses high. It was and is still not clear if women's soccer is a profitable enterprise, a great one yes, a profitable one maybe not. To API it seemed the right thing to do for the game's development in the USA but a poor decision financially.

No longer "World Champions" the USA team needed redemption. It was to appear in the form of that greatest of all American sporting achievements, Olympic Gold. With girls making up 45 percent of the 16 million kids playing soccer in the USA it was almost unconscionable that women's soccer would not be allowed in the 1996 Atlanta Olympics. Akers, Foudy, Hamm and others set about changing this and by mobilizing thousands of freckle-faced pony-tailed kids to send petitions, letters and make calls to their senators, the International Olympic Committee, not surprisingly, relinquished. Remembering how successful soccer had been in 1984 and just how spectacularly the 1994 World Cup had been hosted, it was not a stretch for them to decide in favor. It was also a great move for the self-interest of the team, as I am sure they felt they had a great chance of winning. Nothing in American sport seems as important to Americans and their families as winning an Olympic Gold medal, it's part of the American psyche. Give most Americans a chance to win a World Cup winners' medal or Olympic Gold and they would opt for Olympic Gold every time. Victory at Atlanta would put pressure on the US Soccer Federation to increase funding for the Women's Team program. Throughout the nineties the women players were not given salaries, were not compensated for lost wages, and were not provided with health-care benefits. While this was okay for those players still at college, for senior players such as Michelle Akers and Mary Harvey – players who had to pay a mortgage or raise a family – it was tough. Very hard choices had to be made, would they follow their passion to train and play with the USA or give up their dreams and go about their lives? Akers did eventually get an Olympic stipend that allowed her to continue and she would go on to lead her team to its greatest successes.

It's fair to say that Silver was not an option the USA contemplated, no longer World Champions, they needed Olympic Gold. They had battled both personally and as a team to get women's soccer into the Olympics and had succeeded; it would be a huge disappointment if they now lost. Although NBC in their wisdom decided not to air women's soccer, an embarrassment to both the network and the Olympics, the US Team stormed to Gold in front of 76,489 screaming fans (see Table 8.1), the lack of television however hindering their marketability and awareness.

Once again the most successful team in soccer would have to wait for riches and respectability. Olympic bonuses were still a thing of the future and the girls were left negotiating with US Soccer for a new deal that would recognize their talents and allow them to pay their rent. Eventually in 1997 an agreement was reached to pay the players a $3,150 per month stipend and $150 per game win bonus meaning that a player such as Mia Hamm, the most recognized and popular women's player in the world, was earning less than $40,000 per year. But what it did was allow the team to stay together and train together as a "club" as they prepared for World Cup 1999, a critical and, in the end, decisive benefit. During this period, the girls decided it might be a good idea to find themselves an agent to handle their collective rights, which is always a sign a sport is growing up.

Hiring John Langel, a Philadelphia lawyer, they set about improving their "lot". Always cognizant that the Men's Team seemed to have more, a dangerous precedent in gender-equity

Table 8.1 Games that convinced Hendricks to launch WUSA

Olympic Gold again		
Opponent	Result	Crowd
Denmark	3–0	25,503
Sweden	2–1	28,000
China	0–0	43,525
Norway	2–1	64,198
China (Final)	2–1	76,489

Source: US Soccer.

America, their first move was simple. Noticing in a video that the women were carrying their own equipment, the question was asked as to whether the Men's Team did the same: the answer was no – strike one. Asked if the Women's Team had permanent trainers, the answer was no, the men of course did – strike two. Asked if the women were put in the same grade hotel as the men, the answer, again, was no – strike three. While the economics of men's soccer were infinitely stronger it mattered nothing in American society, and, less than nothing to the agents representing the girls. For while the Federation were not obliged to follow Title IX (as it did not receive government funds) it could not ignore the power of the team and the popularity of the personalities leading it. This was an important step for the psychology of the women's program and a quick shot across the bow for US Soccer. With trainers and equipment managers in tow, and nicer hotels to sleep in, they set about winning the 1999 World Cup.

Chastain places the ball on the spot – she steps up

Sometimes a moment of inspiration can do more than all of the clever multi-million dollar marketing campaigns in the world. What price the front page of every newspaper in America? Coverage on every news and sports broadcast network in the country and appearances on David Letterman, Jay Leno, Good Morning America and CNN? What price a Disneyland parade, the cover of Sports Illustrated, a visit with President Clinton and a private plane to NASA with front row seats to the Shuttle take off? What price 17.9 million Americans, the largest TV audience in US Soccer history (men's or women's), tuning in to witness the moment? What price the impact on the hearts and minds of millions of young pony-tailed girls in shocked awe at the performance of their sporting idols? The answer, of course, is that it was immeasurable and incalculable.

At precisely 6 PM on Sunday, 10 July, Brandi Chastain hammered a left-foot penalty high to the Chinese goalkeeper's left to win the 1999 Women's World Cup for the USA. In a now iconic sporting moment she ripped off her shirt and slid to her knees in celebration, sending the media into a frenzy of flashing cameras and overhyped commentary. Within minutes, the images would be sent hurtling around the world, hitting the morning papers, news magazines and breakfast shows. It wasn't just a winning goal and it wasn't just the culmination of a great game: it was a statement made to the watching world that women can do anything they want and anything a man can do on the sports field. It was one of the social sporting statements of its time. Empowering and emotive, defiant and challenging Chastain let the world know that anything Beckham, Klinsmann or any other male soccer star could do, they could do. The US Women's Team delivered when it had to, won when it said it would and backed up the promises it made to every young soccer player that idolized them. Team USA became a "brand" that day, a brand that embodied everything every young girl in America wanted to be. They wanted to dribble like Mia Hamm, fight like Michelle Akers save like Briana Scurry and hammer in the winning penalty, slide to their knees and rip off their jersey like Brandi Chastain. This was Girl Power indeed.

Women's World Cup 1999: the girls of summer

It wasn't a stretch for anyone around the soccer world to appreciate that the decision by FIFA to grant the 1999 Women's World Cup to the USA was a wise one. Coming off the spectacular success of the men's 1994 event and the dominant position the USA held in the world, it was a sporting no-brainer. What no one could have expected though was just how successful the event would be and how much women's soccer would capture the attention of an entire nation. Call it confidence, arrogance or blind hope but the mindset of the World Cup 99 organizing committee was that, as with the men's event, do it big, do it right or not bother. With World Cup 94 alumni at the helm it was no surprise. Initially FIFA felt the event should be hosted in small college and sports venues on the East Coast. Rothenberg and Steinbrecher however were having none of it: it was big stadiums or nothing. FIFA eventually relented but only on the understanding the USA took all the financial risk. The rest is history.

The final was of course an event in itself but who would have thought the overall average attendance for the tournament would reach 35,000. It's almost beyond sporting comprehension to forecast how 65,000 would show up to see Brazil versus Italy, 23,000 for Japan versus Canada, and 34,000 for Ghana versus Sweden. Not meant to be condescending but there is no doubt that 95 percent of the crowd could not name a single player on any other team except the USA. It is possible, however staggering, to understand that the USA could draw crowds of 78,000, 65,000 and 50,000 for its first three opening-round games against Denmark, Nigeria and North Korea respectively. In the quarter-finals smart marketing put on double headers ensuring big turnouts with 54,000 plus to see the USA take on Germany. The stand-alone semis telling a slightly different story with 73,000 showing up to see the USA beat Brazil in Stanford California but just 9,000 in Boston to see China defeat Norway. It was however 4 July, so maybe the thought of spending it supporting China or Norway seemed oddly strange. Overall, television attendances through the semi-final stage had been impressive if not blockbuster. The USA's opening game against Denmark attracted 1.7 million households, 1.6 million for the quarter-final victory over Germany and 2.9 million homes for their semi-final win over Brazil. The final however drew an astonishing 17.9 million viewers, with 32 percent of all TVs that were on during the time period tuned into the game, which was a simply staggering achievement. When you think the first World Cup in China drew an average 19,615 fans (many bussed in) and Sweden averaged only 4,316 it was clear that women's soccer in the USA was on a different level both on and off the field.

The genius of the attendance records for the 16-team tournament was of course the implementation of the same grass-roots ticketing blitz that so successfully served them in 1994. Tickets were sold field by field, state association by state association and girl's team by girl's team. World Cup staff and players attended youth matches, tournaments and clinics in all the designated World Cup cities and beyond. They reached out and touched the people they knew would make or break the event. They collected names, handed out bumper stickers and ticket information and enjoined them into the movement that was women's soccer. As with the Men's World Cup, ticket sales were viral and grass roots with 500,000 pre-sold before a ball was kicked. Focused, direct and almost missionary sales zeal mobilized an army of pony-tailed girls along with their moms and dads to commit to a three-week celebration of girls' soccer and female empowerment. The USA grass-roots soccer engine had been revved up again and delivered again. Of course everything depended on the USA team making the final which they duly did, but not without almost faltering against the Germans in DC. Had they done, so the world would have been a different place for the "girls of summer" and the event. For while most tickets were pre-sold, 17 million would have not tuned in, Chastain's jersey, or lack of, would not have made world news and many of the 2,000 media outlets scheduled for the final would have been checking the cancellation policies on their hotel rooms and airline tickets, all of which, fortunately, were not necessary.

Sponsors of course were beating a path to the door, who would not want to be part of the biggest girls' empowerment movement since the Spice Girls told them what they "really want". Millions of young girls who "spend" their pocket money at the mall, alongside millions of mothers who control the nation's household expenditure dragging along millions of dads who will do anything for their little girls. The women's world cup became one of the greatest father–daughter dates of the summer. Hyundai, Coca Cola, McDonalds, all wrapped their marketing arms around the movement. Gatorade utilized Mia Hamm with Michael Jordan, Budweiser utilized Julie Foudy in a national commercial for the first time ever and Adidas and Nike fought it out for the hearts and feet of the masses.

Expected to lose money, the 1999 Women's World Cup turned a reported $3.5m profit on total revenues of close to $40m, which was handed over to the United States Soccer Foundation, an organization set up after World Cup 94 to manage and distribute the $60m financial legacy the men's event generated. At the time the women were only earning their regular monthly stipends and win bonuses. However, in recognition of the tremendous success of the event, the World Cup board led by Marla Messing, Rothenberg and Steinbrecher voted a special non-contracted bonus of $750,000, recognizing the incredible feat they had achieved.

Standing in front of the 90,000 fans, holding the World Cup aloft with cameras flashing and media fawning, the team felt vindicated. They were World Champions again and despite feeling they were poorly paid and constantly having to accept being second fiddle to the men's team, they had come through and won. They had delivered profits, delivered fans and delivered media along with television ratings beyond anyone's dreams. This was their moment and their time and they knew it. What could possibly go wrong?

Well it took just a day to find out. Unbeknown to the Federation, the women had contracted with SFX, a leading sports marketing company, to appear in a 12-city indoor arena victory tour, the dates announced just a day after the Rose Bowl final. US Soccer immediately filed a legal sanction threatening to sue the team and its representatives and blocking the tour. The players claimed the Federation had been informed, with the Federation refuting. Acrimonious meetings ensued but ultimately the tour went on, as a settlement was reached. The women were clearly stretching their wings, enticed by the guaranteed $1.2m the players got to share and the additional $500,000 they received for licensing memorabilia. Whatever the truth of the matter, ultimately, the players decided to take care of themselves. US Soccer however felt betrayed and aggrieved. The tour itself was a phenomenal success and gave thousands of kids a tremendous experience. I took my two daughters to the Philadelphia event and to a person the team smiled, signed autographs and made each kid feel special: at the end of the day, the only thing that really mattered.

The women were taking charge of their own future and seeing just how far their new found stardom would take them. They had their own tour but now wanted more, they wanted their own league. As they say, be careful what you wish for.

The girls go professional: anything men can do, girls can do (more expensively)

It seemed a natural sporting progression in the minds of the USA women's team that the next step in the evolution of Women's Soccer had to be the formation of a new Division One outdoors professional league. The men of course had one so why not them? It was the least they deserved, it was what the women's sports movement (which they championed) deserved and it was surely what the world of women's soccer wanted. The World Cup had proven their case. Television ratings were great, attendances huge, media coverage stratospheric and sponsors loving it. Everybody was in love with women's soccer and everyone was in awe of the girls of summer. If this was not the right time to be launching a new league, then frankly when would it be? Three years and $130m in losses later, they would realize that it was, but they blew it.

There seems an inextricable link between the Olympics and soccer's development in the USA. Just as 1984 convinced FIFA that the Men's World Cup might work, the 76,000 that turned up to see the US Women win the 1996 Gold Medal convinced the Chairman of the Discovery Channel, John Hendricks (a father of two daughters who played the game), that professional women's soccer could be a successful business venture, and the right thing to do.

So as with MLS after 1994, who was going to invest in the risky endeavor of starting a new professional soccer league, particularly seeing the challenges facing MLS at the time? Fortunately, WUSA had a great champion in the form of John Hendricks. Openly admitting that the women's victory at the Olympics in Atlanta was the catalyst for his belief that women's soccer could be successful, he first approached the league in 1998 but was turned back by the Federation who wanted to wait until after the Women's World Cup in 1999 to consider any launch. The Federation knew the stakes were high and knew that whatever chance a women's league would have of surviving would be greatly enhanced by a highly successful 1999 World Cup, just as it had for Major League Soccer. Anything sooner would be foolhardy. Of course 1999 succeeded beyond anyone's imagination and just heightened the intensity and interest in getting a new league up and running as quickly as possible.

With a group of powerful investors in tow and a $40m war chest raised from some of the most powerful cable and media companies in America they set about forming "The Women's United Soccer Association" (WUSA), America's first ever Division One Women's Professional Soccer League, just like the men. Taking their lead from MLS they formed WUSA as a single-entity Limited Liability Company, with investors taking ownership for the overall success (or failure) of the league while also operating their own local team. The ownership group on the face of it could not have been stronger with Hendricks calling upon his colleagues in the cable industry to pony up alongside him. Time Warner, Comcast, and Cox Communications represented some of the strongest players in the country. Very quickly the league struck a deal with Turner Broadcasting and CNN/Sports Illustrated (both owned by Time Warner) to air their games and the league was looking like becoming the next big thing on the sporting landscape. Turner even agreed to use its internal sales force to sell the league inventory. Sponsors, sensing momentum, lined up quickly with Hyundai, Johnson and Johnson, Gillette, and Proctor and Gamble coming on board early. It clearly looked like the league had put together a strong platform on which to launch, with impressive television coverage, cable marketing partners, who if they wished could reach millions of consumers through television and print. Imagine a WUSA ticket offer in every billing statement and sponsors baying to reach the female demographic they delivered. What could possibly go wrong? Unfortunately a lot and in just three years the league would collapse.

Where's Mia? Star power and super heroes

No one was in any doubt that when MLS started, the league would not be populated with the best players in the world, but this was clearly not the case with WUSA. Almost every leading player in the world would be appearing for one of the eight teams in the league when the season kicked off. This, however, was a league based on the appeal and drawing power of US stars Mia Hamm, Brandi Chastain, Julie Foudy, Briana Scurry and the rest of the 1999 World Cup winning team with everything resting on their ability to put fans in the stands. Every other player in the league was relegated to the chorus line, but with average salaries of $24,000 to $40,000, it was a not unprofitable role. WUSA became the Holy Grail for every women's soccer player in the world, players that were typically treated as second-class soccer citizens in their homelands, patronized by a male-dominated sport with little serious interest in the women's game. Playing in America, the Disneyland of women's soccer, where anything was possible and gender equity mandatory and being paid to do so, represented everything they could possibly have hoped for when they first laced up a pair of boots and began embarrassing the boys with their skills. The final icing on the cake was that as players, they were also given a percentage ownership in the league.

The business plan for the league projected that they would break even if they could attract 6,500–7,000 fans per game for a 22-game season and generate around $20m per year in national and local sponsorship. They ended their first season in 2001 averaging just over 8,000 fans per game, inflated somewhat due to the double headers with MLS, though the women would claim the fans were coming to see them. They had a rating of 0.4 (450,000 households) for their broadcasts, half of what Turner had hoped for, but at the time almost double what MLS were achieving, even though the broadcasts were typically scheduled for early afternoons when presumably their audience was out watching or playing. WUSA had set their stall out early on, painting MLS as a Hispanic-driven adult demographic, insisting they would be attracting a different, more classic, minivan-driving surbuban mom and kids demographic. Season ending research supported this showing their fan base to be 66 percent female, with an average age of 33 from households with an average income of $80,000, otherwise known as "soccer moms".

On the surface, the first season of WUSA was looking like a great success with crowds exceeding expectation and television ratings more than they should really have expected. This however was as good as it was going to get with the glow of "girls of summer" at its strongest and the initial fascination of a new league at its most appealing with "pats on the back for all", positive press releases from the commissioner's office and the promise of "it's just the start" from the faithful players, all pretty typical of any opening season of a league. However they had one very big problem, an "800lb gorilla in the room problem" for, in relative terms based on their resources, they were spending money faster than a Russian billionaire at Harrods, managing to spend the entire $40m of reserves earmarked to cover five years of losses in just the first nine months of the league. Their second season advertising message for the league centered on the phrase "it's on". Which it most certainly was.

First, the television contract between Turner and WUSA came to an abrupt end. Ostensibly the league argued that the early

Saturday and Sunday afternoon time slots were hurting TV ratings, as most of its audience were out playing games at that time and pressed Turner for better programming. Unable to reach agreement they parted company, this was even though Turner's parent company was an investor in the league. The more likely issue however was the mistake the league made in placing its sponsorship and advertising sales in the hands of Turner in the first place. The sales were nowhere near the $20m the league needed to survive. With a multitude of other properties to sell, and a sales force that knew or cared little about soccer, the sponsorship and advertising sales for the 11 games they aired nationally were more than disappointing. Handing over control of key sponsorship revenue sources to a cable advertising-driven sales force was fatal. Soccer in the USA never has and likely never will be a ratings driven "spot" buy, it's an emotional life-style driven sale that needs very careful pitching and presenting. At least by switching from Turner they could reclaim back the rights, the problem however was that they jumped into bed with a new network, PAX Television, which while it reached 80 percent of US homes was an unknown start-up whose only other major property was the senior PGA Tour, hardly complementary programming. PAX of course wanted to reduce the average age of its viewers from comatose to the young active American families advertisers desired and WUSA wanted a regular 4–6pm afternoon regular time slot for its games.

They therefore entered their second season with major challenges ahead of them. First, they had to stem the bloodbath of financial losses. Second, they had to renew all of their sponsors due to the change in television partners, which to their credit they did, and third, they had to face the inevitable second-year attendance slump that every league faces. Offices were moved to Atlanta from New York, and staff reductions made (including the removal of their CEO). As expected, the second-year attendance slump arrived, with crowds falling 14 percent to around 7,000 per game. The television move to PAX was a disaster with ratings falling by 70 percent to 100,000 households for each of the 22 national broadcasts. The logic that fans would race home from the soccer fields and tune in to the later 4–6pm slot was left in tatters. Falling crowds and plummeting ratings hardly impressed sponsors enticed to the sport by images of the 1999 World Cup. The shine was off, the US women were less intriguing and the televised games were often of suspect quality and exuding little in stadium atmosphere. This was not destination television, for even the most die-hard of fans, even those that did know where to find PAX on the remote. As the second season came to an end the league was reeling, the numbers not pretty and despite valiant efforts at cost cutting, losses of $25m were reported. Something was clearly still wrong with the business model.

The fact they made it to season three was more a testament to blind faith and no one wanting to throw the towel in on the great experiment of launching women's professional soccer and the empowerment of women in sport. No one wanted to tell Mia, Julie and the pony-tailed millions that the "game was up". Crowds however fell again by another 14 percent, to 6,700 (see Table 8.2) and with television ratings still in the cellar, the investors made the announcement on 16 September 2003 to "suspend" operations. This was heartbreaking to the players, who had given their all, and devastating to female players around the world who looked to the USA to lead them to the promised land of professional women's soccer. And it was a huge disappointment to millions of young girls in the USA, who would now not have a professional career option to inspire and motivate them but who, ultimately, went on playing as usual, still unsure where PAX was on the dial.

It was equally a massive blow to the previously untarnished reputation of the "girls of summer". For the first time, something that Mia, Julie and Brandi had touched, had failed. They were not after all superhuman, they were not infallible and although they had created miracles in the past, this time they had failed.

Table 8.2 Average attendances for WUSA 2001–03

Where were the 90,000 fans and 17m viewers?

League	2001	2002	2003
WUSA	8,000	7,100	6,700

Source: WUSA.

It was to be the beginning of the end for this special group of play-ers who, now aging, would need to make way for the younger, faster and fitter players coming through – players inspired to play by the women they would replace. It was not however how the women wanted to go out or be remembered but just when they thought it could not get any worse, it did.

The timing for the collapse of the league could not have been worse for US Soccer, coming just weeks before the hastily rearranged 2003 Women's World Cup, scheduled to be hosted in China but falling to the SARS outbreak, moved at the last minute to the USA. It was hoped that another home-based World Cup would re-ignite enthusiasm for the league and give it a second wind. If the league could have just hung on for one more season the impetus gained by again repeating as World Champions might be the catalyst for its survival. What if they could capture lightning in the bottle twice? The harsh business reality was they were not going to be given the chance.

So what went wrong? And what lessons could be gleaned that could be used for the next attempt because if one thing was certain there would be one?

1 Whether it was defiance, arrogance or feminism it was pretty clear that WUSA was not interested in talking to or learning from what was happening at MLS. Their feeling was that the league was not exactly a shining example to follow, awash with losses, struggling for crowds and not reaching the very fan base they believed they owned, the affluent suburban soccer family. Adopting a "go-it-alone" stance they did not feel it necessary to seek financial or marketing advice from the very people who had spent the past five years trying to sell professional soccer. The parallels however were there for all to see. Had they not seen how tough it was to get fans to attend games or watch soccer on TV? Or how sponsors retract after World Cups? Had they not seen how MLS overspent in year one and struggled to keep costs in check? Sadly they were not interested in asking, let alone learning. Swept up (almost who could blame them) with the ego of their own success and the desire to prove they knew more than the men, they were either too proud or too entrenched in their beliefs to seek

help. It was a mistake they were to rue, for while they did not have to merge with MLS they should have had the smarts to learn from it. (Interestingly it was Mark Abbott from MLS who devised the original business plan for WUSA made at the bequest of US Soccer. This plan recommended a smaller-scale launch and significantly lower operating costs, not necessarily what the new investors or players wanted to hear.)

2 What were the investors thinking in allowing the league to run up $50m losses in year one and where did the money go? My sense is their costs were major league and their income minor league. The best hotels, the best air travel, high initial players' salaries and highly paid management teams, supported by low ticket revenue, low sponsorship and no television income, seems to fit the profile. Over-expenditure in almost every area doomed the league to failure and destroyed the confidence of investors. Even reducing the losses by 50 percent in year two and another 20 percent in year three was not enough as the damage was done. It was always going to take four or five years to build and stabilize a fan base so blowing through a $40m budget in nine months that was supposed to last five years was unforgivable. With losses in year three of $20m the league was never going to be given the opportunity to survive.

3 If sponsorship income was the critical source of income for the league then they needed to hire a top-level experienced soccer-sponsorship team to sell it, and not hand the responsibility to a television advertising sales group and hope for the best. While good at what they do they are commission driven, have little expertise in the area and will always take the lowest hanging fruit when it comes to a sale, and I guarantee that fruit is not soccer.

4 Over-pricing and under-delivering on sponsorships. Crowds of 7,000 and television ratings of 100,000 households do not command sponsorship fees of $2.5m per year however noble the cause. The business model for the league called for eight partners spending this amount per year. While big name sponsors were announced, they were not paying anywhere near this amount with much being provided in kind: services and marketing and media support. While it sounded good on paper and kept the "value myth" alive it does not pay the

bills. The two major contracts with McDonalds and Coke that were announced at $2m, actually brought in closer to $1m with just $250,000 each in cash and $250,000 in marketing support. At best, the league might have been generating $8m a year against a budget of $20m. Add this to the overspending and the picture starts to become clear. The bottom line was that a sponsorship of WUSA was never worth $2m. Take out the the intangible value of the "girls of summer" and packages were worth no more than $300,000–$500,000 and that would be generous. (I had spent years selling the US Soccer and US Youth Soccer programs, programs that also included the Women's Team. We were very lucky if we got deals over $500,000 per year and not to boast but we were very good at what we did and had a proven track record. Selling soccer was and still is a tough business.)

5 Much was made after the collapse of the failure of corporate America to get behind the league. WUSA failed to understand that companies do not buy corner kicks and penalties or indeed pony tails. I doubt any of the sponsorship money came from the philanthropic budgets of Hyundai Coke or McDonalds. WUSA had to pass the test of delivering at the cash register or offering outstanding value in its sponsorship packages. It failed on both fronts.

6 Hendricks, an impressive and highly successful entrepreneur and a committed supporter of women's soccer, did what no other person could probably have done which was raise $40m to fund the league. Unfortunately it was delivered by huge remote media corporations that had little feel for soccer and even less for the local operations of a small league. If they signed because they felt soccer would garner great ratings they were wrong. MLS could have shown them that. If they signed on to reach young families, WUSA was small potatoes. WUSA was just not big enough or important enough to earn their attention. This is the only reason I can see for how costs got so quickly out of line.

7 Giving the players a share of the league, while socially laudable, was in hindsight probably not a smart move. To allow them to sit on the board and influence operating decisions affecting crucial decisions regarding the league's marketing,

sponsorship, television, travel policy, hotels, expenses, salaries
and more was a major mistake. Could these players objec-
tively analyze a balance sheet, profit and loss or cash flow
statement? Would they really vote in favor of moving players from the Hilton to Motel 8, or taking connecting flights
instead of directs? I might be doing a disservice here but
I doubt it. Add to this the fact that many of the other board
members were slightly intimidated by being in the presence
of Mia, Julie and Brandi, women who were role models to
women and young girls everywhere; again the only reason I can
see why the normal, rational business heads from highly
successful business people were left at the door. I am sure everyone got a picture and autograph but for $130m I would want
a little more. What about labor negotiations and how could
WUSA negotiate from a position of strength when the players
sat in on all management meetings? Would the women really
vote for reducing their team mates' salary or slashing benefits? (They did take pay cuts in year three but they had hit the
iceberg by then and even the band was preparing to jump.)

8   They made a mistake in thinking MLS were not after the same
suburban family as they were. Only 30–40 percent of MLS
were Hispanic and while MLS and WUSA agreed a fuzzy
"lets help each other" relationship, general managers and ticketing directors could see that a ticket sold to a WUSA game
was potentially one less that would come to a MLS game. It
was not always a zero sum game but selling group tickets to
local youth soccer clubs could often represent 40 percent of the
attendance – someone was going to win and someone lose.

9   Moving from Turner to PAX decimated their television audience. They should have realized 450,000 was a very decent
rating number at the time. Something tells me Turner was not
happy with the revenue potential of soccer and pulled the plug.

10 While formed and funded by Hendricks and partners, WUSA
was guided, influenced and took its lead from the leading US
National Team players. They were world-class brilliant soccer
players and tremendous social role models and idols to millions.
They were however woefully ill prepared to make decisions
on launching and running a professional sports league in the
toughest and most unforgiving sports market in the world.

Wiser heads should have prevailed. Had they done so and invested the now $103m carefully, the league might be flourishing today (Table 8.3).

Just when the women thought it could not get any worse, it of course did. Just weeks later they would lose their crown as World Cup Champions making 2003 a year they would all rather forget!

Clearly FIFA now had tremendous confidence in the USA as a venue for staging its most important tournaments and turned to them when the SARS outbreak forced China to withdraw. Given just four months notice it was a monumental task, but one, again, the USA executed almost flawlessly. Operating with a much smaller budget than in 1999, estimated at around $15m, they turned to MLS markets and potential MLS markets to pull it off. By this time also Soccer United Marketing owned the television rights to the tournament having purchased them in the overall 2002–2006 Men's World Cup rights deal. Of course thrilled that from a commercial standpoint the event was in the US, they smartly set about doubling the standard rates earning a healthy $8m in incremental revenue. The organizers also made the smart decision to schedule the US Women's team to play at least once in each of the six cities hosting games, providing them with a private plane to ease the burden. The event was never going to capture the excitement and hype of 1999 and with an aging US team losing 3–0, the end of the road for the girls of summer was at hand. Crowds of 34,000 turned up to see them beat Sweden in the opening game, 31,000 in Philadelphia to see them beat Nigeria and 27,000 to witness their semi-final loss to Germany. The event itself came and went and once again proved that women's soccer has a huge and involved fan base in the USA with over 650,000 fans pouring into stadiums to see the 32 matches. Had WUSA

Table 8.3 WUSA losses 2000–03

A financial bloodbath

2000	2001	2002	2003	Total
$6m	$57m	$23m	$17m	$103m

Source: Compiled from private source. Some say the total was closer to $130m.

survived who knows what the 2004 season might have delivered? Had they repeated as Champions, the season-ticket boost may have saved the league? We of course will never know and always wonder what might have been. It was clear however that the fans had not deserted the Women's Team and came out in their thousands to support them.

The good news for US Soccer was that the event made an $11m profit; over three times what was made in 1999. Underwritten by FIFA and supported by the new sales team at Soccer United Marketing, the event was a financial bonanza.

With WUSA gone and the team no longer champions the US National Team players went back into residency and back on the payroll with US Soccer, which at around $50,000 a year (with all the women getting paid the same) plus bonuses, helped ease the financial pain of the collapse. A lost World Cup and collapsed professional league is not how these women wanted to, or should, be remembered and as US soccer began the process of rebuilding a new team, Hamm, Foudy, Chastain, Scurry, Lilly and company would be provided one last chance to go out on the high they deserved. The opportunity was seized with both hands as a mixture of fresh youth and experience led the team to its second Olympic Gold medal at the 2004 Athens, Greece Olympics. They returned to complete a 10-city "Fan Celebration Tour" that would mark the farewell games for Mia Hamm, Julie Foudy and Kristin Lilly, retiring at the end of an 18-year run that changed the face of US Women's Soccer.

In 2005, US Soccer and the Women's Team representatives sat down to negotiate a new deal through the 2012 London Olympics that would go on to make the US Women's Team the most highly paid players in the world. Guaranteed a constant squad of 20 players year round with salaries of $45,000–$70,000 based on their tier, along with win bonuses of $1,250–$1,500 per game (which if they played 30 plus games a season could generate an additional $30,000) they could earn anywhere from $70,000 to $120,000. If they win an Olympic Gold or the World Cup they receive an additional $1.2m bonus plus a guaranteed victory tour for which they would be paid an additional $1.2m: the 2008 Gold medal in Beijing earned the women close to $300,000 each for the year. With a 25 percent escalator built into the contract, Gold at the London 2012 Olympics could be worth as much as $1.5m to $2m depending on whether the team wins the 2011 Women's World Cup in Germany. A fresh-faced college kid breaking into the team at the 2012 Olympics might find themselves going from eating "top ramon" (a cheap noodle-based soup, which is the staple of broke students everywhere) to banking $250,000–$300,000 if Gold is won, a life changing amount for a 22-year old.

They were not however to cash in on a $1.2m bonus for the 2007 Women's World Cup in China as a young USA team were thrashed 4–0 by Brazil in the semi-finals, causing headlines on the sports pages of newspapers throughout the country. Reporters discussed and dissected the coach's decision to drop Hope Solo, their young new keeper, for Brianna Scurry, who had not played all tournament, but had more big game experience. It mattered not really, because Brazil would have won anyway but the point is that it caused a furor of media attention and upset the fans knowledgeably and sometimes passionately discussing who should be in goal for the Women's National Team.

Built into the new player agreement was also the clause that allowed the National Team players to compete in the newly formed Women's Professional League launched in 2009. As I said early in the chapter these women cannot be stopped.

Almost immediately following the 2003 World Cup loss, Julie Foudy led a group that formed the Women's Soccer Initiative Inc, dedicated to re-launching Women's Professional Soccer. Both FIFA and US Soccer agreed to invest some of the revenue from the highly profitable 2003 World Cup in support of it and the initiative went about re-igniting interest. By 2007 they would have the framework in place, a new Commissioner in ex-Yahoo executive Tonya Antonucci, and investors including John Hendricks, the perennial optimist and financial champion of women's professional soccer. By 2009 they were back playing again as the Women's Professional Soccer League (WPS) with a new look and streamlined plan for how to eliminate the errors of the past. Gone were the excesses of WUSA and in came rational business sense and financial control. Gone was the single-entity structure replaced by individual local-team ownership. Failing miserably to sell enough sponsorship in WUSA, this time they turned to an experienced and well connected partner in Soccer United Marketing who signed on to sell their packages.

They also were fortunate to benefit from the impact Fox Soccer Channel was having on the soccer television landscape and securing a three-year deal and a solid Sunday night time-slot for matches. Franchises were sold for around $1.5m per team and almost complete control of all aspects of their marketing and local operations. Team salaries caps were set at $565,000 with player salaries averaging around $30,000 per season, with US National Team players earning $40,000 – almost half what they earned in WUSA in the early years, but unlike WUSA, they remained on the National Team payroll. Sponsorship packages were set at a far more realistic, though in today's economy, still challenging $500,000 at the national level and I am sure $25,000 to $100,000 at the local. So on 29 March 2009 the Boston Breakers, Chicago Red Stars, FC Pride, Los Angeles Sol, St. Louis Athletics, Sky Blue FC and Washington Freedom suited up to begin the next great adventure in Women's Professional Soccer. Expansion teams, Philadelphia Independence and the Atlanta Beat, are waiting in the wings scheduled for a 2010 start.

Working much more closely with MLS and with a business plan in line with reality, the league has a chance. Only LA Galaxy owner AEG has stepped up to the plate to actually own and operate a team, another tenant for the impressive Home Depot Center in a Southern Californian market with a huge girl's soccer program. Nothing concentrates the mind and focuses the attention more than having money on the line. Where WUSA had anonymous corporate ownership, most WPS teams are owned by small groups of local investors. Ownership that puts the teams in control of people that live and work in the community, have connections, history and a sense of local pride. This is a far cry from the corporate cable "faces" of WUSA. Once again the world's best players beat a path to the USA, for Soccer Disneyland was open again.

With the first season now complete, the jury is still very much out on whether the league will actually make it (see Table 8.4). It had the terrible misfortune of launching in the middle of the worst financial crisis since the great depression and the toughest sponsorship environment in decades.

The final between the Los Angeles Sol and Sky Blue FC drew a respectable 7,216 fans with 80,000 television homes tuning in to watch. For the 21 regular season matches aired on Fox

Table 8.4 First season attendance WPS

A new approach

Team	Total	Average
Boston Breakers	46,651	4,665
Chicago Redstars	49,276	4,928
FC Gold Pride	36,666	3,667
LA Sol	62,980	6,298
St. Louis Athletica	38,326	3,833
Sky Blue FC	36,513	3,651
Washington Freedom	57,466	5,747
Total	327,878	4,684

Source: WPS.

Soccer Channel they drew an average of 32,000 households which compared to the initial WUSA season that had 450,000 viewers tuning in to watch Hamm, Foudy and the rest, shows that the WPS have much to do to elevate the product and create the level of star power that will sustain interest. For purposes of comparison, MLS on ESPN 2 draws an average of 255,000 viewers, while on the same Fox network MLS draws an average of 50,000 viewers. Losses for the first year varied from $1m to $2m per team which considering they were projected to be closer to $500,000 is a little alarming. With an already scaled-down operating model and part-time players it's hard to see where major cuts can be made. First year start-up costs were, as usual, more than expected and sponsorship and attendance levels, less than expected. Sponsorships in particular are very weak and an ominous sign unless the economy changes.

The proverbial and unavoidable second-year slump will occur in 2010 and we will see just how patient and deep-pocketed their critical investor pool is, as it highly unlikely that ratings, attendance or sponsorship will take a quantum leap, potentially quite the opposite. The future of professional women's and indeed national team soccer in the USA rests on it producing a new era of talented players who can continue to win Olympics and World Cups. No disrespect to the men, but this is a team that has to be winning Gold medals and World Cups, as semi-final losses and Silver medals represent a step back, a step back from the glory days both on and off the field of Mia, Julie and Brandi. To be successful, the USA team has to create their own identity their own post-"girls of summer" history and reputation. Not an easy task. Women's soccer needs more than a winning team, they needed a winning team with identifiable and marketable star players that can bring out the fans and elicit the interest and Hollywood-style stardom the team once exuded. With money and resources provided by US Soccer, the USA national team will unfailingly produce great players and great teams but as they know only too well the world has caught up and they no longer dominate.

Sport is of course cyclical and with millions of young girls playing, the next Mia Hamm or Kristin Lilly is surely lacing their cleats up on some soccer field somewhere ready to lead the Red, White and Blue to glory. In many ways because of the USA, there will be young girls in Brazil, Mexico, England and countries everywhere doing exactly the same. For one of the greatest contributions US Women's Soccer at all levels has given to the game is a global one. That there were 91,185 spectators and 17.9 million television viewers for a women's soccer game was an incredible message of women's empowerment that echoed around the sporting world, forcing federations to look close to home at just how they treated the women's game, resulting in increased funding and resources.

The USA has seemingly often led the way in the fields of women's rights and gender equity and the increasing power of women in American society mirrored closely the rise of women's soccer in the past 20 years. There are many contributors to this success:

- the United States Soccer Federation who funded programs and these days Nike for pouring millions into US Soccer to support it;
- the "girls of summer" who won when they had to, created a generation of young soccer fans and fought for everything they and future players would get;
- SUSAP, who originally packaged and sold women's soccer to corporate America, staged games and produced broadcasts;

- the 1999 and 2003 World Cup Organizing Committees that ran first-class events, filled stadiums and beamed high-quality television images around the world of women's soccer and FIFA for knowing a good thing when they see it;
- John Hendricks for his perennial optimism in the future of professional women's soccer, only time and the economy will tell if he is right but the fact that the world's young girls can dream of playing professional soccer in the USA is special;
- finally, and most importantly, the millions of soccer moms and young girls who, swept up by Mia mania, forced corporate and media America to accept women's soccer as a legitimate exciting and hopefully viable sport.

Summary

The defining moment for the team was, of course, the 1999 World Cup when it captivated the hearts and attention of a nation. With two World Cups and two Olympic Gold Medals under their belts, they were without doubt the most successful and respected women's sports team in the world. What Brazil was to men's soccer, the All Blacks to Rugby, Australia to cricket and the USA Track and Field Team to the Olympics, the USA team was to women's soccer. This was a brand that embodied everything young pony-haired girls tearing up the soccer fields of America wanted to be and corporate America raced to embrace.

CHAPTER 9

The "Business" of Youth Soccer

The growth of soccer in the United States is one of the most interesting sporting, social and political phenomena of the past 20 years. From city to city, playing field to playing field, across most geographic and demographic lines, soccer has woven itself into the fabric of American family life. Right up there with apple pie and the pledge of allegiance is the now lemming-like procession to soccer practice, games and tournaments as kids are car-pooled to dusty, bumpy and overused fields to run, kick and play a sport that the world knows as "football". Bewildered parents running lines, trying to understand the offside rule, look on as a game alien to everything they grew up with unfolds in front of their eyes. Mothers, Starbucks in hand, follow every play hoping for a "big kick" or the holy grail "goal" that will send them into joyous rapture while fathers look on with eyes on the game and an earpiece hooked into a radio broadcasting the local baseball or football match.

The simple beauty of a game that allows kids of all shapes and sizes to run around, tackling, passing, dribbling, occasionally heading and sometimes scoring appeals to the senses of new young American parents looking for a healthy, competitive and fairly safe alternative to the bruising reality of American football, the glaring individual spotlight of baseball and softball or the height restricted fairness of basketball. In soccer they have found a sport that embraces boys and girls alike and rewards persistence, effort and teamwork. In a country that gushes over the 250 lb high-school linebacker and 6 feet, 5 inch 13-year-old basketball players, soccer represents the ultimate physical equalizer for the masses and the merits and importance of team over the individual. American parents might not understand and appreciate the game but they absolutely embrace its attributes and the love their kids have for playing it. The numbers do not lie and the growth of soccer over the past 20 years has been nothing short of amazing. Participation has leveled off at an impressive 16–17 million players per year, meaning that in just three decades, soccer is nipping at the heels of both the 100-year-old American football and 130-year-old baseball as the national participatory pastime of a new America.

It would be a mistake however to believe that the sport of soccer in the USA is just a recreational pastime for the masses with little organizational structure or competitive fire. There exists in the USA a highly organized youth soccer network that ensures the sport is played in every city, town, village and suburb in America. The United States Youth Soccer Association alone, one of five major organizations that operate youth programs, has seen its registration grow from 100,000 members in 1974 to 1.7 million members in 1990 and then to peak at just over 3.1 million in 2006, testimony to the explosion of interest that has taken place. The youth soccer club structure in the USA, if recognized, would be the envy of many so-called sophisticated soccer nations and forms the bedrock on which the sport has been built. It is also a $1.1b to $2.5b business and that is billion.

So, apart from the fact that soccer is a fun, easy and inclusive sport, what has driven its growth? First, for 80 percent of the 18 million playing the sport it is just that, a fun, seasonal pastime they will play for 10 weeks and then move on the next in line, be it basketball, softball, lacrosse or baseball: never to think of it again until September comes around and their parents once again sign them up buy them a new pair of cleats and ball and send them out to have fun. For the other 20 percent however, it's a different and more serious matter.

Driving this seriousness is the fact that soccer at the college level in America has undergone a tremendous growth spurt in the past 20 years with a 45 percent increase in those offering men's programs (to 750) and a 220 percent increase (to 930) in colleges offering women's programs. The startling growth of women's soccer was fueled by a Title IX government mandated statute that requires any college accepting public funding to offer equal sporting opportunity to both male and female students. Soccer became a cheap and effective way to meet these requirements and colleges instantly set about issuing scholarships to fill their rosters. Between both sexes, over 40,000 American soccer kids now compete at the college level which is great for the sport and great for colleges, though not necessarily great for the professional game. A college season that lasts from September to December hardly represents the fierce indoctrination and training required to prepare America's best for a professional career.

While not the only reason, the emergence of soccer as a serious and competitive college sport along with associated scholarships has been responsible for the rise of a highly competitive youth club soccer system in America and one that has motivated parents doing everything they can to get their kids to the best money can buy.

That will be $5,000 please

The organization and economic sophistication of the American youth soccer system would shock most of the soccer world. Countries would do well to come and see for themselves a privately run system that creates tremendous competition between clubs and provides enough self-financing to allow the best to employ full-time coaches, assistant coaches and administrators. With no government funding, American soccer has found a way to create the dollars necessary to ensure that youth soccer is a self-generating economic engine that will continue to ensure millions of kids compete and play each season. Thousands of privately run soccer clubs saturate the USA, the best of which play almost all year round (particularly in California) in highly competitive leagues and tournaments. Clubs compete among themselves for the best players, the most motivated parents and of course, for the most prestigious titles and tournaments. The value exchange is simple, the clubs that win the most will attract the most motivated players and most demanding parents, who are willing to pay handsomely to have their kids play for the "best". Their motivation again is simple, if their kids are on the best team there is far more chance they will be spotted by a College or National Team Coach. It's a feeding frenzy of mutual interest. A frenzy that from the age of 10 ensures parents of any player that can kick a ball straight starts a mission to ensure their child plays on the best teams, gets coached by the best coaches and is seen by the most colleges and scouts possible.

In moves that would make Premiership players blush, loyalty to clubs is usually at a minimum (win or we leave), loyalty however to coaches is strong (if a coach leaves a club the whole team might well leave with him). Parents will commit to 8–10 years of club participation and coaching in the hope that their kid might be deemed good enough to gain a college scholarship, or at the worst be deemed good enough to get into the college of their choice (without a scholarship), because the soccer coach needs a "striker". In the hugely competitive college acceptance "jungle" being a 20-goal a season forward might be enough to tip the balance in your favor, over a smart, studious, library frequenting applicant with two left feet. Not necessarily fair, but I used the world jungle for a reason! With the college carrot always present, leading clubs can afford to pay their coaches anywhere from $100,000–$150,000 per year supported by parents who are prepared to pay anywhere from $2,000 to, in some cases, $10,000 per season in fees and travel expenses. On average, parents might pay $1,500 to register, $250 on required uniforms and training gear, and a further $250 to underwrite the cost of attending key tournaments (excluding the travel and hotel expenses incurred from actually playing), and this is just for regular clubs. The super-elite clubs might charge anywhere from $5,000 to $10,000 to be a part of the program.

A quick back of the envelope calculation gives you an idea of the revenue some of these clubs, as illustrated in Table 9.1.

The king's shilling

It is not a one-way street though. To justify such fees, clubs do need to provide what the parents perceive as "top class" coaching,

Table 9.1 Sample of youth soccer club revenue potential

It's big, big business

Club	Teams	Players	Cost	Total
Club A	10	15	$2,000	$300,000
Club B	20	15	$2,000	$600,000
Club C	30	15	$2,000	$900,000

the problem being that most parents would not know a top class soccer coach from a top class chef and so their opinion is based solely upon whether their team wins or loses, which can be a flawed concept. If English Premiership Academy soccer coaches refuse to allow scores to be kept or results posted for their young teams, preferring instead to concentrate on seeing how individual players develop, then why are American coaches so hooked on ensuring the under-10 Ohio Blue Stars crush all before them (usually due to the fact that they have an early maturing 9-year-old who scores five goals a game)? It's either the coaches' ego or the parents' uneducated demands and most probably both. Either way it's killing the "development" of American soccer players and robbing players of many of the innate skills they need to learn at a young age, skills that will need to be second nature by the time they are 16 if they are ever to become professionals.

There are of course many excellent coaches in the USA and that's not surprising. A Director of Coaching might earn $130,000–$150,000 per year at a club and an assistant director $50,000–$80,000 per year. Clubs then supplement their staff with individual team coaches who typically operate on a contract basis earning around $1,200 per month per team (many take on two or three teams). Coaches will also supplement their income by providing private lessons to players (read parents) looking for that extra edge. Charging anywhere from $30 to $50 per hour and often requiring a minimum of four players per session, a comfortable $150 to $200 per hour can be earned. A fact that if known might convince a few dentists and doctors to switch trades. It's a tough job however and for taking the "king's shilling" coaches are expected to produce winning teams, handle awkward parents, get their players selected for State, Regional and National teams and most importantly, earn college scholarships for as many of their players as possible. Failure to do so results in a set of very angry and vociferous parents.

Year-round commitment

To ensure, or chase success, major clubs will undergo a very stringent season of games and tournaments supported by three intense practice sessions per week, with the best including speed, strength and explosion sessions favored by NFL Teams (I said they were serious). For many of America's best youth clubs and players, the commitment is year round. Try-outs and summer tournaments consume June to August, with "fall" leagues beginning in September. A short break for Christmas and the best will return in early January to prepare for the all important (in their minds) State and National Championships, success in which will determine whether players and parents return to try again or journey down the road to a "better" club. To put the finishing touches on the competitive season, newly emerging spring leagues consume the Easter months after which players are granted a well earned six-week break for the batteries to be recharged. Come June it starts all over again! As a result, the top (or most affluent) American youth players are competing on a calendar schedule almost on par with Barcelona and Manchester United. In fairness, the above really applies only to the top echelons of the sport and the Premier Level clubs that dominate it. Of the 3.1 million registered members of the United States Youth Soccer Association only 20 percent would be deemed serious club players, with 20 percentof these elevating to Premier and elite-level play. For the majority (80 percent) of those involved in organized soccer in the USA the sport is a recreational pastime played from September to December each year in parks or high schools across the country.

The American Youth Soccer Association (AYSO) represents probably the ultimate recreational soccer program in the USA, with mission statements and soccer ethics to match. Every kid is guaranteed to play 50 percent of the game with a huge volunteer parent body coaching and administrating at the grass-roots level. It is however professionally run, highly organized with a multi-million dollar budget and national sponsors such as Herbalife and FC Barcelona, and which generates up to $90m per year in registrations. Its mission statement is not about developing world-class players but rather enriching the lives of kids, a far more noble and worthy cause, but not one that will win the US a World Cup. (Cobi Jones and Landon Donovan both, however, got their first introduction to the game through AYSO before moving on.)

Table 9.2 gives a breakdown of organized soccer in the USA and the level of seriousness and financial commitment made.

Table 9.2 Estimates of registration income for organized soccer in the USA

$2.2 billion business

Category	%	Players	National	Player	Player	Total (m)
National Level			Fee			(m)
US Soccer		4,093,000	$1.00			$4.09
US Youth Soccer*		3,100,000	$1.00			$3.10
US State Associations		3,100,000	$12.00			$37.20
US Amateur Association		273,000	$15.00			$4.09
AYSO		600,000	$8.00			$4.80
SAY		150,000	$9.00			$0.96
US Club Soccer		200,000	$2.00			$0.40
Total National Fees						$54.64

State and Local Level		Players	Fee		Total	
			Low(m)	High(m)	Low(m)	High(m)
US Youth Soccer	100	3,100,000				
US Youth Rec	80	2,480,000	$100	$300	$248	$744
US Youth Club	20	620,000				
Club Travel	80	496,000	$600	$1,500	$297	$744
Club Elite	20	124,000	$2,000	$5,000	$248	$620
AYSO	100	600,000	$50	$150	$30	$90
SAY	100	150,000	$50	$150	$6	$90
Amateur Association	100	273,000	$100	$150	$27	$41
US Club Soccer Org.	100	200,000				
Total Players		4,093,000			$856	$2,329

Notes: All clubs have to submit a portion of the registration fee paid by their players to their national organizations. So everyone in the food chain gets paid. Members of the USYSA clubs typically send $10–$12 to their State Association, who in turn submit $2.00 to the USYSA, who in turn pay $1 to US Soccer.
*Numbers vary from state to state

The best clubs in America also stage lucrative tournaments that generate not only thousands in additional revenue but also enormous prestige. The quality of entrants and number of college coaches attending are a measure of the club's standing. Tournaments give the clubs the opportunity to charge team entry fees, and sell tournament merchandise including the all important "must have" tournament T-shirt (no one in the world produces as many "event T-shirts" as the USA). Leading clubs need to win the most prestigious tournaments to ensure the continued patronage of their parents and to establish the highest possible ranking for their club programs. Most tournaments attract domestic teams but some of the largest including the Dallas Cup draw teams from all over the world, including powerhouses such as Manchester United, Real Madrid and Boca Juniors. Soccer tournaments are a way of life in the USA and a very lucrative one too.

If it's not a soccer tournament the kids are playing, the chances are they are off to a soccer camp. Almost a uniquely American experience the three-month school summer break affords American coaches and "stars" the chance to run very profitable summer camps, designed to either improve skills or give parents a welcome break. From the highly visible and tempting David Beckham Academy to soccer the "Foudy way", soccer the "Brazilian way", soccer the "English way" or soccer the everyway, coaches and players throughout the country run profitable, and for the most part professional and entertaining, camps for players of all ages. (David Beckham's LA-based Academy quietly closed down in 2010, a victim of the recession).

So what is the end result of the US Youth Soccer phenomenon in the USA? It's certainly very well organized, increasingly profitable and growing in geographic reach each year. Parents are content to pay thousands of dollars to get their kids to the right clubs and camps and are willing to sacrifice their weekends, Easters, summers, Thanksgiving and Christmases to watch their kids compete in the best tournaments. They are equally quite prepared to pay for private lessons and the latest hot shot $200 cleats that just might give their kid that extra advantage, that extra goal that catches the college coach's eye. Most of course will not catch any one's leg let alone eye, but the race to impress and the hope of successfully doing so, fuels top-level youth soccer throughout the country. Fortunately, like the tide, the players keep coming as millions of fresh faced 5-year-olds, first soccer ball in hand and $20 cleats on their feet take to the fields each year replenishing the millions of 12-year-olds that leave to pursue other more lucrative sports or 18-year-olds that begin college or adulthood. The fact that American kids love to play soccer is not in doubt, but the two questions that need answering however are, first, is America breeding a nation of soccer fans and consumers, and second, are the players that youth soccer is creating any good? The answers of course are subjective but the analysis underscores some of the tremendous challenges soccer in the USA faces but which, in my view, it is gradually overcoming.

It would not be wrong to say that most parents of gifted soccer players around the world would want their kids to sign for Manchester United or Barcelona or at least a professional soccer team of some description. Primarily a working-class sport, soccer represents the classic escape from poverty for many cultures around the world with the opportunity to play for a professional team offering a route to riches and social elevation beyond their wildest dreams. In the USA however due to the highly educated and affluent nature of the soccer demographic, the road to riches is already mapped out: High School, College, and then marketing, accounting, investment banking or graduate school for law or medicine. For one of the greatest challenges US Soccer faces in developing players that can take on the world is the fact that most of the kids they currently target are not hungry, young ghetto kids fighting their way out of the streets, willing to sacrifice all for a chance at the big time and knowing that failure means a future down a coalmine or some mind-numbing existence in a factory. It is quite the opposite for most American players because if soccer doesn't "work out", their future is most likely a four-year college education, skipping classes and chasing girls. This is not a criticism or envy, just a fact. What is also a fact is that the USA will never win a World Cup if this continues.

For the most part, soccer in America is a clean-cut, middle-class suburban sport populated with families earning in excess of $80,000 per year – parents with college degrees, parents that have aspirations for their kids that center on attending college and gaining an education rather than sending their kids to toil on the training grounds of professional soccer clubs, in the "hope" that a career emerges. Playing soccer in America is seen primarily as a route to college rather than a pathway to a professional career, the complete opposite of every other soccer playing nation in the world. Once again, this needs to change if the USA is to produce world-class players. (Frankly it only has to change for the very highest elite players as for the rest, college is by far the best route.) There are signs that this mentality is changing with kids coming through the system who dream of playing professionally in the MLS or Europe. For most however, the risk of losing a valuable college scholarship keeps them and their parents from taking the risk and overall, despite all of soccer's gains, it will take a cataclysmic change in the psyche of middle-class America to alter this.

As ever the only thing that will change this is money, and even then this is not certain. Richard Motzkin, agent to many US players, said it best when he says the starting point for any agreement, for a player thinking of passing up on college and signing with a professional club, should be the cost of four years' tuition at the college of his choice, if his career fails. This is smart advice, but again not the mentality of 99 percent of the world's best players, most of whom have no plan B.

It will take one American-bred star to rise to the heights of a Messi, Beckham, Torres, Rooney or Ronaldo for young players and their parents to take a chance on soccer. It will take stories of $30m transfer fees and $200,000 per week salaries to salivate the pallets of young athletes that have phenomenal soccer potential at age 12, but switch sports to follow a more lucrative career in the traditional established American sports. That player will of course emerge, as surely as LeTissier scored from the penalty spot. (Matt Le Tissier spent his career with Southampton and from 1986–2002 scored 48 out of 49 spot kicks.) Who would bet against it? In what sport has America not created a world class superstar – Tiger, Jordan, Lewis, Sampras, Phelps, to name a few. While the current development system might not be conducive and the current professional climate not financially attractive, it is only a matter of time before this improves. Brad Friedel, Kasey Keller, Tim Howard, Clint Dempsey and Landon Donovan represent the best of the current era and have laid down new standards of American excellence. The world of soccer now expects raw unfinished quality from America allied to an impressive work ethic and willingness to learn. Forces, however, are coming together that makes it a distinct possibility that somewhere on the bumpy dusty soccer fields of America a star is emerging. Why am I so confident? First, the demographic composition of American is changing dramatically and will continue to do so over the next 20–30 years. Soccer-mad Hispanics, America's fastest growing minority, will number 6 million by 2020, accounting for 18 percent of the population and overall by the year 2040, 50 percent of the US population will comprise ethnic minorities, many of whom will be from countries where soccer is the dominant sport.

As a result, it is not untoward to think that in the next 10–15 years an incredible young American Hispanic, Russian, Asian, African or African-American kid raised in the USA will emerge and change the face of soccer in the US forever. One thing seems certain though, the breakthrough player will not be a clean-cut suburban college-bound kid whose family arrived on the Mayflower and it certainly won't be someone focused on getting a liberal arts degree and attending frat house parties at some four-year college. When the player does arrive however, the question still remains as to whether the current structure of player development in the USA will (a) identify him and (b) develop him correctly. Again I am no coach, but the USA has yet to develop such a star and with the resources and human capital available to it, hard questions need to be asked as to why?

A quick kick around

Soccer clearly has become a dominant sport for all kids in the USA and in particular at the local organized youth-club level and indeed college. Interestingly in most countries in the world it is "pick up" soccer where the skills are learned and "hours" put in. Casual soccer however has not taken root yet as a cultural phenomenon in the USA with basketball and touch football dominating weekend pick-up sports. Basketball is the ultimate "pick up" game in America and the equivalent to soccer world-wide. The NBA is fueled with kids who learned their skills playing eight hours a day, "winner stays on" pick-up basketball on inner city courts against

Table 9.3 General participation numbers for US sports that have major professional leagues

Soccer participants need to turn up

Player Type	Soccer	Football	Baseball	Basketball	Ice Hockey
Total players	16m	9m	16m	24m	1.8m
Core players	9.5m	6m	12.1m	18.8m	1.1m
College	41,500	62,252	28,767	31,662	5,700
Youth organized	4m	225,721	4.1m	240,000	355,156
High School	715,631	1.1m	478,842	1m	43,305
Casual pick up	21%	37%	25%	45%	47%
Pro League attendance	3.5m	17.5m	78m	36m	21.1m
Average attendance	37%	291%	644%	191%	1927%

Notes: Average attendance percentage reflects amount of core fans who attend as a percentage of total attendance for league. Football also has 12m "Touch Football" recreational players.

Interestingly each season 21 million hockey fans attend professional NHL games yet the total core playing population is only 1.1 million (see Table 9.3). It's a completely unscientific comparison but sort of shows that you do not necessarily need to be playing the sport to be a fan of it.

Source: Compiled: 2006 Sporting Goods and Manufactures Association.

players five years older and ten times tougher. The skills learned and mental strength developed in this Darwinian world provided players with the tools needed to survive the tough road to a professional contract. Unfortunately, soccer in America has yet to develop a similar culture. Life is just too planned for most suburban kids with calendars filled with regimented school and social activities. American soccer kids are over-coached and over-organized and unfortunately it shows! Things are slowly changing and you are starting to see far more soccer balls on school playgrounds and in family backyards, but the US is a long way away from Sunday afternoon 15-a-side games, lasting four hours with the first to 30 crowned winner, unless of course you're Hispanic (but that's a different and later story).

I would argue that the past 20 plus years in American youth soccer have been all about getting as many players as possible involved in the game and fortunately it looks like this has now been achieved. The United States Youth Soccer Association (3 million members), American Youth Soccer Association (600,000 members) and other smaller organizations, do tremendous work in ensuring the game is delivered to American families and their kids, and long may they do so. But if soccer in America is to move forward, then the next decade needs to be about the "quality" of players produced, rather than the quantity. America needs to develop world class players that not only drive MLS to become the best professional league in the Americas but also populate leading clubs around the world, both of which will drive money into the sport and hence attract the best athletes. To achieve this the status quo and insular nature of American soccer needs to change, with new structures and a new focus considered.

There are some signs that changes are afoot with the leading clubs stretching their wings and assuming greater control over their destiny. Most top clubs are now members of the newly formed US Club Soccer a break-away youth soccer organization created by the clubs themselves. Unhappy with the restrictions placed upon them by their governing body and recognizing that 80 percent of the 3 million members registered to youth soccer are recreational, the top clubs combined to create their own "soccer world" dedicated to servicing the demands of the best teams and best players. It's early days but the route to quality has to run through top youth clubs and Major League Soccer, with highly qualified (international standard) coaches developing players under a national coaching syllabus, developed in conjunction with MLS, US Soccer and the National Coaches Soccer Association. I would suggest stealing the best ideas from Brazil, Spain, Argentina, England and Italy adding a US feel and creating a syllabus that all top college and MLS coaches sign up to and ask (insist) that all youth soccer coaches embrace. From the age of eight, every kid in the Boca Juniors system knows what is expected of them, what skills and understanding of systems they need and what, by the age of sixteen, they should have innately mastered and can replicate at will, for only then will they have any chance of getting a professional contract. The USA needs to do the same for its top players and needs to engage everyone involved in the game to establish what this needs to be. As a quid pro quo, top American youth and college coaches should be offered the opportunity, and financial support, to gain the very highest coaching qualification and training in the new system and be engaged and consulted in shaping the future of the game. The silos that divide soccer in America need to be pulled down for the good of the player, the professional game and ultimately the US National Team and by doing so everyone in the game will benefit. America's youth and college coaches can play a critical role in developing the quality of player that will propel the US National Team and Major League Soccer to new levels, but they need to be guided and to embrace and share the vision. The best way to do this is to have them part of the process of developing it.

The National Soccer Coaches Association (NSCAA)

With 30,000 members, the NSCAA is one of the largest coaching organizations in the world and the envy of many leading soccer nations. Most leading college, high school and premier youth club coaches are members and its annual gathering represents a meeting place for America's most committed and dedicated soccer teachers. It is once again testimony to the great organization and infrastructure of youth soccer in America and provides an insight into why the participation levels are so strong. The biggest question surrounding the organization is not their commitment or passion but rather is the organization working together with US Soccer and Major League Soccer in a unified way for the ultimate good of the American player and coach? Organized youth and college soccer has grown enormously over the past 20 years and in each of these years over four million kids are in the controlled leagues and games. America still however has not developed, and in fairness not come close to developing, a world-class star. Is this because of the structure and environment, the standard of coaching or the quality of the raw material, namely players?

The bottom line is that there are 16 million players but no world-class stars, and something needs to change. Switzerland has just won the under-17 FIFA World Cup, has a total population of just 7.8 million, is covered in snow for most of the year and has pitches sloping down the side of mountains (the last bit not exactly true but you hopefully get the point.) If Ghana, Nigeria, Switzerland and others can develop players that can win a youth

World Cup, why not the USA? The NSCAA has just appointed a new Executive Director: Joe Cummings, a long time soccer man and veteran of Men's and Women's soccer in the States. His coaches sit across all the political, geographic and business divides in the USA and if mobilized can seriously impact soccer on every level. If I am MLS, US Soccer, US Youth Soccer and AYSO, I am looking at the best way to work with them. On the reverse side, if we assume that the NSCAA coaches represent most of the colleges in the USA then they can also do American soccer a great favor. It is absolute nonsense that if Manchester United invite a 17-year-old American for a trial and so much as buy him a cup of coffee it could jeopardize that kid's eligibility for a college scholarship. This one NCAA rule prevents the majority of players even attempting to play abroad, with parents mortified at losing out. This rule was implemented to stop college alumni buying cars and jewelry for football and basketball players as inducements to join their program. It has no relevance in soccer. The NCAA just might be American soccer's greatest challenge and a battle worth fighting.

CHAPTER 10

Viva Futbol/Viva Mexico!

American soccer should wake up every morning and say "gracias" to the 48 million Hispanics that call the USA home. It should further mount a statue with a huge sombrero, soccer ball and flag in honor of the Mexican-American community that constitute the majority of this demographic and who have played a vital and incredible role in soccer's commercial growth. The US Census predicts that by 2030, 20 percent of the US population will be Hispanic, rising to 25 percent by 2050 and as such they represent a core and critically important group for developing and expanding the sport (see Table 10.1).

Before looking at the Hispanic community it's important to distinguish between soccer Hispanics and non-soccer Hispanics for America has both. Mexicans (64 percent), Central Americans (7.6 percent) and South Americans (5.5 percent) are all deemed to be soccer friendly. Puerto Ricans (9 percent), Cubans (3.4 percent) and Dominicans (2.8 percent) are primarily baseball fans. Therefore, whenever we discuss numbers it's important to remember that only 80 percent of Hispanics living in the USA are what we would call soccer friendly. (And if you are thinking of buying a team in Miami, it's important.)

Table 10.1 Growth of soccer Hispanics 1990–2050

Soccer mad and growing							
(m)	1990	2000	2010	2020	2030	2040	2050
US Population	241	281	308	335	363	391	419
Hispanic Population	22	35	48	60	73	88	102
% Hispanic Population	9.1	12.5	15.5	17.9	20.0	22.5	24.3
Soccer Hispanics	18	28	37	46	56	67	79
% of population	7.5	10.0	12.0	13.7	15.4	17.1	18.9

Note: Soccer Hispanics defined as Mexican, Central American and South American.

Source: Compiled from US Census.

However, it's not their numbers, while important, but their passion and unbridled patriotism for both the game and their country that has helped shape soccer in the USA, for above all, Hispanic America is a colorful, passionate community born and raised with soccer in their blood and "futbol" in their hearts. The business press is full of stories about the incredible emerging $1 trillion buying power of the Hispanic community and indeed this has convinced many American corporations to pour millions into the game. They also talk about their rising wealth and education, which is also relevant (indeed the first ever Hispanic Supreme Court Judge was appointed this year). However the greatest and most important lesson the Hispanic community has taught America about soccer can be summed up in one word: "passion", for wherever and whenever their teams appear in the USA, you can be sure that thousands of their fans will descend upon the stadium, turning it into a cauldron of flag waving, song singing, and patriotic fervor. None more so than when the incredible fans of the Mexican National Team arrive to support their "gods". It's a sight to behold and the most exciting atmosphere in American soccer to witness the unshakeable and unbreakable bond that exists between the Mexican community and its national team – a bond every true soccer fan can admire, and one that American soccer fans need to emulate.

The best supported team in America: Mexico

It is one of the strange anomalies about soccer in the USA that there are 30+ million fans living in the country that support America's biggest rivals Mexico, Honduras, Guatemala and El Salvador. When the USA plays these teams on American soil it might as well be an away game and none more so than when the mighty Mexico arrive. It is the Mexican National Team and its now ferocious rivalry with the USA that is one of the key drivers for the future of the sport.

Great sports are all about great rivalries and fortunately Mexico versus the USA has become a beacon around which US soccer fans and the American media can congregate. No one wants tepid friendly relationships in the sporting arena and fortunately the rivalry between USA and Mexico is fast becoming as fierce as some of the greatest soccer rivalries in the world (not yet in numbers of course but certainly growing in intensity). It takes fierce competition and "history" between the teams to nurture and fuel this level of "intensity", a history that fortunately has evolved between the two North American rivals as it has between bordering countries for centuries.

Most England fans loathe the Scotland national team, weary of them marauding through London in their kilts with rebellious intentions and plans afoot to invade the sacred home of English football (Wembley), steal the turf and rip up the goalposts (which they successfully orchestrated in 1977) after a 2–1 victory. It's a rivalry and history that goes back decades and, at deeper levels, centuries. For the thousands of Scots pouring over Hadrian's Wall the feeling was intensely mutual, their pilgrimage a celebration of patriotism, culture and identity. (It was also payback for centuries past as Americans who watched "Braveheart" will understand!) It may all sound very dramatic and histrionic but it is these rivalries that are at the very heart of soccer's popularity, and fuels a level of intensity few Americans understand. Real Madrid versus Barcelona, Liverpool versus Manchester United, Celtic versus Rangers, Riverplate versus Boca Juniors and Chivas versus Club America are all games that keep fans coming, people talking and traditions passed down. The Boston Redsox versus New York Yankees might go some way and many college football rivalries are deeply engrained but nothing beats soccer and its national and club rivalries. Fortunately USA/ Mexico is well on its way to establishing a soccer "history" between its teams and a rivalry that will hopefully get more intense as the years pass. There is no love lost between the competing players or the opposing sets of fans with the US dominating on the field and Mexico in the stands. (There is however a sense that a new Mexican team is emerging that will challenge the USA's recent dominance, hopefully throwing more fuel on the fire – fuel ironically paid for, in part, by the vast dollars generated marketing Mexico in America. An interesting point of discussion!)

The great rivalry between the USA and Mexico teams began of course only when it became clear the USA could actually compete with them, by beating them at the 1991 Concacaf Gold Cup. Prior to this the USA was a minor soccer irritant whom they beat at will, in fact losing only twice in 54 years and 27 previous games (with one of those being in 1930).The soccer field was the one place they could exert dominance over the political and economic superpower to their north, for when kickoff time came there was only one "superpower": Mexico. Until 1991 and Bora, that is. In much the same way that the Ryder Cup only became important to Americans when the "Brits" joined up with the Europeans and started to beat them (regularly), the Mexican media and population only began their intense scrutiny and rivalry once the USA started winning. Since that victory in 1991 the USA has played Mexico 18 times on USA soil, and they have won nine, lost just three and drawn six. Importantly, when the real pressure was on and the key battle for supremacy fought, the USA prevailed, knocking out Mexico in the round of 16 at the 2002 Korea/Japan World Cup. This defeat, above all others, ratcheted up the rivalry. The game itself was watched by 6.5 million viewers in America (4.2 million of them Hispanic) and millions more in Mexico. The result let the world (and more importantly Mexico) know that the balance of power had shifted in North America, and that the high ground belonged to the USA. It has to hurt that Mexico has not beaten the USA in a World Cup qualification match on American soil for 20 years and neither by the way has the USA beaten Mexico on Mexican soil (see Table 10.2).

The rivalry is also great for the cash register with games between the two rivals being by far and away the best attended matches in the US Soccer calendar, as can be seen in Table 10.3.

A $2m loss

The average attendance for the USA–Mexico games however is hugely understated due to the fact that from 2002 onwards a

Table 10.2 USA versus Mexico: head to head

A new sheriff in town

	1930–91	Post 1991	Post 2000
Games	27	30	16
USA win	2	13	10
Mexico win	22	8	4
Draw	3	8	2

Source: Compiled as at December 2009 from US Soccer.

Table 10.3 Average attendance for USA National Team games by category of match

USA Mexico dominates

USA games	All Game Average	World Cup Q 1998	World Cup Q 2002	World Cup Q 2006	Word Cup Q 2010	USA v. Mexico
	25,869	38,959	35,276	19,519	18,696	53,551*

*Misleading, read heading "a $2m loss"
Source: Compiled from US Soccer.

conscious decision was made by US Soccer to make World Cup Qualifying matches against Mexico (and other teams) as uncomfortable as possible (as is their right). As a result, many of the games were staged in the small compact Columbus Crew stadium, a 24,000-capacity concrete stadium in the cold and inhospitable winter of mid-west Ohio. It works every time and three points are as certain as the freezing weather. Financially however, it's a huge loss for US Soccer with close to $2m in revenue left on the table. The games could easily have been played in Los Angeles, Houston, Dallas or any other city with a major Mexican population. Sell-out gates would be assured, but the USA would be handing the Mexican team the atmosphere they crave and thrive on and that is the last thing you want to hand your biggest rival.

There might have been a time when US Soccer would have needed to make a financial rather than soccer decision but fortunately those times have passed. Beating Mexico and qualifying for the World Cup is now a US Soccer "mantra" and every advantage is taken to ensure it is achieved. The powers-that-be recognize the importance of doing both and are prepared to sacrifice immediate revenue to achieve this. Of course the financial payoff for qualifying is enormous but with that said, not many sports organizations in America would walk away from a $2m pay day. Just to reinforce the point, the last two Mexico versus USA games played at the Rose Bowl in Los Angeles averaged 92,000 fans each (90 percent of them Mexican, of course). The best thing about the rivalry however is that it now transcends "money", US Soccer truly just wants to beat and if possible "hammer" Mexico – it's now about pride and patriotism and not dollars, as it should be.

In a broader sense, the Hispanic fan base in America has played an incredible role in shaping the sport and to a degree "teaching" the newly forming US fans just exactly what is expected of true supporters. It is they that sing, bang drums, dance, congregate behind the goal and berate or applaud their team. Soccer to them is a touch point to their culture, heritage and identity, particularly when it comes to their national teams appearing in the USA. There has been an explosion in the US Hispanic population over the past 20 years and in particular with those arriving from Central America. As with earlier immigrant groups from centuries past, they had to enter the workforce obtaining whatever manual labor and menial jobs they could find and toiling almost anonymously in communities across the country. (It is an interesting fact that although today Irish heritage is the most beloved of all ancestries in America, in the early 1900s this was not the case. Factories and stores displayed signs proclaiming "no Irish need apply". It is almost a rite of passage in American culture that early immigrants have to work their way up the economic ladder and millions of Hispanics are attempting to do so.) When their national soccer teams arrive however, it becomes an opportunity to step out of the shadows, celebrate their heritage, their passion and culture and to remind themselves and everyone around them that although they work and live in the USA and appreciate all it gives them, they are (particularly when it comes to soccer), first and foremost Mexican, Honduran, El Salvadoran, Guatemalan and more.

America has always celebrated its multicultural diversity and soccer, more than any other sport, embraces and enhances it. Passionate, crazy, loud and colorful, these fans create the atmosphere that soccer thrives on. The manner of the support is however unique. Hispanic fans might berate the US National Team which is their right, but rarely, if ever, do they berate the USA, which is an important distinction. Go to many USA versus Mexico games and you will see joint USA and Mexico flags and kids with the Mexican flag painted on one side of their face and the Stars and Stripes on the other, proud to be Mexican Americans. Sure they will support Mexico when they play the USA but will support the USA when they play Honduras, El Salvador, Guatemala or any other country. The ex-President of Univision, David Downs, recalls going to see the USA play Panama in the final of the 2005

Gold Cup, and with a film crew in hand noticed a group of fans with USA and Honduran banners, who, when asked why they were there and who they were supporting, replied "the USA of course" (a little surprised), "it's our country as well you know". This sums it all up really and gives a great insight into soccer fans in the USA. It is their country and they are proud of it, but by the very nature of the country, it is okay to feel proud of your ancestry and support the country of your birth. (By the way go to Mexico City for a World Cup qualifier however and it's a completely different matter entirely and as hostile and rabid an experience as you might experience as a USA fan.) Over time it remains to be seen if the second and third generation kids are as fervent soccer fans as their parents but the growing evidence is that Hispanics, while taking the best of what America has to offer, also wish to maintain and indeed intensify their links to their culture and identity. The buzzword for this is acculturation, defined as "maintaining a native culture while acquiring a new one", rather than assimilation, "replacing a native culture with a new one". In our world this means ditching soccer for American football, basketball or baseball. But it's not happening now and not likely to in the future as the ties are too deep and too historic: put the LA Dodgers up against the New York Yankees on the same day as Mexico versus the USA and there would be few sombreros to wake up for the seventh innings stretch.

Had a trial for Boca!

Representing such a vast section of the USA soccer market and with a passion nurtured through generations, it is disappointing that not more of them are coming through the ranks to MLS or the US National Team program. Reasons abound, but they are primarily economic and cultural. First, while many of the early Hispanic youth and adult clubs were part of the US Soccer Federation program, they gradually drifted away feeling that the return they received on the obligatory registration fees was not worth it. Feeling under-served and under-appreciated, they came to the conclusion that the Federation offered them little they could not do for themselves and equally imposed reporting and insurance requirements they would prefer to do without.

As a result they formed their own autonomous internal leagues and competitions that sat outside the US Soccer organizational structure, operating in a Hispanic soccer netherworld with rules, fees, and programs unique to them. In a further nod to the nature of the Hispanic community, most teams organized along ethnic lines: Mexicans with Mexicans, Hondurans with Hondurans and El Salvadorans with El Salvadorans. As ethnic communities sprung up around America, migrating in good economic times from the usual traditional centers in California and Texas to places such as Philadelphia, Columbus and Boston, so too did their soccer teams. In Southern California alone there are over 250 leagues each with 1,500 players each that compete each weekend, representing 375,000 plus players: interestingly, following the South American model of two seasons, the "Apeturer" and the "closure". Registration fees run at $100 per season, uniforms, usually unbranded, are acquired "across the border" or locally at exceptionally good rates and should a player suffer an injury the rest of the team will "chip in" to offset medical fees. Uninsured players are not something that sit well with US Soccer and many teams drifted away from the oversight of a Federation that demanded compliance.

The leagues themselves however are equally independent of each other and rarely compete, making the whole grass-roots Hispanic market very tough to reach for the business community and hard for coaches and scouts to identify players. There is little doubt that some very exciting talent is competing in these leagues, talent that if discovered and nurtured could well produce an American superstar that changes the game. Unable to afford the registration fees for the top clubs they never appear on the radar screen of US coaches and MLS scouts. Teams and clubs are reaching out, but lack of funds and even the requirement of many young Hispanics to work at weekends and nights to help support their families makes it tough to get these players through. There is little chance these kids can afford the $5,000 plus that the elite players spend to get noticed. MLS and US Soccer try to counter this with open try-outs throughout the year and while good talent might appear there is always the paunchy out of shape 40-year-old with new boots trying convince the scouts he once had a trial for Boca Juniors and still has what it takes to dominate MLS, but again that's what we love about the game, the legs might have gone and certainly the waist but the "soccer brain" still tricks us.

Concacaf: Trump Tower please

It's almost a rite of passage for all organizations in the North American soccer arena to have to overcome severe financial obstacles and political upheaval to survive and The Confederation of North, Central America and Caribbean association football (Concacaf), the controlling authority for soccer in the region, is no different. Encompassing the two powerhouses, USA and Mexico, its remit also covers 38 other countries ranging from Honduras, El Salvador and Guatemala to Jamaica, Costa Rica and the Cayman Islands, countries with vastly disproportionate populations and economic fortunes. The challenge for Concacaf however is to assist the sport's development across this wide spectrum. Ultimately, as with most countries, it is qualification for the World Cup that drives it forward and with four places on offer, the Concacaf teams have much to play for. Many smaller Concacaf countries how-ever have enough trouble rustling up 11 players and coach let alone putting together a program capable of getting to South Africa 2010. Countries such as Martinique, Belize, Antigua, St. Kitts, Barbados and Guyana have little hope of matching up against the might of Mexico and the USA (unless of course it's at cricket) and so it's usually a quick home leg, away leg and back to the beach – unfortunately with little cash to show for it. For the USA however, the Concacaf group represents an almost assured trip to every World Cup Final and indeed since 1990 it has made them all. Frankly, it would be a disaster and public humiliation if it did not qualify, the qualifying group is not that tough and to not make the top four would be inexcusable.

Concacaf's development has in many ways mirrored the growth of US Soccer and indeed in the late 1980s, the money was as tight and the politics just as fractious. The pending changes at the top of US Soccer were however child's play compared to the battle for control of Concacaf taking place in Mexico. Jack Warner (now President) was barred from the meeting hotel and received reported death threats before unseating the incumbent Joaquin Soria Terrazas in 1989 with FIFA President Havalanche having to fly in to restore order, serious stuff indeed. Change was however secured and ex-US Soccer aficionado Chuck Blazer installed as General Secretary. Affable and smart, Blazer was to become the face of Concacaf in the USA, calling upon all his years as a corporate marketer and soccer administrator to drive revenue into the organization's coffers. Blazer's approach was strikingly similar to that being undertaken by US Soccer, that is, to bring together the region's best teams to play in the USA and wrap, not necessarily the Red, White and Blue of the USA, but the Green of Mexico, the Blue of Honduras and the Red of Trinidad around them. To achieve this, in 1991, he launched the bi-annual Concacaf Gold Cup, a European Championships-style event with leading Concacaf countries. The first event was a low-budget low-key affair based solely in Los Angeles and remembered mainly for the fact the USA beat Mexico in the semi-finals and went on to win the final. It should also be remembered for the low crowds, just 4,797 to see Mexico beat Canada and 6,344 fans to see USA beat Guatemala with the only USA fans being the team staff. Gates did improve for the semi-final with 41,103 fans showing up to see the USA beat Mexico (41,000 of whom went home very unhappy) and 39,873 to see the US beat Honduras in the final: 39,500 of whom, left mightily depressed. It was however a start, and with the USA winning, a good one for Bora and his team. It wasn't however profitable.

Looking to make a little more money, the 1993 event was staged in both the USA and Mexico and while crowds averaged just 15,000 in America, 130,000 fans turned out in Mexico City to see Mexico defeat the USA in the final, restoring what in their eyes was the "natural order" of things. To keep it fresh, in 1996 Concacaf invited (and of course paid) Brazil to compete and 88,000 poured into the Los Angeles Coliseum to see Mexico beat them in the final. By 1998 the event was clearly growing in stature and importance, and a staggering 91,000 turned up at the Rose Bowl to see Mexico defeat their nemesis the USA. Just when the event could seemingly do no wrong, Mexico began crashing out in the early rounds, sending the event into a tailspin of falling crowds and financial losses. It would be too cynical to suggest that independent promoters were reaping the rewards of staging individual games for Mexico in the USA and as such a "free" appearance in the Gold Cup was counter-productive, but whatever the reason, it was catastrophic for the event and brought it to its knees. And not helped by the fact they also decided to stage the first ever Concacaf women's Gold Cup to capitalize on the phenomenal success of the 1999 Women's World Cup (I think they are still counting the losses!)

Miraculously when the event returned to Mexico, the team's performance improved dramatically, resulting in another final success over Brazil at the Azteca. Back in the USA in 2005 and Mexico again crashed out in the quarter finals, this time to a Colombian side that would go on to lose to Panama in the semis. All fun and games. In 2007 with Mexico now represented by Soccer United Marketing they stormed through to the final losing to SUM'S other key client, the USA, in front of 60,000 at Soldier Field in Chicago. The victory was enough to send the USA to the 2009 Confederations Cup in South Africa, where they incredibly beat Spain 3–2 in the semi-final and took a 2–0 lead against Brazil before losing, 3–2 in the final, performances which elevated the status of American soccer around the world. This was quickly undone however by a 5–1 thrashing by Mexico in the final of the 2009 Gold Cup in front of 79,000 Mexicans in New York. The USA put out a young and inexperienced team, but to the majority of the American media the result said it all. Concacaf of course are neutral when it comes to results, but Mexico versus the USA is always the preferred final with a 79,000 in attendance representing a great pay day! With the 2009 event, Concacaf had the best of both worlds as Soccer United Marketing staged, managed and sold all the sponsorships to the event (the hard stuff), while Concacaf Marketing and Television (CMTV), its in-house marketing division, formed after the financial debacles of 2000 and 2002, controlled and sold all of the television rights (the easier stuff). I told you Chuck was a smart guy! (See Table 10.4.)

With the Gold Cup secure and cemented on the calendar, Concacaf have recently launched its own version of the Champions League (without of course the mega millions, teams are getting just $30,000 a game to cover travel costs and keeping their

Table 10.4 Concacaf Gold Cup record 1991–2009

Battle for Confederations Cup place

Year	Average	Final	Total Gates	Winner
1991	22,947	39,873	160,629	USA
1993	58,618	130,800	527,566	Mexico
1996	32,117	88,155	321,174	Mexico
1998	35,849	91,255	573,587	Mexico
2000	24,173	7,000	265,901	Canada
2002	18,498	14,432	184,979	USA
2003	23,883	80,000	382,128	Mexico
2005	26,164	31,018	340,129	USA
2007	37,598	60,000	488,772	USA
2009	34,402	79,156	860,046	Mexico
Percentage increase	49.9%	98.5%	435.4%	

Source: Concacaf Research Department.

own home gate revenue). Twenty-four club teams from the region including Major League Soccer and the Mexican First Division compete against each other in group format to be crowned the region's best, with the winner earning a place in the very lucrative and prestigious Club World Cup and a possible match with teams such as Barcelona, Manchester United or Boca Juniors.

The strength of Champions League Soccer in Europe is the incredible quality of the games, the fanatical atmosphere of the stadiums and of course the multi-camera digital high-definition broadcasts. Which is great if your games are at Old Trafford and the Nou Camp but is not replicable if your games are at second division stadiums in Puerto-Rico, Guatemala or Honduras, where finding a plug socket can sometimes be a challenge. To overcome this, Concacaf has built a first-class digital television studio in its New York offices to ensure the quality of its broadcasts and has implemented a consistent look and feel surrounding the presentation of its games. The commitment to delivering their brand to the highest possible standards highlights just how far they have traveled, how financially secure they have become and how marketing savvy they are. Launching new high-quality websites with streaming video, designed to provide their smaller events with world-wide exposure, again shows a Confederation on the cutting edge of technology with an understanding of how to maximize the economic value of the content they possess.

As ever in North American Soccer it's been a long tough road with some dark financial days and potentially catastrophic moments for Concacaf, but come 2010 it is a vibrant and financially secure organization with meaningful events and programs and a firm grip on where the future of its soccer is heading. While it might on paper look like a confederation responsible for shaping the fortunes of (with all due respect) soccer lightweights such as Aruba, Grenada, Guadeloupe and Panama, its operation and vision would put many so-called soccer heavyweights to shame, and some of the largest confederations in the world would find a trip to Concacaf's offices in Trump Tower, New York both an enlightening and worthwhile experience.

CHAPTER 11

Young Americans: Transfers and Lost Dollars

Now here opens a can of worms in American soccer. Just how good are the USA players, how good the system producing them and how proficient the coaches developing their skills? I do not purport to be an expert coach or skilled manager but all I know is that I have followed and watched soccer for over 45 years, know a good player when I see one and a promising kid when exposed to one. I have followed American soccer since 1989 and my gut tells me the USA has lots of promising players, in fact a decent level of good players but nowhere near enough great players! For the purpose of this book and its focus, great players are those that the top European clubs would pay good money to buy. For until America is producing players and enough of them that are good enough to play for Manchester United, Barcelona, AC Milan and Real Madrid it will never win a World Cup. Because teams that do have players populating the top leagues in Europe. For America to compete it will have to adopt a systematic, professional and far-reaching player development system that discovers talent on par with the world's best. It may not be easy but is necessary and actually can be done. Steve Heighway, the Liverpool youth team coach, who developed Owen, Gerrard, Carragher and Fowler and spent many years coaching youth soccer in Florida, once told me that he thought the talent pool he left behind was better than the one he inherited when he returned to Liverpool. A frightening thought really but also an optimistic one.

There is not a kid growing up in any soccer-mad country in the world that does not dream of being scouted, signing for a professional club and eventually securing the big money transfer or salary that will change their lives forever. For most teams around the world, finding, developing and transferring talent is as much a part of their profit and loss statement as the attendance at the gate or sponsorship sales, and forms a significant portion of board meeting discussions. The reality is that 95 percent of the teams around the world "survive" by their ability to identify and sell talent. Completely alien to traditional American sports (where the players control their own fortunes, and "transfer fees" are non-existent), it should and will become an important part of the business model for Major League Soccer and its teams over the next 20 years.

Some of the top soccer countries in the world have no problem in exporting their talent, as can be seen in Table 11.1. Brazil who have gone on to win the World Cup five times, followed by Argentina who have won it twice, France who have won it once and Uruguay who have won it twice, all make a point of selling their best players. The movement of players from the South American countries has always been for economic reasons with clubs surviving and prospering by their ability to find and develop

Table 11.1 Number of foreign players in top leagues and their source

Right up there with the Ivory Coast

Rank	Country	England	Spain	Italy	Germany	Total
1	Brazil	14	27	33	33	107
2	Argentina	5	36	33	6	80
3	France	34	14	12	7	67
4	Holland	14	7	3	10	34
5	Portugal	7	15	4	3	29
6	Uruguay	0	13	11	2	26
7	Switzerland	4	3	5	11	23
8	Serbia	4	4	6	8	22
17	Cameroon	4	4	1	4	13
18	Ivory Coast	4	5	0	4	13
19	USA	7	0	1	5	13
29	Mexico	3	4	1	1	9
47	Honduras	3	0	2	0	5

Note: Numbers as at 30 October 2009. Altidore was sold by MLS to Villarreal in Spain but loaned by them to Hull City.

Source: Compiled from online research.

new talent. The economies of the South American countries mean that the leagues, while popular, cannot compete for salaries so they become net "exporters". The players prosper and succeed because they are "schooled" and "developed" for the purpose. If MLS intends to do the same then they need programs to develop these players in a similar manner. Finding and selling talent is a business and needs to be treated as such.

With Major League Soccer teams now keeping around 70 percent of all transfer fees from the sale of players they find and develop, there may well be far more opportunities for players in the USA to find either an MLS, or international club, or even a combination of the two. Certain MLS teams are tying in with local youth clubs to identify and develop the best talent and "cutting them in" on any "sell on" transfer fees they generate. This has potential on many levels: (1) it ties the local youth clubs closer to their MLS team, (2) it provides a potential clear path for youth players with embedded contacts and programs and (3) puts young kids on notice very early on that if they are good enough there is the potential for a career. In this scenario the local youth system and the MLS club work closely together on developing the best players to the mutual benefit of all parties. Young players have to see a clear pathway through to the professionals wherever that might be and Major League Soccer could take the lead on this by working with the top international leagues and clubs to develop them. They could bring in leading clubs and host both seminars and potential courses in what it takes to be a professional player in both the USA and Europe. Players such as Keller, Harkes, Reyna, could be used by the league and teams to speak to, and mentor, young professionals. The clear route to professional soccer should be through MLS organizations working in conjunction with the leading players and clubs. Equally the program should be open to players not in the youth systems, those that might be playing in ethnic leagues around the country. An interesting question in developing young talent for professional clubs, either in the USA or abroad, always come back to how committed the player and or parent is to let their kid go abroad.

As discussed previously, the vast majority of suburban parents want their kids to get a classic high school and then college education, not necessarily conducive to developing the next Messi.

Maybe a hybrid system might work where players spend time with their local MLS team but then get a chance to spend time with leading European teams. Players around the world usually develop in and around a professional club setting, whether it's a small Spanish, German or English club. Here they learn what it takes physically and mentally to be a professional soccer player. American kids need to be around such environments to improve and develop. To benefit financially from developing young talent either for themselves or to "sell on", MLS Clubs need to develop programs to identify, develop, and prepare kids for life as a professional. It's how some of the most successful soccer countries and teams in the world do it. They start preparing their kids at an early age to be professionals and enjoy tremendous financial rewards from doing so, either in "saved" expense because they have developed their own talent or in transfer fees because they have developed a bright young talent. It's organized, it's systematic and it's a key part of the business model. There is of course the argument as to why export your top talent when MLS needs to improve its overall quality. The answer is that you need to first have a system that finds, develops and prepares "professional quality" young players and you want international leagues and teams fighting for your best prospects, because if they are, it means there is a clear financial path and reward for young American players and athletes.

If MLS does develop strong programs and controls the flow of talent, it will strengthen its hand in the global game. Ultimately there is no reason why, with the economic power the USA can bring to anything it ultimately decides to commit to, it cannot compete for quality talent and become a net importer of players, indeed it will need to do this to drive the league forward and raise the standard of play. Every country will ultimately lose its very best "superstar" players to the Manchester Uniteds and Real Madrids. The key for MLS is to keep developing new young talent, bring in the best players and stars it can afford from around the world and make it financially attractive enough for those Americans that can't sign for the top European clubs to stay.

The question of course is, can the USA develop enough professional quality talent? On the face of it looks like the USA, with seven players in the English Premiership, is creating players, but three of those are goalkeepers and not one is playing for what any of us would call a top team. Smaller countries, such as Ecuador with four players including Valencia at Man United, Honduras with three players including Palacios at Spurs and the Ivory Coast with four players including Drogba at Chelsea, are all developing players that leading clubs want and play. As MLS develops and the professionalization of the sport increases there is no reason why it cannot provide the resources and programs to identify and develop players the world wants. It first, however, needs to develop the programs. This is the domain of dedicated soccer coaches rather than myself but let me raise some questions that beg answers.

In 1991 at the under-17 FIFA World Cup, the USA team beat a very strong "Sebastian Veron"-led Argentina team 1–0, a very impressive result against a perennial world soccer powerhouse and a nation that prides itself on developing and selling great young talent. It would probably be a reasonable guess to say that the USA team must have been pretty good and contained players who, with the right development, might have gone on to have decent careers in soccer either in the USA or around the world. However in 1991, the "stock" of USA born soccer was not very high and international teams not really willing to risk or even contemplate signing young American talent. For most of the team, it was on to college and then five years later a career with the fledgling Major League Soccer. But what of the team they beat that day: Argentina? Well over the next ten plus years, those players went on to generate over $200m in transfer fees and have successful careers playing in England, Spain, France and of course at home in Argentina. Veron alone transferred for over $170m to teams like Lazio, Manchester United and Chelsea. The situation for USA young players was not much better in 1993 when they tied with a strong Czechoslovakian team 2–2, a team that went on to generate over $30m in transfer fees and play for the likes of AC Milan, while the US team again headed off to college. It was clear however that the tide was starting to turn and the world was starting to take notice. The under-17 "school" of 1999 that beat Uruguay 1–0 in the World Cup secured transfer fees of $10m with Beasley ($4m), Onyewu ($3m) and Convey ($3m). The Uruguayan team they beat that day "sold" for over $24m, but it was a start. Over the past ten years the world's best leagues and teams have started to cast their net far and wide for raw (and hopefully inexpensive) young talent and the USA has come into focus as potential source. The 2005 under-17 team that beat Italy 3–1 has accumulated $18m in transfers to date with Joze Altidore's $10m transfer to Spanish Club, Villarreal (now on loan at Hull City) being the largest in US history (Figure 11.1).

The other $8m of that $18m however brings into question a whole different area of discussion and draws a light on just whether US Soccer and its coaches are doing everything in their power to ensure that the best possible players are identified and "secured" for the US National Team. Remember to win a World Cup in the next 20–50 years it "only" needs 11–15 top-class quality players

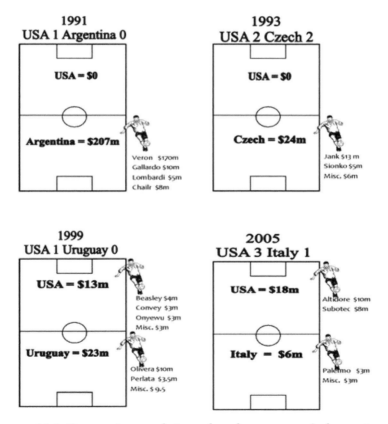

Figure 11.1 Comparison of transfer fees earned from teams competing against the USA in U-17 World Cup finals

arriving on the scene and available at the same time, with enough in them to win seven games over a three-week period. It can be done, look at Denmark in the 1992 European Championships, and again Greece in the 2004 tournament, not the World Cup, but a "tough as hell" tournament to win. Both teams were from small countries, hopelessly out-resourced by the rest of Europe, with, at best, average professional leagues. But come the day come the tournament, they put it all together and with the soccer gods on their side achieved an incredible upset. They did not however achieve this by letting their best players slip out of their hands.

Earlier in the book I made the case that the type of players the USA will need to develop to win a World Cup will probably come from the newly emerging ethnically diverse American demographic, particularly from those families with a strong soccer heritage: Hispanic yes but also European and eventually African-American. Let's look at two players that highlight a weakness that needs to be fixed.

Nevan Subotic: let's play Botswana

Subotic was actually identified by US coaches and not only played for the US under-17s but also the under-20s before going on to play at University of Southern Florida. With no sign of being picked for the full US National Team (and indeed being dropped from the under-20s), he joined the German team, Mainz, where his performance soon led to an $8m transfer to Borussia Dortmund in the German Bundesleague, where he is now a stalwart of their defense and also scoring six goals in the 2008 season. Still just 20 he was then identified by the Serbian National Team who quickly called him into their squad. Starting all seven games of Serbia's impressive World Cup 2010 unbeaten qualification campaign, he has quickly drawn the attention of leading Premiership Clubs who are circling for his "signature", which will likely come after the 2010 South Africa World Cup. This, of course, begs the obvious question: how come this guy isn't the anchor of the USA defense for the next 15 years?

Frustratingly Subotic was in the system, his family had left Yugoslavia during the "crisis" and headed for Germany but were forced to leave after five years when their authorization expired. They then headed to the USA where they were taken in and looked after. He has much to be thankful for to the USA, for he represented the Red, White and Blue at two different age groups and he is quoted as saying he considered himself American. He now however plays for Serbia. It is said he "chose" Serbia over the USA but we need to get real here. He should have been recognized as an emerging talent, brought into the full National Team squad at 17 or 18 and given a game, even an arranged game against Botswana. Had they done so, he would now be secured, forever, as a USA National Team player. The USA does not have the luxury of missing these opportunities and needs to get ruthless in how it secures such talent going forward, as the rest of the world does. Judging players is subjective, but losing out on a 6 foot, 4 inch young goal-scoring center half that was in your system is not good! If they are good enough, they are old enough but I sense the USA has such a rigid "age appropriate" system or mentality that it will continually miss out. Every good business secures its best assets and talent and the USA National Team needs to do the same, whatever it takes.

Giuseppe Rossi: the New Jersey "traitor"

Rossi represents a different issue that faces American Soccer, that of a Newark New Jersey born 12-year-old deciding that he needed or wanted to go to Europe to develop as a player rather than stay in the USA. (Rossi ended up scoring two goals for Italy against the USA in the recent Confederations Cup.) With Italian heritage and strong roots he moved to Parma to become part of their youth system. He holds both Italian and US Citizenship but went on to represent Italy at under-16 and now at full national team level. It tells you two things. First, we do have a raw talent pool in the USA that can, if developed correctly, go on to play for the very best teams in the World (Rossi was at Manchester United, now at Villareal and of course played for four-time World Cup winners Italy). Tim Howard and Brad Freidal would both be in the English (and just about every other international country's) squad. Second, the USA needs to find a way to keep these types of players at home or "fund" their development abroad while keeping and committing them to play for the USA.

Rossi took a brave and very risky path to compete in one of the toughest and most competitive leagues in the world. He moved out of his comfort zone where he could have won multiple State Championships, made the Olympic Development team and been courted by UCLA and Indiana University, but then he wouldn't be playing for Italy. The USA needs 15 Giuseppe Rossi "mentalities" except they need to be called "Bobby" and they need to want to play for the USA and if necessary they need to be funded and supported. A USA team entering the 2010 World Cup with Howard in goal, Onyewu and Subotic at the back, Bradley in midfield and Altidore, Dempsey, Rossi and Donovan up front (the spine of the team) would be an interesting and exciting proposition. Of course this is all hypothetical and too late, but over the next 10–20 years, the USA needs to do whatever is necessary to identify and "secure" its talent pool. A partnership between MLS/US Soccer and top European Clubs that saw America's best young talent spend time both abroad and in the USA might be a model worth exploring. These need to be kids like Rossi who have no other desire but to be a professional soccer player. A tough group to find in the "college" dominated mentality of American Youth Soccer, but maybe then we are fishing in the wrong pool or need to widen it?

The mentality is changing and there are kids now that want to play abroad but parental influence and college will always stand in the way. It is clear that many Hispanic and ethnic families are not fortunate enough to be able to afford the college route and so there is less resistance to moving abroad or uprooting. As a business it makes sense to focus on these markets, or identify those in the "anglo" market that have no desire to go to college. Unfortunately to win a World Cup or to populate a top league you are not looking to find socially well rounded and educated upstanding citizens, you need individuals whose only thoughts are to play professional soccer, win a world cup and make a lot of money.

Was Freddy much "adu" about nothing?

Before leaving the issue of securing players, a quick note is worthwhile about Freddy Adu. Hyped as the next Pele by an uneducated American media and paraded on talk shows and television commercials, he quickly became one of the highest earning players in US history and according to some the future of American soccer. A great player but young and never able to live up to the enormous expectations placed on him, but he did enough to convince Benfica to pay $2m for him. No one apart from Alexis Lalas and Mia Hamm generated more in sponsorship support or media exposure. Unfortunately, off-field success should never be earned before on-field performance deserves it. Unbelievably Freddy is still only twenty and may well end up being a great player. He is learning his trade in Europe with Benfica, which has placed him on loan lately with Greek club Aris. He may never play regularly for Benfica but one thing is for certain, he will be a better player for it, maybe learning at 17–20 what he might have gained at 14–17 if he was in a European club environment and not shooting commercials with Pele.

CHAPTER 12

Soccer on American Television …
It's Bigger than American Idol!

Well, according to Univision, it is in Houston when Mexico is playing the USA in a World Cup qualifier for South Africa 2010 and the Spanish language network is airing the game live! This tells you a lot of what you need to know about televised soccer in the USA and the focus of the business dollars that drive it. First, that Spanish language television has been a dominant and consistent force in driving soccer forward as a TV product in the USA and second, that the World Cup itself has been the catalyst for soccer's growth as a televised sport across all markets. The match referred to above was USA versus Mexico World Cup Qualifier played in Columbus Ohio, February 2009, which drew a record-breaking average of 5.9 million Hispanic viewers, beating out "American Idol" in Houston and running it close in other key Hispanic markets. That 5.9 million audience represented close to 20 percent of the US Mexican population, numbers that would be impressive for any soccer nation. The same game on ESPN attracted 1.2 million English language viewers, which for soccer represented a very strong audience (higher than both a National Hockey League playoff game and Tennis Grand Slam event). Although in the grand scheme of ESPN television ratings this represented only a small percentage of the overall American population and certainly not a "must see" blockbuster sporting event, this one example highlights the reason why advertisers are prepared to commit millions of dollars to Hispanic coverage of soccer and in particular World Cup coverage, understanding the singular passion of its audience and the incredible depth of its support for the Mexican Team and Mexican Soccer.

It is probably fair to say that you are not regarded as a "big" professional sport in the USA until American television tells you so! Your importance and "arrival" are represented by the size of the check that the networks are willing to write and the promotional support they are prepared to put behind it. The measuring stick for success is the simple currency of ratings and demographics, with no hiding place for sports that fail to deliver on either. The story of soccer as a television product in the USA has been woven throughout the book and highlights the challenges it has faced establishing itself and the still immense challenge ahead of it to gain respectability, ratings and most importantly the "rights fees" that underpin every other major sport. The $4b a year paid to the NFL, $1.2b a year to the NBA, $640m to Major League Baseball and $250m plus to the NHL underwrite the finances that allow these leagues to attract and pay the very best talent, players that drive attendance, TV ratings and sponsor support. The networks invest so heavily that they scream from the rooftops the importance of their coverage, the excitement of their games and spend millions in promotional support urging viewers to tune in. It's a symbiotic relationship that if it exists can fuel incredible growth and prosperity for all but if absent can break a sport in two and subject it to a long, lonely and financially painful struggle. NBC's partnership with the Olympics, Fox Sports with the NFL and NASCAR and ABC/ ESPN's with the NBA and CBS's with the NCAA Basketball are others, all networks and sports working together to mutual financial benefit.

So where does soccer fit in all of this? Where is soccer's "network sugar daddy"? Unfortunately nowhere to be seen for 20 of the past 25 years and if professional sports supposedly live and die by how well they do on television, soccer should be long dead – but it isn't – but in fact is in the midst of establishing itself as an increasingly valuable and prized addition to the sports television landscape. The driving force is the emergence over the past 20 years of the FIFA World Cup Finals as a "must watch" television sports event and a highly competitive "must have" property for American networks. Viewership since 1990 has climbed 625 percent and "rights fees" paid have ballooned 566 percent for English Language coverage and an incredible 3,400 percent for Spanish, as shown in Table 12.1. These increases can only occur if something fundamental is changing in American soccer, which of course it is.

Table 12.1 Growth in World Cup rights fees 1990–2014

World Cup	English ($m)	Spanish ($m)	Total
Italia 1990	7.5	5	12.5
USA 1994	11	20	31
France 1998	22	50	72
Korea Japan 2002	20	75	95
Germany 2006	20	75	95
South Africa 2010	50	150	200
Brazil 2014	50	175	225
Increase %	566.7	3,400	1,700

Note: **Three times the fee for Spanish**.

Source: Compiled from private sources and interviews.

There now exists 24/7 penetration of international soccer on screens throughout the country, whether it's World Cup qualifiers, European Championships, English Premiership, Serie. A, La Liga, Argentinian, Brazilian, Mexican, Russian or French – if it's being played, the chances are it's on American TV somewhere, and almost certainly live! Domestically, all US National Team games are covered with huge emphasis on World Cup qualifiers and in particular the USA versus Mexico game. Major League Soccer is aired on ESPN, Fox Soccer and Univision with supporting pre- and post-game shows, highlights and talk shows such as "Super Sunday Plus" and "Fox Football Phone in". The USA Women's team gain extensive coverage (and still hold the record for the most watched soccer match in American history, the 40 million audience for their Women World Cup Final win against China in 1999) along with the fledgling Women's Professional League (WPS) which is aired weekly in season. College soccer, semi-professional soccer, indoor soccer and even youth soccer all make it on to American television screens in one form or another. So no one should feel sorry for soccer fans in America, for in 2010 they probably have the opportunity to watch more soccer than any other country in the world. Some of the many questions to be answered however: Is anyone actually watching? Is the coverage any good? Is it improving the sport's popularity? How does it compare against other American sports? And is it improving the value of MLS Teams?

Is anyone actually watching?

This depends entirely on the game's importance and the network covering it.

Over the past twenty years, soccer has had to rely on two major networks to advance it with ABC/ESPN dominating the English language coverage and Univision its Spanish. These have been joined over the past five years by the Fox Soccer Channel, which while still small and relatively new compared to the others, has become soccer's "local": the place you go each evening to meet your friends after a long day, knowing both that they will be there and that they want to talk "soccer". Sometimes the beer's bad, the opinions varied and there is always someone you don't agree with, but to soccer fans in America it's a friendly "home" and safe haven in a television world of touchdowns, free throws and home runs.

Between them these three soccer media partners, all of whom have come to the sport for different reasons and motivations, are changing the face of soccer in America and their continued support is critical to its future. But in the television landscape nothing has been, or will be over the next 10–15 years, more important as coverage in America of the FIFA World Cup.

At the heart of soccer's emergence as a broadcast sport is the World Cup and America's growing love affair with it – Table 12.2 highlights just how much it has grown in the past 20 years. While the number of viewers for the 1990 World Cup from Italy cannot be accurately measured due to lack of Neilson ratings the analysis of TNT's coverage (Turner Network had paid $7.5m for the English Language Rights but aired just 23 of 52 matches) indicate that approximately 2.7 million viewers tuned in to the final in both English and Spanish. Sixteen years later in Germany all 64 games would be aired live on ABC /ESPN and the France versus Italy final would be watched by 17 million viewers (representing a 625 percent increase in viewers). Equally according to Nielson ratings, 90 million Americans, almost a one-third of the population tuned into at least part of one game, a staggering number considering that in 1988 Americans could not have cared less.

Table 12.2 USA television viewers for World Cup Final Match 1990–2006 (English and Spanish)

Must watch TV

Final Viewers	1990*	1994	1998	2002	2006	1990–2006
English	1,518,440	14,509,777	8,623,943	3,932,338	11,961,318	687.7%
Spanish	1,200,000	3,551,000	4,346,000	2,882,000	5,041,000	320.1%
Total	2,718,440	18,060,777	12,969,943	6,814,338	17,002,318	625.4%
Hispanic	44.1%	19.7%	33.5%	42.3%	29.6%	

With increased interest comes increased support from sponsors and subsequently increased demands from the rights owners for higher fees. Overall between both parties the $425m paid for the rights to the 2010 and 2014 World Cups represents the highest fee paid to FIFA by any country in the world! A nail in the coffin of those that claim soccer will never catch on in America!

English language coverage of the World Cup Final itself has become "must see TV" over the past decades with a 687 percent increase in viewers since 1990, which tracks the growing development and interest in both the USA National Team and the international game in general. The numbers of course peaked at World Cup 94, hosted in the USA, when "big eventism" was at epidemic levels, but later finals established the true measure of support culminating in 11.9 million English and 5 million Spanish viewers tuning in to see Zidane head butt Mazeratti for insulting his sister, and of course Italy win the Cup. This 17 million number stands up very favorably against other major "American" sports and in fact if compared to the 2009 television audiences would beat out finals in Baseball, the NBA and the NHL, losing only to the power and might of the NFL (Table 12.3).

Finals of course are the showpiece of any tournament and attract the biggest audiences but what about the regular World Cup games that, to a degree, reflect the core key soccer audience,

Table 12.3 TV audience for major finals, 2009

2nd to the Super Bowl

SuperBowl	World Cup Final	World Series	NBA Finals	NHL Finals
98,732,391	17,002,000	15,812,282	14,347,021	3,211,572

those that engage in the entire event and tune into early round games (Table 12.4).

Once again the numbers show an impressive increase in viewership with a 571 percent increase in English language viewers and a 194 percent in Spanish language for a 387 per cent overall increase. In 2006, games aired on ABC would draw around 4.8 million viewers which put it ahead of the ratings achieved for the NBA playoffs, coverage of Golf's "Majors" and the NHL Stanley Cup Finals for the 2009 season. If the Spanish language viewers tuned into Univision are also included the total audience of 6.7 million viewers would also place World Cup games ahead of Nascar and Major League Baseball playoffs (see Table 12.5).

What also needs to be taken into account for the above comparisons is the fact that the World Cup ratings for many of the

Table 12.4 USA viewers for regular World Cup games, 1990–2006

Core fans tune in

Network	Italy	USA	France	Korea/ Japan	Germany	%+/−
	1990*	1994	1998	2002	2006	1990–2006
ABC	713,000	7,527,638	3,559,868	1,977,990	4,790,743	571.2
Univision	680,000	1,308,000	1,243,000	846,000	2,002,000	194.4
Total	**1,393,000**	**8,835,638**	**4,802,868**	**2,823,990**	**6,792,743**	**387.4**
Hispanic %		14.8	25.9	30.0	29.5	

Notes: *ABC did not cover the 1990 World Cup; Turner Broadcasting ratings for regular games averaged 713,000 viewers.

Table 12.5 TV audience for playoff games versus World Cup regular games, viewers

			It's bigger than you think			
NFL	Soccer*	Nascar	MLB	NBA	Golf	NHL
Playoffs	W Cup Regular	Cup	Playoffs	Playoffs	Majors	Final
29,910,358	6,792,743	6,543,177	6,535,611	4,789,129	4,107,392	3,211,572

Note: *English and Spanish language viewers.
Source: ESPN and Univision.

regular games are impacted by the time zone differences between the USA and the World Cup venues: brutal, middle of the night and early morning games from Korea and Japan in 2002 and late morning and mid-afternoon games from Europe. Measure this against the "prime time" evening slots for most of the traditional American professional sports and the soccer numbers are even more impressive.

So what of the USA National Team in World Cup Finals, and how do they stack up against other major US sports and indeed against other games in the World Cup itself? Clearly it is important that the USA team performs and the country is kept engaged, but the numbers also indicate that supporters of the US Team are also supporters of soccer in general, the average for general games matching closely those achieved for US Team games, except for key meaningful matchups (Table 12.6). In fact the World Cup games give an excellent indication of the true level of support the team has in the USA. Every soccer fan knows the most important matches a country can play take place at a World Cup and no true fan will miss a critical, or indeed any of their team's games. Countries close down, streets are empty, wars are halted and politicians and kings are glued to their sets as their nations do battle in search of the ultimate soccer prize. Not quite at this level in the States yet and I think it's fair to say that Obama will continue his work, Wall Street will still open and I can almost guarantee that Secretary of State Hillary Clinton will not be slipping into a bar in Algeria, Slovenia or indeed England to "catch the game".

Table 12.6 Viewers for key USA World Cup games

More than a game

Games	Italy	USA	France	Korea/Japan	Germany
ABC	1990*	1994	1998	2002	2006
USA Game Average	*	8,962,155	4,227,488	2,827,441	4,435,428
Key Matches					
USA v Brazil		13,694,155			
USA v Iran			5,496,382		
USA v Mexico				2,935,232	
USA v Germany				5,334,936	
USA v Italy					6,732,655

Note: *ABC did not cover the 1990 World Cup.
Source: ABC/ESPN.

Clearly the viewership numbers for the 1994 World Cup were swayed considerably by the fact the tournament was hosted on home soil with an average of close to 9 million viewers per match for the US games and 13.6 million for the USA versus Brazil round of 16 match on 4 July, the power of the Red, White and Blue combined with "big eventism" displayed in full force. The disaster in France 2008 was probably a truer reflection of the fan base with just the core fans left standing numbering around 4 million, though interestingly the highest viewed game of their campaign came in their final group match when 5.4 million Americans tuned in to see them take on their political foes Iran, and lose. Not a result that endeared the sport to the average American but a game that captured the imagination of the American public and once more emphasized the fact that international soccer is always more than just a game.

The time zones in Japan and Korea for the 2002 World Cup were always going to be tough but a respectable 2.8 million viewers tuned into the USA games with a very strong 5.3 million viewers for their quarter-final match against Germany (with thousands more watching in bars representing the real story of the Korea/Japan World Cup in the States). Germany 2006 represented a return to "normal" viewing hours for American fans and subsequently viewership increased 57 percent, this even though the team's performance left much to be desired. The first match 0–3 capitulation to Czechoslovakia drew 2.7 million which while a little disappointing, was probably for the best. This was boosted however by a very impressive 6.7 million viewers tuning into watch the USA battle ferociously against Italy in their second group game, earning a much deserved 1–1 draw. The final "must-win" game, but 1–2 loss, against Ghana completes the story of the numbers with 3.8 million fans tuning in, a number that probably highlights the true fan base the team enjoys. It has to be assumed that the USA versus Italy match probably attracted a large number of Italian fans to the broadcast resulting in strong numbers. This would not have been the case for the must-win match against Ghana which to true fans was more important than the Italy game, as the fate of the USA's progress in the Cup rested on them winning. If one assumes that no true fan would miss this critical final group stage match then the viewership number of close to 4 million might be that number. Interestingly Czechoslovakia and Italy were the USA's first two opponents in the Italia 1990 World Cup and a measure of the new found interest in the team is the fact that 6 million more viewers watched the same match in 2006 over the 1990 game: a good indicator of just how far the sport and World Cup itself has come as a television product in the USA (Table 12.7).

The 2010 World Cup from South Africa will represent a watershed moment for the coverage of soccer in the USA with unprecedented exposure and promotional support from both

Table 12.7 Viewers for group games, Italia 1990 versus Germany 2006

Huge growth in US support			
Game	1990*	2006	Difference
USA v Czech	713,000	2,754,724	286.4%
USA v Italy	713,000	6,732,655	844.3%
USA v Austria	713,000		
USA v Ghana		3,818,906	435.6%

Note: * No Nielson rating verification available for 1990 numbers, average from TNT.

ABC/ESPN and Univision – exposure and coverage that might well change the face of American soccer forever. More later in this chapter on this, but first let's look at the reasons why two of America's leading television and nedia companies have embraced the World Cup and indeed soccer in general and the journey that has led them to the summer of 2010.

Univision: the network that soccer built

The check for $10.00 arrived on the desk of Mal Karwoski, at the Spanish International Network (SIN) on 1 July 1986 and attached to it was a simple handwritten note from a soccer fan in Washington DC thanking them for their coverage of the 1986 World Cup from Mexico. The amount of the check was irrelevant and hardly likely to make a dent in the cost of coverage, but the sentiment was a telling insight into the passion of the dedicated soccer fans in the USA, and just how thankful they were to see top-class soccer on television in the 1980s. It was also a $10 check upon which Univision, now America's fifth largest broadcast network, built a $12.9b Spanish media empire, which in part was built on the back of passionate American soccer fans, their love for the sport and their absolute "stop at nothing" passion for all things "World Cup".

While the world of televised soccer in America has changed dramatically in 2010, back in the late 1980s it reflected everything most Americans felt about the sport, a game that appealed solely to Hispanics and European immigrants and so ignored by just about every major network. Soccer fans' savior during this time was an emerging Spanish language network seeking to expand its footprint in the USA and prepared to use the power of soccer to do so. Formed in 1955 with just one station in San Antonio in Texas, it became SIN in 1961 when Emilio Azcarraga, the Mexican entertainment mogul and later owner of Televisa, acquired a stake. Building and expanding the network station by station over the next 20 years, SIN's love affair with soccer gradually began to bear fruit, and while in the 1970s the Mexico, Germany and Argentina World Cups were aired on close circuit television in places such as Madison Square

Garden, New York (under a wholly owned subsidary of SIN called Magna Verde), the demand and interest for the games convinced executives that not only could broadcast coverage of games be sustainable, it could also be used as one of the pillars upon which to build a network.

With this in mind and in a move that all soccer fans living in the USA, whatever language they spoke, applauded, SIN's love affair with soccer was consummated with the airing of all 52 games from the 1982 World Cup in Spain. (The newly formed ESPN aired just 7 games.) There were no scientific or measurable metrics for how many people were watching games in Spanish, but every true soccer fan was! Understanding they had a tiger by the tail, they set about using their new-found position to quickly grow their network across the USA using the 1986 and 1990 World Cups as leverage to convince cable stations, particularly in the notoriously tough Midwest States, they should carry the now named "Univision" (renamed following their 1986 acquisition by a partnership of Hallmark Cards and Televisa). The tactic was quite simple, to tour the United States visiting grass-roots soccer organizations of all ethnicities, convincing coaches and players that if they wanted to see the World Cup in their market they needed to write to their local cable company and have them "carry" Univision. Pretty basic and extremely focused, it gambled everything on the passion of soccer fans and won! Thousands wrote in and Univision's march to national coverage exploded. (A strategy by the way not dissimilar to Rupert Murdoch and SKY who purchased Premier League Soccer rights to drive satellite dish sales for his fledgling sports network.) Very quickly Univision became the *de facto* home for World Cup Soccer and aficionados of all ethnicities and languages tuned into to watch what was deemed "real and commercial free" coverage of games presented by commentators who clearly knew what they were talking about, even if most of us didn't understand a word they said!

With the arrival in the USA of World Cup 94 soccer was clearly on the "up" and Univision stepped up with a $20m rights fee to ensure they had a seat at the table. In fairness, while the event represented a monumental sea change for US Soccer and indeed ABC and ESPN (who covered all 52 games for the first time), for Univision it was something they had known for years, the "World Cup was the biggest of all sporting deals". The biggest difference, the incredible rise in advertising revenue brought about by the influx of new sponsors to the sport. Viewers, now covered by Nielson, would show double-digit increases over English language coverage, with the final attracting a 24.5 percent rating against 9.5 percent for ABC.

The 1990s would be good to Univision with the growing power of soccer allied to a 60 percent increase in the overall Hispanic community that would see 13 million more soccer-friendly fans call the USA home. On the back of the financial bonanza in 1994 they stepped up with a $50m bid to secure the rights to the 1998 World Cup from France and coverage that would embed soccer into every aspect of their coverage, from news, to talk shows to the weather! World Cup soccer never perceived as an intrusion to an audience with soccer in their blood and of course Mexico in their hearts. In much the same way (maybe less schmaltzy) as NBC pull at the heartstrings of Americans' love for the Olympics, Univision in 1998 began a style of coverage that would tap into the patriotic fervor of soccer fans and of course the wallets of the myriad of advertisers looking to reach them. Although the poor performance of the US National Team drove down ratings on ABC and ESPN from France, Univision reported significant gains with overall numbers three times that of their English language counterparts (22 percent to 7 percent for the final).

The Univision Coca Cola commercials for the 2002 World Cup from Korea/Japan showed a Hispanic man cycling in the dead of night with a six pack of coke under his arm arriving at a friend's house to watch a world cup game. Two things are striking about this image: (1) we all know in real life it was a six pack of Budweiser! (2) it really happened. The "night time" World Cup was to test fans' resolve throughout America on all sides of the ethnic divide. The first games of the day airing at 2.30am on the East Coast (11.30pm Pacific) and the final game usually 7.30am East Coast (4.30am Pacific), found fans sleeping, or sleep walking through work all day and watching soccer all night. While no productivity studies were run you have to believe anyone employing a "soccer nut" was being short changed that month. American soccer fans of all persuasion stepped up to the plate but once again the Hispanic community led the way. With Hispanics congregating in western states such as Texas and California the 11.30pm–12.30pm time slot was actually not too bad resulting in viewers increasing over the 1998 day time (and hence work time) broadcast times from France, buoyed by an increasing television universe and growing population. The ratings actually fell slightly but actual viewers increased by 10 percent for the final and 17 percent for regular games. Quite the opposite effect occurred in the English language broadcasts where the middle of the night time slots sorted out the die-hards from the "regulars" with 6 million less viewers tuning into the final and 2.8 million less for regular games. The truer story for the English language coverage was the massive viewing parties and gatherings of fans in bars, soccer clubs and at professional grounds around the country that captured the media's eye. The biggest game of the 2002 World Cup in the USA was the round of 16 shoot-out between Mexico and USA, a game for all the marbles and bragging rights in the North American soccer landscape. The result a 2–0 win for USA on the field and victory for Spanish language television ratings off it. While ABC had a 2.3 rating, about 2.9 million viewers, which was strong, Univision had 4.2 million viewers, allied to the fact that 66 percent of all Hispanics' TV sets on at that timeslot were tuned to the game, once again highlighting the incredible passion of the Mexican fans. For advertisers of course it re-affirmed their decision to spend millions on sponsoring the World Cup as a way to reach this community, for in the land of Hispanic America, soccer is king and Mexican National Team soccer is the King of Kings.

The above goes to the heart of why, when it comes to rights fees for the World Cup, Univision are prepared to pay three times as much as ABC and ESPN, and rightfully so. Ratings of 42 percent clearly excite advertisers, letting them know they are reaching a very specific targeted market with programming the audience cares about. Even though the number of total households carrying Univision might only number 12 million it accounts for the majority of Hispanic households in the country, and therefore when 42 percnet of them tune in you know soccer is important. ABC/ESPN on the other hand are measured against a whole different level of household numbers – 90 million for ESPN and 110 million for ABC – and while the World Cup is important, it ultimately is just one of the many huge events the networks cover and this is reflected in the advertising dollars corporate America is prepared to pay. Univision likes to call it "share of heart" and outside of family and religion, soccer captures a huge portion. Not so in the general market where there are a lot more forces culturally fighting for a piece including perennial behemoths basketball, football, baseball, hockey, college sports, golf and more. Buying Hispanic soccer in America however is akin to buying the Premiership League in England, La Liga in Spain and Serie A in Italy, it drives everything.

In another nod to the power of soccer and especially World Cup Soccer, Univision used the same 2002 World Cup to launch Telefutura, a new sister network. By immediately re-broadcasting all of the live games during the day, Hispanic fans not blessed with insomnia could watch a repeat of the games at a civilized if less exciting time. The matches were all still compulsive viewing and helped cement Telefutura as a new network that now reaches 89 percent of all Hispanic homes, achieved with a huge kick (excuse the pun) from soccer (see Table 12.8).

Viewership numbers for the final in 2002 highlighted again just how much more important soccer is in the Hispanic community compared to the general population, with 42 percent of the 6.8 million viewers being Latino. This number is normally closer to 30 percent proving that to Hispanics the time zone difference from Koreas/Japan had less of an impact and was certainly not going to stop them watching the Brazil–Germany final.

Everyone however was thankful that the World Cup in 2006 meant the end to a nocturnal life style and never-ending tests of loyalty to one's teams. With games mainly airing in mornings and afternoons it still posed problems for anyone with a real job but as they always do, fans found a way to watch and ratings and viewership skyrocketed 75 percent for the final and 136 percent for regular games. Once again Univision immersed the entire network in the event and was rewarded with strong viewing numbers and advertising support buoyed the easier time zones from Germany.

Advertisers covet the male 18–34 audience and a quick look at the television universe in the USA highlights the fact that 1 in 5 of the population in this important segment are Hispanic – it's closer

Table 12.8 Spanish language viewers – Univision

Every home a fan

	Hispanic P2 +	Hispanic P2 + 2	Hispanic P2 + 3	Total US P2 +
Spanish language viewers	**1994**	**1998**	**2002**	**2006**
Number of games	52	56	64	64
World Cup Final (000)	3,551	4,346	2,882	5,041
World Cup regular ames	1,308	1,243	846	2,002
Households	**1994**	**1998**	**2002**	**2006***
Number of games	52	56	64	64
World Cup Final (000)	1,617	2,004	1,918	2,915
World Cup regular games	767	843	610	1,338

Note: *In 2006 Univision ratings estimates were set against the total US Television household universe.

Source: The Nielsen Company, NPM and NPM-H, Live + SD data; live games only; 2006 and 2002 World Cup live games aired on Univision and Telefutura.

to 1 in 4 for the equally important male 18–24 segment (Table 12.9). Sponsors line up to reach them and soccer is of course their preferred vehicle for doing so. Reaching the "Anglo" 18–34-year-old male is a far trickier proposition as their loyalties are divided among many competing sports and hence both expensive and tough to reach. Put your latest advert inside a Mexico versus "anyone" World Cup match and you are guaranteed to reach a prime advertising market and lots of them, underpinning the reason why some of America's top sponsors fight for space and brands like Budweiser and Honda have been with Univision World Cup coverage for over 20 years.

It would be unfair to just characterize Univision as a bandwagon World Cup media partner, for soccer flows through and provides much of the lifeblood for the network itself. In fact many games involving Mexico in the Copa America actually outdraw their World Cup coverage due to the fact that games are aired in evening time slots and the event is a 100 percent Hispanic affair.

Table 12.9 Why soccer is important to Hispanic advertisers

	Young and growing demo		
Demographic	Total USA	Total Hispanic	% Hispanic
TV Households	114,500	12,660	11
Adults 18–24	28,790	6,099	21
Adults 18–34	68,170	13,928	20
Adults 18–49	131,970	22,678	17
Men 18–24	14,550	3,295	23
Men 18–34	34,270	7,455	22
Men 18–49	65,680	11,981	18
Total Persons 2+	289,950	43,303	15

Source: Univision Corporate Research: Neilson Television Universe Estimates 2008–9.

Their approach to soccer is much akin to coverage you would see in "true" soccer nations like Brazil, England, Italy and Argentina, where the sport is woven into the fabric of everyday life and coverage. Daily news coverage is delivered through shows such as Republica Deportiva, La Jugada and Accion. Weekly games are delivered through Futbol Liga Mexicana, MLS, Superliga and the Concacaf Champions League. Big events like the Copa America, US National Team games, Gold Cup and Confederations Cup are secured and of course the ultimate event of all the World Cup, qualification and finals, are a staple of their sports coverage and delivered with the reverence and depth it deserves.

How powerful is professional weekly soccer from Mexico in the USA? Games typically draw anywhere from 1.5 to 3 million viewers and are so important to Spanish networks that when the "door was opened" to acquire rights following a dispute between Univision and Televisa, NBCs Telemundo, ESPN's Deportes and Fox Sport Espanol all seized their chance to grab a piece of the "golden goose" or *ganso de oro* as they say in Tijuana.

ABC/ESPN

Not quite as romantic a tale as Univision's love affair, soccer's acceptance as a viable sport inside of ABC and ESPN has been a tougher and more challenging journey and one that has needed "soccer believers" on the inside to succeed. Fortunately at key moments in its evolution, American soccer has had them. When soccer needed someone to step up and broadcast the 1994 World Cup, David Downs convinced the network and then the sponsors that it was a worthwhile venture. (David by the way is a committed Arsenal fan.) When in 2006 MLS and Soccer United Marketing found themselves being ambushed by NBC for the rights to the 2010 and 2014 World Cups, John Skipper, Executive Vice President of Content, mobilized ABC and ESPN in support of a last-minute bid that fought off the NBC approach, paying $100m for the privilege. (John by the way is a Spurs fan.) The irony is that two Americans, both of whom support opposing North London bitter enemies, yet are responsible for helping secure the broadcast future of soccer in the USA and committing over $425m in the process. (David Downs left ABC/ESPN in 1989 to become President of Univision. He led the negotiations in 2006 for their $325m offer for the 2010 and 2014 rights.) People do change the course of events and soccer, in order to progress, has certainly needed every friend it could muster in the USA.

John Skipper came to the sport as a soccer coach for his kids, without ever having played (a not untypical occurrence for many in the USA) but then falling in love with the game. Charged in 2001 with taking over Soccernet.com, a recent Disney acquisition, he ventured to London to learn more and became hopelessly hooked, the atmosphere at his first game, Arsenal versus Charlton, was unlike anything he had previously witnessed. Further visits to watch Charlton, Fulham and Tottenham provided him with enough to make an educated guess as to where his allegiance would be given. As he describes it "years of continual disappointment followed by bouts of inexplicable hope"; it could of course only be Tottenham, and a Spurs fan it was to be, as Arsenal at the time was too much of a front runner and perennial winners, while Charlton and Fulham lacked the storied history. An English major at College, the "Hotspur" name evoking images of Harry Hotspur who led an unsuccessful rebellion against Henry IV in 1403, was enough to earn Skipper's lifetime allegiance. (I guarantee the only Spurs fan to come to the team through the history books.) It mattered little, what was important was that in 2006 when soccer needed a "friend" inside ESPN it helped that the guy making the decision had become a passionate and fanatical one.

His mortal North London rival and Arsenal fan, David Downs, President of Univision, came to his fandom in a more traditional manner. Born in Holland, he grew up with a love of soccer and both played and coached the game and administered the sport in the USA throughout the 80s and 90s, becoming immersed in the US youth soccer culture and American soccer landscape from a very early age. Again when it mattered most, both at ABC/ESPN and Univision, American soccer found itself with a "champion" when it needed it most and fortunately one who had the power to decide. In 2006 between them Skipper and Downs committed not only $425m to World Cup coverage but also an additional $18m plus per season in contracts to cover MLS, US Soccer, Mexican and certain international games for the next eight years, ESPN paying $8 million and Univision $10 million per season, two North London rival fans committing over half a billion dollars in support of soccer in the USA.

It's all very well being a fan but the management and share-holders of both companies of course needed to see a strong business case for why soccer was worth supporting. Clearly evident within Univision, it was not so clear at ABC/ESPN, where the competi-tion for TV time and ratings was and is far stronger and more diverse. The simple point of the matter was that soccer has never been a "must watch" or "must buy" sport on English language television and only the World Cup itself has lifted the sport to ratings that matter to advertisers and consequently, manage-ment. ABC/ESPN has had a long history of covering the event going back to the 1982 World Cup in Spain where it aired seven matches, followed by Mexico 1986 where 15 games made it. Absent in 1990, when TNT acquired the rights, they returned in 1994 to cover all 52 games, a commitment they have continued in all subsequent World Cups. The disastrous performance of the US Team in 1998 (an event they paid $22m to cover) set the sport back immeasurably inside ABC/ESPN, so much so they did not bid for the 2002 or 2006 event, leaving Soccer United Marketing and MLS to fill the void. American audiences witnessed the games on the ABC and ESPN but the rights and production fees were firmly in the lap of someone else. All of this changed after the 2006 World

Cup and for the first time since France 1998, ABC and ESPN now owned all of the English language rights directly and will for the first time cover an overseas World Cup with all studio broadcasts originating in the host country and all 64 games called live in stadium, supported by over 150 in country staff. The promotional campaign hoping to drive viewers to their sets in the USA is the largest ESPN has ever undertaken for any single sport: ever!

Tremendous news for soccer in the USA but why the sudden increase in interest and full court press on World Cup Soccer and indeed to a degree soccer itself? Here are five reasons in no particular order:

1 ESPN's growth aspirations are international. There is no sport in the world more popular than soccer and no event more important than a World Cup. By immersing themselves in World Cup, Premiership, La Liga, Champions League, MLS and US Soccer they have become a soccer broadcast "brand". The strategy no different to Nike's or Budweiser's: if you want international brand strength and recognition you have to be in soccer.
2 Germany 2006 proved there is a strong and growing market and understanding for international soccer in the USA along with an increasing awareness and support for the USA Team. The 10.9 million viewers for the final ranks it above many major sporting events including NASCAR and Baseball play-off games and the 4.5 million average viewers for a game ahead of key golf and regular baseball games and on par with NBA playoff games.
3 Live sports: how much log rolling from Wisconsin, world's strongest man from Oregon or truck pulling from Utah does America really want to see? Because for a while in the early part of the decade, the afternoon and early morning weekend fair of ESPN delivered multitudes of this mind numbing programming. Tune in today and chances are it's live soccer from somewhere in the world, with big crowds, excellent broadcast quality and a clear sense of something "big" and meaningful taking place. Premiership soccer from England on Saturday mornings, and Champions league mid-week afternoons (until the recent loss of the rights to Fox) from some of the best stadiums and leagues in the world. Sure there are still body builders and

lumberjacks searching the dial and quickly flicking past Real Madrid versus Barcelona but until 70,000 turn up to watch them chop wood it's not a sad loss.

4 8,760: television lives by this figure as it represents the number of broadcast hours each network has to program each year (24 hours x 7 days x 52 weeks). With ESPN 1 and 2 this represents a lot of programming. Soccer by its very nature has "tonnage" meaning there is a lot of it. It's also currently pretty economical as its rights fees, even for a World Cup, make it fairly cheap television compared to other sports. Equally, apart from MLS or US National Team games, the matches take place at times that complement rather than compete with their other broadcast commitments.

5 Competition. NBC bidding for the World Cup rights was a shock to the system and one that certainly quickly focused minds. Controlling both the Olympic Games and the FIFA World Cup would have meant the two most important sporting events in world sports would have been on a competing channel. Add to this that NBC also controls Telemundo, its Spanish language partner and a direct competitor to ESPN Deportes and it becomes clear why the $100m check was written. Fox Soccer Channel has also now established itself as a fierce competitor for soccer rights in the USA and has become the home for many MLS, English Premiership and Women's Professional soccer league games. It also won the rights to air Champions League soccer from 2010 onwards beating out incumbent ESPN. For the first time in the history of soccer in America there is real competition for the key soccer "rights", not so great for ESPN but great for soccer in the USA.

So this brings us to the summer of 2010 and the South Africa World Cup an event that many feel might be a significant moment in soccer evolution in America.

World Cup South Africa 2010: the tipping point?

In 2010, both ABC/ESPN and Univision will unleash on the USA the largest and most impressive coverage of a World Cup ever aired on American television with a promotional campaign whose reach and expense will be unlike anything previously seen in America. In fairness, Univision's coverage will be much as previous cups, not a criticism and in fact a compliment – sure there will be far more online coverage and video on demand, but improvements in what is already authentic and immersive coverage is measured in small increments for Univision. The real sea change however will be in English language coverage and this will be quantum. I sat down with ESPN Director of Marketing Seth Ader in New York in early 2010 and I have to admit I was incredibly impressed by the thought process, planning and listening that have gone into developing ESPN's approach to their SA 2010 coverage, representing an understanding and empathy for the sport, an event I have not witnessed with ABC/ESPN in 20 years of being involved in televised soccer in the USA. It has nothing to do with the amount of games covered – all 64 in HD and up to 25 in 3D – it has everything to do with the fact that after almost 30 years of involvement with the World Cup and soccer in general, ESPN finally "gets it" and let's face it while grateful that the games are covered, ABC and ESPN have always danced between getting it right and unfortunately horribly wrong.

There is a very thin line between delivering an average and great television fan experience in America and the sensitivities that let true fans know whether they are tuned into a broadcast and talent that "knows their stuff" and "gets it" or a network that is just looking to sell advertising and "make a buck", and believe me "getting it" in soccer is everything! For example, in 2006 soccer fans tuning into an ESPN game were often brought into the broadcast with the ball in the center circle and teams ready to kick off – no pre-amble, no coverage of the gladiatorial march of the players into the arena, no sweeping shot of the stadium with flags fluttering, faces painted and songs echoing, in fact missing everything that the game is about: an international battle of soccer-warring nations, the likes of which no other sport can deliver. ESPN's delivery was more akin to contractually delivering 90 minutes coverage than immersing themselves in the meaning and passion of the game, failing to understand that to the fans tuning in this was a game that reached into their soul, their heritage and their very being. Thankful of course but equally disappointed and a little insulted, they were left wishing they were there in person or watching in a country that respected fully the magnitude of the event and convincing many to flick the remote to Univision and watch in a language they little knew, and didn't need to.

In 2010, ESPN will not miss a walk, not miss a furtive glance as players size each other up and not miss one look of pride and passion as the national anthem echoes around the stadium.

2006 also witnessed overbearing graphics fawned over in American sports, frowned on in soccer, and detested even further in World Cup matches, where it's akin to selling advertising on the front of the Church pulpit and make no mistake to true fans watching, the game is a religious experience. Finally, soccer fans smell authenticity, or lack of it, at a thousand paces, which considering most would be sitting just five feet from the screen was a major problem in 2006. Ader admitted that their strategy of trying to appeal to the masses backfired horribly (sound familiar?), alienating and upsetting true fans in a attempt to draw in big event and bandwagon general sports fans and assigning talent and approaching the broadcast to achieve this. If you have gotten this far in the book you will understand the fatal flaw in this plan and the reaction of millions of core soccer fans who swore they could give better insights, call the game clearer and explain just why their team won or lost with a lot more depth and clarity. Some of course actually could, many couldn't but all were left disappointed and therein lies the issue and if there is one word that everyone working in American soccer should tattoo on their forehead, it is authenticity. Thankfully this is a different dawn at ESPN.

Following a year and half of market research and an inclusive soccer summit involving industry experts, journalists, players and fans the penny dropped. Just airing games is not enough, appealing to the masses an errant strategy and shortchanging the core is a recipe for failure. The World Cup is just too big an event to "skate" and the fan base too passionate and emotional to not know everything about them and deliver exactly what they crave. Fortunately for all of us, from what I have seen, the ESPN's build up and coverage from South Africa will represent the most authentic, immersive and "fan" friendly coverage of a

World Cup seen in America to date. Promotionally they will run two campaigns, the first targeted at the "core" soccer base and placed in soccer-specific shows, events, newspapers, websites and radio shows. The adverts will be filled with authentic messaging and respectful education, their print campaign a country sensitive set of soccer drawings created by a collective of Cape Town artists, every picture a meaningful and relevant soccer story created by someone who clearly "knows the game". Core fans will see the ads that reflect the power of "10", the number worn by many of the "greats" including the likes of Pele, Platini, Baggio, Zidane and Maradona, the playmaker and game changers. In Basketball that number is 23, the jersey number worn by Michael Jordan and every "wannabe" since. Slip it on however and you had better deliver. The point again, advertising and messaging that "gets it" is a quantum leap forward and sea change in ESPN's understanding.

The second campaign is aimed at the armchair "big event", bandwagon fan and the very fact it's a separate campaign is an evolutionary step forward for both soccer and ESPN. This campaign airs in major sports events such as the NBA Finals, the Masters Golf, College Basketball and Football Finals, targeting those viewers who move in and out of "big TV events" whatever the sport. The message is a simple one, that the FIFA World Cup is not just a big event, it's an enormous global tournament: bigger than the Super Bowl, the Kentucky Derby, the Masters Golf and more, combined. Condescending to the core fan base of course who already know and would be insulted if you preached this to them, but educational and hopefully persuasive to bandwagon fans, and bandwagon fans do help pay the bills!

Coverage of the games themselves will feature Martin Tyler, one of the world's most respected and authentic commentators, and importantly to millions of younger Americans, the voice of EA Sports FIFA 2010. All 64 games will be aired live in High Definition with up to 25 of these in 3D and all studio shows will emanate in-country from within South Africa itself, a first time occurrence for World Cup coverage. Many of the games will air online live on ESPN360.com, appear on Video on Demand and be broadcast live in ESPN radio. Equally up to 40 matches will air in Portuguese on ESPN Deportes including the much anticipated Brazil versus Portugal match (representing a direct head to head battle with Univision for viewers, ESPN ceding the ground to Spanish speaking Hispanic homes but clearly battling for the rest).

Billboards on freeways in key cities will keep drivers up to date with live scores, online widgets will inform office workers unable to call in sick and phone "apps" will mean 24/7 "anywhere" reach to a world that goes nowhere without one and finally World Cup sweepstakes forms will make their way by the hundreds of thousands into offices and clubs nationwide, replicating the iconic March Madness College Basketball Sweepstakes that is a staple of USA sports.

A $50m rights fee for the coverage, tens of millions of dollars in marketing spend, the largest single promotional campaign for any sport ESPN has ever covered and it is hard not to get excited about what is happening with soccer in the USA this summer and the impact it might have. For six months in 2010, ABC and ESPN will scream from the rooftop to anyone with a pulse and a TV set that soccer is a huge sport and the World Cup the biggest of all sporting events. To a changing American society, a grow-ing MLS investor and fan base and an emerging soccer educated youth, having one of the most influential media companies in the country supporting the sport is invaluable.

The proof of the pudding will be in the eating as measured by the television audience for the Saturday 12 June game between the USA and England, the first game for each in the 2010 World Cup and the beneficiary of six months of promotional build up. No true USA fan will miss the game, no general soccer fan should miss the game, with Mexico not playing, no Mexican American should miss the game either and equally, if you are just into big sporting events, there is no bigger show on earth to watch that day. Numbers should surpass the USA Brazil 1994 game (13 million) and should even surpass the World Cup final itself in 2006 (17 million). It will be a day of reckoning for USA Soccer as a TV sport in America and I have a sense it will be a spectacular success.

The World Cup finals represent the pinnacle for television audiences in the USA but what about the other three years and eleven months when fans are looking for their fix. As stated earlier there is certainly plenty of it, but on all levels this coverage has yet to cross into mainstream America and by its very nature maybe never will, nor need to. The future of soccer on television in America is delivering an authentic product, relevant and meaningful to the core soccer audience, however small and niche at this stage that market is. It is only by providing an experience these fans crave can it hope to build and grow a sustainable viewership base. It might end up being slow and incremental growth, but it will be reliable, sustainable and ultimately valuable.

Not surprisingly the USA National Team represents the most significant audience on ESPN for soccer broadcasts as it should be, with USA Mexico being usually the most important game of the year. In 2009 however, the USA's remarkable run to the Confederations Cup final culminated in 3.9 million viewers tuning in to see them take a 2–0 lead but ultimately succumb 2–3 against Brazil, a number that put it ahead of the Stanley Cup Hockey final and laid testimony to the four million number that seems to be the core base.

The 2009 Champions League final between Barcelona and Manchester United lays testimony to the fact that US soccer fans appreciate the best with 1.4 million viewers despite the fact it was an afternoon work day kickoff on the East Coast and a midday one on the West. Regular MLS, English Premiership and Champions leagues matches all draw similar viewers and ratings but it would be interesting to measure the crossover of fans. Certainly, it is unclear if those tuning into the English Premier and Champions League games are the same as those watching the MLS (see Table 12.10).

It has been a tough road for Major League Soccer when it comes to television ratings and certainly one it needs to improve on if it is ever to realize its full potential and generate anywhere near a meaningful rights fee for its games. The good news is that at least it now gets one, courtesy of ESPN and Univision, and for the first time in the league's history it is being paid for its product.

There might be a sign ahead that MLS's fortunes as a televised product are on the upswing with 2009 playoffs delivering ratings and attendances that surpassed everyone's expectations,

Table 12.10 Average soccer broadcast ratings in USA, 2009

Quality of game matters

Matches	Viewers	Households	Ratings	Channel
USA Mexico WCQ	1,190,598	794,760	0.81%	ESPN 2
USA WCQ	734,461	521,712	0.53%	ESPN
Champions League Final	1,400,000	1,070,000	1.1%	ESPN
Champions League Reg	310,470	256,712	0.26%	ESPN 2
MLS Final	1,140,714	778,542	0.79%	ESPN
Mls Playoffs	391,908	298,774	0.30%	ESPN 2
MLS Regular	298,897	225,426	0.23%	ESPN 2
English Premiership	243,430	199,063	0.20%	ESPN 2
Fox	142,000			

Notes: Certain Premiership games faired higher Liverpool v Villa August 24th 398,391 viewers Arsenal Tottenham Sat Oct 31st 325,187.
Fox Soccer Chelsea Tottenham Sunday September 20th 296,000.
Fox Soccer: Man United v Arsenal August 29th 2009 295,000.
Source: (epltalk.com.)
Source: ESPN.

the LA Galaxy versus Houston Conference final drawing 537,683 viewers and 1.1 million viewers tuning in to watch the MLS Cup final itself. Not SuperBowl numbers, but increases over previous years.

It is all about meaning, relevance and promotion and for the first time probably since the opening season there was a sense that the MLS playoffs were important events as witnessed by the outstanding crowds and tremendous atmosphere in the stadiums, particularly those experienced in Chicago and Los Angeles.

Allied to all of these has been a quantum increase in the broadcast quality, commentator analysis, pre- and post-game shows originating in Europe and indeed the USA with a World Cup, Champions League or English Premiership game now every bit the equal of any NFL or NBA broadcast – a very important point in soccer's development as a broadcast property. Often not economically feasible for Major League soccer games, the emergence of High Definition television and digital production facilities is leveling the playing field somewhat as highlighted by Mike Cohen, head of broadcasting for MLS, stressing that the fan experience for televised games, once limited by the amount of cameras they could afford and broadcast trucks they could roll up, is immeasurably enhanced by digital capabilities that allow for multiple replays of goals, offside decisions, penalty shouts, red cards and more, all orchestrated at the press of a button. It may sound simplistic but it's critically important to the dedicated fan and vital to enticing new ones.

Soccer has also learned that fans want analysis and replays, chat shows and "phone ins", radio coverage and online interaction. They have opinions on whether the USA team will beat England, whether Kansas will make the playoffs, whether Ronaldo should be sold or Chelsea buy Gerrard. In the past five years, soccer at all levels has reached into the American fan base and been rewarded with an educated, passionate and excited response. There is a growing thirst for involvement and participation from an increasing core audience, the numbers are not huge yet but they are solid and they are growing and they will be sticking with the sport.

Clearly soccer, on a day to day basis, has a long way to go to challenge the might of the big American sports but on its day, when the big games are played, it can draw audiences that show just how big the sport could be. Table 12.11 highlights just where soccer audiences would rank against the staples of American sports broadcasts.

Table 12.11 Soccer broadcasts compared to other USA sports

Meaningful games matter					
Event	2009* viewers	Combined soccer	English language	Spanish language	Game
NFL SuperBowl	98,732,391				
NFL Playoffs	29,910,358	17,900,000	17,900,000		USA V China WWC Final ('99)
BCS Bowls	17,597,386				
MLB World Series	15,812,282	17,002,000	10,900,000	5,041,000	World Cup Final (06)

(Continued)

Table 12.11 (Continued)

NFL Regular	14,632,546		13,694,155		USA Brazil (94)
NBA Finals	14,347,021	8,734,655	6,732,655	2,002,000	USA V Italy(06)
NCAA Tournament	8,928,482	7,435,232	2,935,232	4,500,000	USA V Mexico (02)
NASCAR Sprint Cup	6,543,177	7,336,936	5,334,936	2,002,000	USA v Germany (02)
MLB Playoffs	6,535,611	7,090,598	1,190,000	5,900,000	USA v Mexico (09)
NBA Playoffs	4,789,129	6,792,743	4,790,743	2,002,000	World Cup Regular Game (06)
Golf Majors	4,107,392		5,496,382		USA Iran (98)
NHL Stanley Cup	3,211,572	3,900,000	3,900,000		USA Brazil (09)
NBA Regular	1,940,813	3,760,861	3,760,861		Euros Final 2008
MLB Regular	1,628,934	2,100,000	1,400,000	700,000	Champions League Final (09)
Tennis Grand Slams	1,038,044		1,140,714		MLS Final 09
NHL Playoffs	929,503		734,461		US World Cup Qualifiers
NHL Regular	492,739	921,476	700,479	220,997	LA Houston Conf Final
Champions League	310,470				
MLS Regular Season	298,897		391,908		MLS Playoffs Average
English Premiership	243,430				
Women's USA Team	400,000				
Women's Pro Soccer	42,000				

Source: ESPN Research Department, Univision Research Department.

In 2010 it is fantastic for those of us that live in the USA and love soccer to be able to watch just about any major game we want and for me personally, especially the "back-to-back" coverage both Saturday and Sunday (and Monday) of live games from the English Premiership League. Fox Soccer and ESPN spend millions of dollars in rights fees for the privilege along with millions more for coverage of other leagues. As a measure of the progress achieved in the past 20 years, in 1991 as publisher of Soccer International Magazine I owned the rights to air English First Division (now Premier League) soccer in the USA and paid the princely sum of $2,000 per week to do so. The sad fact was I still lost money!

CHAPTER 13

The Making of a Soccer Nation

If those of us in soccer had $1 for every time we have heard the question "when will soccer catch on in America?" we would all be in the Cayman Islands now with a cool drink and a satellite dish. The answer of course is that soccer in America has already "caught on". How else would 93,000 fans came out to watch Barcelona play the LA Galaxy, 72,000 to watch Real Madrid play D.C. United, 66,000 to watch Chelsea play AC Milan or 79,000 to watch Mexico beat the USA in New York? Soccer equally was the first sporting event to be played in the new $1b Dallas Cowboys stadium, selling out all 82,252 seats for a quarter-final Gold Cup Match. During what was marketed by Soccer United Marketing as the 2009 "Summer of Soccer" over 1.9 million soccer fans poured through the gates of 98 soccer matches, 68 of which were broadcast on national television. Games included 15 MLS Teams, 14 national teams and 10 international club teams. Record attendances were set in Los Angeles, Seattle, New York, Toronto, San Francisco and Washington DC. So let no one tell you that America is not a soccer nation.

The following league (Table 13.1) would keep the NFL up at night.

Just for fun and to make a point: if a September to January eight-home-game season was held with the world's leading soccer power houses listed above playing with all of their superstar talent, the crowds would match and in most cases beat those of the NFL and decimate those of baseball. It wouldn't match them on television (though on Univision they would) but would where it matters most for true fans, in the stadiums. The reality is that in America today Real Madrid versus Barcelona would "out draw" any Giants game in New York, Bears game in Chicago or Cowboys game in Dallas. The crowds might come from different audiences but soccer fans would outdraw them. Why? Because the hard core "Anglo" soccer community would attend,

285

Table 13.1 Hypothetical international league USA

It's about quality

Home Team	Away Team	Gate
Real Madrid	Barcelona	90,000
Chelsea	AC Milan	65,000
Manchester United	Chivas Guadalajara	75,000
Club America	Inter Milan	65,000
Juventus	Liverpool	65,000
Boca Juniors	Bayern Munich	50,000
Arsenal	Porto	50,000

Note: Author's speculation.

European, African, Asian and Middle Eastern fans would attend and the enormous soccer rabid Hispanic soccer community would attend; add in Mexican powerhouses Chivas Guadalajara and Club America and the die would be cast. No sports league in America would like to see this league sailing over the horizon. Fortunately for them the above "scenario" is only "hypothetical" but it makes a point. A league comprising the world's best "club" soccer teams pitted against the world's best football and baseball teams, on American soil, would send shock waves through the American sporting landscape. I know for a fact that soccer is the only sport that would give the NFL sleepless nights should they get it right.

Anecdotal but incisive, Doug Quinn, ex-President of NFL International and now President of SUM, relayed a story to me about when he introduced the President of FC Barcelona to the NFL executives at a recent SuperBowl. Not wanting to miss a classic photo opportunity the executives posed together holding both an NFL and Barcelona jersey: "you know what" extols the NFL executive "soccer is the one sport that scares us if it ever gets a foothold. 3" Well the NFL is clearly not in any imminent danger nor may it ever be, but soccer is certainly on the move. It is engrained in the social culture of America and playing it a "rite of passage" for most young children growing up, girls and boys alike. The commercial growth of the sport however will depend on it converting these participants into serious players, avid fans and regular television viewers. It's not an easy task, but one that in 2010 is a much more certain and achievable one. I would certainly rather be trying to launch soccer in America than attempting to sell the NFL around the world. They have no participation base and unless they are close to an American air force or army base, few indigenous followers. Soccer in the USA on the other hand is one of the country's largest participation sports, has 35 million soccer-mad Hispanics in the country and has the world's most popular sport backing it to succeed.

According to recent Neilson television reports over 90 million Americans, close to a third of the population, tuned in to watch at least part of a game from the recent 2006 Germany World Cup. I always feel that soccer is trying to storm the gates of traditional American sports, searching for ways to get on the inside to share and indeed seize the wealth they are amassing from television, sponsors and fans. Well if that metaphor stands up then 38 million soccer Hispanics and 16 million participants is a very sizeable Trojan Horse to have on the inside. We just need to decide when the right time is to let them out and steal the city! My sense is it will come with fans. America has some great entrenched sports leagues that over the years have become incredible sports business machines. But increasingly that's what many of them are becoming, machines, slightly soulless and increasingly corporate. Give a new generation of American kids a "game" experience at Barcelona versus Real Madrid or Manchester United versus Liverpool and a game experience at Redskins versus Giants, or Yankees versus Phillies and I would bet heavily that soccer would win their allegiance. When delivered correctly and embraced fully by MLS Teams, the soccer-fan experience is soccer's overwhelming advantage and one that can lead it to prosperity. Soccer doesn't have to topple the NFL to succeed, which is just as well, due to the size and multicultural mix of many US cities – Real Madrid versus Barcelona would sell out even if played at the same time as the New York Giants versus Dallas Cowboys. For while America is most certainly an entrenched "football nation" it is also increasingly becoming a "soccer nation".

There is no doubt that it has been a long and tough road for Major League Soccer and one that has left its scars and wounds. The legacy of the battle has left many in the soccer community disenfranchised or disinterested, whether because they felt they were treated badly or because they just do not accept the league (more typically their local team) as being of sufficient quality, either on or off the field, to warrant their support or interest. It is an unfortunate fact that Major League Soccer is just not that important in the lives of many people involved in soccer in the USA, particularly at the youth level. This needs to change and fortunately there are strong signs emerging that it can. Make no mistake a professional first division league in the USA is critical to the future and growth of the sport at all levels and MLS is the one and only chance the USA has of establishing one. Those that bury their heads in the sand and believe things are fine as they are and that US soccer can survive and prosper as a recreational participant sport, need to wake up and see the bigger picture. Sure the league is no EPL or Serie A, sure the atmosphere at some stadiums is not like Old Trafford or the Nou Camp and definitely the players are not Messi, Rooney or Ronaldo. I have to admit I have been a critic of many games and teams since the league started in 1996 and tried to watch games on television that were frankly unwatchable, due to the quality of play, the atmosphere in the stadium or football lines on the field and often in the early days all three. But this is 2010, the league has survived despite millions in losses saying it should not have, and is now positioned to become the bedrock and platform on which the commercial success of soccer in the USA will be built. The first fourteen seasons have been about survival, the next twenty will be about sustainable and profitable growth, the successful execution of which will provide opportunities and pathways for many in the game. Major League Soccer has no innate right to expect the support or allegiance of anyone in American soccer and must earn every ounce of respect it craves but equally the soccer community has to recognize the importance of it succeeding and the benefits to soccer as a whole in helping it do so.

In my view, the next fifteen years will be exponentially better than the last and the league will go from strength to strength. There are a few reasons why.

1 It *is* all about the money
   At the end of the day it is all about money. Without Phil Anschutz, supported by the Krafts and Hunts, Major League Soccer would

have collapsed in 2001 and the lights would have gone out on the professional business of soccer in the USA, maybe forever. (If it couldn't survive after hosting the 1994 World Cup then when could it?) Without their deep pockets there would be no new soccer-specific stadiums underpinning the sport's future, no World Cup 2018/2022 bid, no career path for young soccer players, no major corporations pouring in millions of sponsorship dollars and the USA's reputation in the global soccer world would be on the floor. It took the financial strength and business courage of "gambling" $70m on the 2002 and 2006 World Cup rights for a league that had just lost $250m to survive. It took, as Tim Leiweke, President of AEG, stated, a need to make the problem "bigger in order to solve it", in fact $70m bigger and this you don't do without strong financial backing. Make no mistake it was close, Leiweke thought it might go, Jonathan Kraft thought it might go, but the plan Garber put forward and the ultimate commitment of Phil Anschutz ensured it did not.

The decision had been made that the league alone could not survive as a stand-alone business proposition and without branching out into the commercial rights, game promotion and sponsorship sales industry, the game was up. It was the commercial upside potential of the US "soccer market and industry" that saved the league, saved the players, saved the coaches and back-room staff and saved the President and General Managers from disaster. The play on the field of the US National Team at the 2002 World Cup gave investors a much needed confidence boost and belief that the market for soccer was potentially there, but it took hard cash and courage to take the risk and this takes strong owners.

The current ownership group of Major League Soccer between them control all or part of some of the most significant sports properties in the USA indeed around the world, providing the league with not only strong financial backing but also the sports business experience to guide it to greater things.

2 Stadiums are up ... the bet has been made

The difference between soccer in the USA today and at any time in its past is that for the first time in the sport's history, soccer-specific stadiums have been built. Previously a "renter" soccer

Table 13.2 Other sports properties owned in full or part by MLS owners

Not just Soccer

Owners	MLS Team	NBA	NFL	MLB	NHL	Misc
Anschutz	LA Galaxy	Lakers			Kings	
Hunts	Dallas and Columbus		Chiefs			
Krafts	New England		Patriots			
Kroenke	Colorado	Nuggetts			Avalanche	Arsenal
Checketts	Real Salt Lake				Blues	
Maple Leaf	Toronto				Maple Leafs	
Red Bull	New York					Formula 1
Chang	D.C.United			SF Giants		
Vegara	Chivas					CD Chivas
Lew Wolff	San Jose			Oakland As		
Roth et al	Seattle		Seahawks			
Mallet et al	Vancouver			SF Giants		Derby County

Source: MLS net and online research.

team is now in many instances a "landlord" and therefore in far greater control of its own destiny. Teams control important revenue streams, play when they wish and deliver their own "brand experience" to fans that have their own home. No American Football lines, no vacuous stadiums and not having to vacate the stadium while other sports play. The future of soccer in the USA rests with every team having its own stadium and the league is on its way to achieving this. The Home Depot Center is a $150m investment, RedBulls Stadium $200m, Real Salt Lake $110m, Colorado $84m, Philadelphia $156m, Toronto $62m, Chicago $90m, FC Dallas $80m and Columbus $25m. With hard-core real-estate commitments like this, soccer is here to stay.

3 Profitability

It has been a very tough ride for most teams in Major League Soccer and in particular the "founding" teams upon whose backs the league has been built. As often occurs, the early pioneers are the ones who end up with "arrows in their back" while the new arrivals benefit from the path cleared and the battles fought. Major League Soccer is no different. On the backs of the failed teams of Tampa and Miami and the long struggles for stadiums, fans and television ratings by those that lasted, has emerged the profitable new models of Toronto FC and the Seattle Sounders, two new unscarred clubs that had the benefit of hindsight and the "smarts" to learn from it. Seattle's 2009 launch has been one of the most successful launches of any professional sports team in recent history: period. With over 22,000 season tickets and average attendances of 32,000, Seattle will be operationally profitable in its first year. Toronto FC launched in 2008 to similar success selling out their 20,000-seat stadium from day one and delivering a fan base of single 18–35 year olds that have changed the future face of fans across all teams in the league forever (Joe Roth, owner of the Seattle Sounders, openly expressing that they used many of Toronto's methods as they developed their own club and fan bases). Along with the new teams' founding owners, LA Galaxy have equally cracked the profitability code, though all of them in slightly different and locally customized ways. Toronto have shown how to do it with few stars, a tight inexpensive urban stadium and fanatical fans; Seattle by commandeering an entire city and listening to and involving its fans and LA by doing what works in LA, an impressive first-class stadium and enormous star power led by David Beckham. Each one slightly different, but effective and importantly establishing an audit trail that shows soccer in American can be a profitable and fruitful endeavor. These new models can be used by league officials to identify where and when to place new teams and then what those teams need to do to ensure success for both themselves and the league as a whole. A track record of profitability within league clubs can only lead to increased club value, greater investment in teams and more interest from cities and investors to join the party.

4 You'll never walk alone

The opening paragraph of this book started with a description of the incredible support the US National Team received in Germany and for good reason. At the end of the day it is all about fans, and the loyalty they withhold or bestow. The USA team is at last off and running with Sams Army and the American Outlaws two groups that would die for the Red, White and Blue. It has taken a long time for America to "get" what being a soccer fan is all about. In many ways it was generational; it took young kids seeing fanatical fans at the World Cup in 1994, and examples beamed into their television sets from English Premier League Soccer and Champions Leagues and of course the experiences gained from attending games. The obligatory chants of "USA, USA" and the annoying "wave" have given way to tribal songs, vehement passion, referee abuse at unfriendly calls and the wearing of the colors, all delivered from the most important vantage point of all for soccer fans, behind the goal.

To this new breed of American soccer fan, winning is everything; sure they want to see a good game but ultimately, whether it's the USA team, Toronto FC or Columbus, they want their team to win. The time has long gone when they came to just see a "good" game of soccer (they hope to but it's not crucial); they come to see their team "win" which represents a big, big difference. I have watched some "rubbish" in my time following Coventry City and I swear I have seen players that make you wonder how they ever got to be professionals, and I have not held back from my uneducated vocal "coaching advice". But you know what, if we won, all was right with the world, and that player, "well he just had a bad day", forgiven until you see him on the team sheet again. The Bara Brava and Screaming Eagles at D.C. United, the Red Patch Boys in Toronto, Hudson Street Hooligans in Columbus, the Loyalist in Real Salt Lake, Emerald City Supporters in Seattle, the Texan Army and El Battalion in Houston, Section 8 in Chicago and Class V1 in Colorado, the Cauldron in Kansas, Midnight Riders in New England, Club Quake in San Jose and the newly formed 3,500 strong Sons of Ben in Philadelphia who will kick off in 2010, all feel the same way I am sure. The numbers are not huge yet but the foundation has been laid and the core established. Over the next 10–15 years, these numbers will increase as the passion grows and the atmosphere becomes contagious.

One of soccer's greatest advantages over every other American sports is its "fandom" and the universal belief that of all sports, soccer fans are the "craziest", even American sports fans will admit to this. The beauty is that American kids are starting to "get" this and like it. It's almost rebellious and counter-cultural to be a soccer fan, but it is also "cool". Soccer is the sport they own, they came to alone – it is in most cases not their father's sport. These fans have little time for football or baseball and in many ways if they were not soccer fans might not be fans of any other American sport. Being a soccer fan and all that it entails is a marketing position that MLS and indeed soccer in general should be all over, for although not everyone can become a professional player, everyone can become a soccer fan and being a soccer fan is unlike anything else in American sports. If every 16-year-old kid in America experienced a game on the Kop at Liverpool, the Stretford End in Manchester or behind the wire at Bombanaro and was then given a Toronto and Seattle-like experience in the USA, the game would be over for most other American sports. How could they go back to listening to the organ player at baseball games or spend three hours at a football game with more time outs and stoppages than action? A new breed of American kids with no allegiances to entrenched sports would choose soccer every time. A quick point on crazy fans: I did once go to a game seven NHL conference final between hated rivals the Philadelphia Flyers and New Jersey Devils, and the Philly fans are definitely crazy, they would grace any soccer crowd and scare a few. The Philadelphia Flyers' fans had a great sense of territorial pride, this was their team, their arena and their city and no one was going to come in and take it over. American soccer fans now have homes worth protecting.

5 If it runs, heads and kicks like soccer …

Don Garber's strategy for saving MLS in 2001 centered on expanding the sphere of influence its owners had over the entire USA soccer market, it saved the league from oblivion then and continues to deliver profits and benefits today. Through Soccer United Marketing it sells the sponsorship rights for most of the country's leading soccer properties including US Soccer, the Mexican National Team and Concacaf. It also runs tours, develops internet strategies and finds a way to profit from most things it touches. It's a great strategy and one that will allow it to continue to compete with the major sports properties.

6 Let's face it … television revenues can only go one way: UP (rewrite)
There is still a huge amount of upside in TV rights for the league should soccer ever eventually begin to capture ratings. The NFL generates $4b a year, the NBA over $1b, baseball $650m but soccer just $22m. To advance soccer in the USA the real increases need to be seen in the rights fees paid for MLS and the USA men's and women's national teams for this is money that goes directly back into the game. Currently both these properties need substantial increases in ratings to achieve significant payments, which is not easy. A US National Team doing well at a World Cup and the residual impact on future qualification games will have an impact. The granting of the World Cup back to the USA would have a huge impact on this and drive up the value for all US Team games as a result. As for MLS, it's still a long road and fees will only rise as the meaning and strength of the league "off the field" increases. As more new teams join the league, those with new fan bases and new impetus, it will elevate the national footprint and create new rivalries and passion. The playoffs in 2009 represented a 95 per cent increase in attendance over 2002 and the atmosphere at some of the games light years more exciting. Over the next 15 years more teams, more games, more rivalries, more in stadium passion and atmosphere and of course more viewers will be needed to prise open the coffers of the networks. The signs are there though that the tide is turning with playoff games at Chicago, LA, Seattle, and Houston creating atmospheres every bit the equal of many around the world and in particular the 21,000 in Chicago that turned Toyota Park into a seething cauldron of smoke, flags and passion, reminiscent of Mexico, Argentina, Colombia and Italy. (By the way merge the Mexican and American Leagues into a new super league and the rights fees' would explode overnight. The good news

for MLS and its owners is that the television rights fees for soccer can only go one way: UP.

MLS 2022: a snap shot

Given the above, and in a perfect world, what might Major League Soccer look like in 2022? The following might be wishful thinking, but here goes. With a model to profitability mapped out by Los Angeles, Toronto, Seattle, Philadelphia and Los Angeles, 24 of the top 50 cities in the country now have teams with stadiums (new or soccer-renovated) close to downtown, preferably stadiums that are built and owned 100 percent by the clubs, but if not, they have operating agreements that give them control of enough of the important revenue streams to ensure profitability. (Free land and a good deal should not be enough to secure or move a team and better no team than one with no hope of making money.) stadiums are designed for 20,000 fans with expansion capabilities for 10,000 more seats. Naming rights are sold at $2m per year (urban location helping), a $2m shirt sponsorship deal is secured and $5m in other founding sponsorships generated. Ticket prices are kept below other major sports and average $30.00 with fans spending a "net" (after concessionaire commission) of $2.50. Fans have representation on the board, voting rights on some key decisions and 2.5 percent of all club profits are placed into a fund to ensure all fans get a birthday card when it's due, a visit from a club official/players if they or their kid is in hospital, free training camps and scholarships for under-privileged kids, and free tickets to fans that lose their jobs. The teams play a minimum of 22 home league or cup games per season and the new $10m salary cap has attracted players and coaches from far and wide. They have a good balance of youth and experience and young American players bypassing college to earn well paid professional MLS contracts with the hope of a big money move to Barcelona on their mind. Rival fans travel in their thousands to "away" games (well those within 300–400 miles) by car, air and bus, with the rivalry in the stands as competitive as that on the field. The Sons of Ben in Philadelphia will invade DC, the Barra Brava of DC will reciprocate, the March of the Sounders will continue past Seahawk stadium and descend on Portland and Vancouver (think about it: how many of Seattle Sounder fans will revel in making the short trip to both these teams to "welcome" their newest and biggest rival to the league?) Television networks vie for the rights to capture the color and excitement paying $75m per year for the privilege. Teams are making profits of $15–$20m with buyers from Asia, Europe and the Middle East circling like vultures happy to pay the $100–$150m asking price for clubs. MLS's future is cemented when the USA defeats Mexico on 4 July in the 2022 World Cup Final at the Rose Bowl in Los Angeles – I did preface this with "in a perfect world".

If the league grows carefully with tight fiscal controls and an eye to profitability over revenue the above scenario is within the realms of possibility. Average gates of 20,000, control of stadium revenue streams, and a healthy but not over burdening $10m salary cap, could see teams generate profits of $15–$20m and as such valuable. I have detailed how the league or conferences might look like and whether it should be two conferences or one 24-team league should be a decision for the fans, after all they are their teams (Table 13.3).

Table 13.3 Possible future MLS Leagues

Room for more?

	Eastern Conference		Western Conference
1	New England Revolution	1	LA Galaxy
2	NY RedBull	2	Seattle
3	Philadelphia Union	3	San Jose
4	D.C. United	4	Colorado
5	Kansas City	5	Chivas
6	Chicago Fire	6	Real Salt Lake
7	Columbus Crew	7	FC Dallas
8	Charlotte City*	8	Houston
9	Atlanta Albion*	9	Portland
10	Cleveland*	10	Vancouver
11	St.Louis*	11	Montreal*
12	New York City*	12	San Diego*

* Author's guesses.

With the above teams in place the following model highlights the potential profitability: (Table 13.4).

Many teams will clearly surpass the revenue numbers detailed above and some indeed do already. The key however will be that the majority of the teams in the league reach profitability and are operating from a sustainable financial foundation. To believe that possible you have to believe that the key drivers can be achieved.

Table 13.4 Proforma profit and loss model for MLS

More teams! More games! More fans!

MLS attendance	20,000	25,000	30,000
MLS teams	24	24	24
Average crowds	20,000	25,000	30,000
Ticket price	30.00	30.00	30.00
Per cap net	2.50	2.50	2.50
Home games	22	22	22
Total league attendance	**10.5m**	**13.2m**	**15.8m**
Games	528	528	528
Numbers			
Attendance per team	440,000	550,000	660,000
Ticket revenue	13.2m	16.5m	19.8m
Per cap	1.1m	1.3m	1.6m
Total game revenue	**14.3m**	**17.8m**	**21.4m**
Shirt sponsor	2.5m	2.5m	2.5m
Naming	3.0m	3.0m	3.0m
Sponsorship	5.0m	5.0m	5.0m
Total revenue	**39.1m**	**46.2m**	**53.4m**
Overhead	15.0m	15.0m	15.0m
Player costs	10.0m	10.0m	10.0m
Profit EBIT	**14.1m**	**21.2m**	**28.4m**
Incremental revenue			
Net player trades	2.0m	2.0m	2.0m
Television revenue	3.0m	3.0m	3.0m
Total	**19.1m**	**26.2m**	**33.4m**

Table 13.5 2009 benchmarks for projections

Not unrealistic

Required	Model	Current as at 2009
Attendances surpass	20,000	Seattle 32,000, Toronto 20,000
Shirt sponsorship	$2.5m	Galaxy $3.5m, Chicago $2.2m
Naming rights	$2.5m	Galaxy $4.5m, most $2m
Sponsorships	$5.0m	Galaxy $5m, most $2m
Player trades	$2.0m	Altidore $10m, Onyewu $3m
Television income	$3.0m	$22m total for league*

Notes: Includes US Soccer games.
Source: Compiled from interviews and MLS.

Fortunately some of these numbers are already being exceeded (Table 13.5).

It's easy to get carried away with analyzing and projecting numbers surrounding professional soccer but the real truth will come in the day-to-day steps that the league and its clubs take to become relevant in their communities and important in the lives of their fans. This is where the true test of whether any of the above will occur. Without developing and executing a model that connects fans it's all just spreadsheets and numbers.

You could make a list under each of the above points and add dozens of tactical steps that could be taken to ensure they are delivered (See Table 13.6.) Ultimately, it is about putting in place a set of best practices and guiding principles, learned from all teams both old and new, and executing against daily.

If the above scenario does play out for MLS, then good things will happen multiplied by a factor of 10 if the World Cup returns.

Move over Italy, move over France

By adding six new teams over the next 15 years and delivering a 20,000 average attendance for 22 home games, the overall season attendance would rise 300 percent to 10.5 million (see Table 13.7) making MLS the fourth best attended soccer league in the world. Most global leagues have already matured as businesses and it's hard to see how they might add new teams or indeed massively

Table 13.6 Some key drivers for MLS teams

It's all about fans

	Driver	Reason
1	Fan integration	Nothing more important: it must become "their team"
2	Urban or "close to": 20–30,000	Our Team, Our City, Our Stadium, Our Sport
3	Focus on new fans 18–35+	Will drive the atmosphere to fuel future fan growth
4	Embrace Hispanic/ethnics	Their sport and increasingly their country
5	Improve quality of play	It is about what happens on the field
6	Respect fans	It costs nothing to do the small things fans love
7	Identify/develop own talent	Save millions, make millions, involve local youth clubs
8	Embrace global, stay authentic	Use every ounce of equity it can milk from it
9	Focus on soccer fans	There's enough out there to support two leagues
10	Controlled growth	Stay alive: get to profitability, it will drive value

increase their overall attendance numbers. It will not be easy to get every team averaging 20,000, but if the World Cup is granted to the USA it will. Even without the World Cup, I would argue that any team that could not achieve these levels should be seriously evaluated.

Being the fifth largest league in the world will certainly help in attracting players, which in turn will excite fans and solidify attendance. Whatever it means for the value of the club, it does little to position MLS in the eyes of American sponsors, television networks or investors. For this the league needs to be compared to the major American sports leagues. Due to the size of stadiums and relative scarcity of games, soccer will never compete with the major leagues for revenues and overall attendance and it will be a long time before television ratings for the domestic soccer league ranks alongside the "big leagues". However, where it does compete is in profitability. Careful financial control, aligned with ownership of stadiums, will place MLS on par with all but the NFL in terms of average profit. If teams in 2022 can make a profit of $19m (see Table 13.8), it would in today's sporting

Table 13.7 Comparison of MLS to other professional soccer leagues 2009–22

4th most attended league in the world

Rank	2009 season			2022 season		
	Top Leagues	**Total**	**Average**	**League**	**Crowd (m)**	**Average**
1	English Premier	13.5	35,599	English Premier	13.5	35,599
2	German	13.0	42,749	German	13.0	42,749
3	Spanish	10.7	28,232	Spanish	10.7	28,232
4*	English 2	10.0	18,026	**MLS**	**10.5**	**20,000**
5	Italian	9.4	25,324	English 2	10.0	18,026
6	French	7.9	21,050	Italian	9.4	25,324
7	Argentina	7.9	20,886	French	7.9	21,050
8	Holland	6.0	19,827	Argentina	7.9	20,886
9	Japan	5.8	19,278	Holland	6.0	19,827
10	Brazil	6.4	16,992	Japan	5.8	19,278
11	**MLS**	**3.4**	**16,460**	Brazil	6.4	16,992

Note: * English Championship.

Source: espn soccernet.

landscape rank MLS teams twentyfifth in the NFL, seventh in NBA, fourteenth in the MLB and the seventh most profitable team in the NHL based on the numbers issued by Forbes Magazine for the 2007–8 season. (Obviously we are a comparing future MLS with current numbers for other leagues but it makes a point that the battle is to be won on profitability.)

Cashing out

If the above is achieved what might be the value of an average MLS team be? It is very challenging to predict the future potential value of MLS teams, as much depends on the league itself being able to build a big enough national footprint to become a relevant competitor to the big leagues. It equally rests on the ability of investors to secure the necessary "downtown" urban sites for stadiums that are at the heart of the new positioning for the league, sites which are notoriously difficult to find and afford. The league will

Table 13.8 Key financial performance numbers for major USA leagues

For MLS it's about profitability

	Highest Revenue	Low Rev	Avg Rev	Player Salaries	% of Avg revenue	Average Player Salary	Profit High	Profit Lowst	Average Profit
NFL	345	208	234	$142m	50%	$1.1m	90	−5.7	32.0
NBA	209	91	126	$78m	37%	$5.4m	51	−7.4	7.7
MLB	375	139	194	$146m	44%	$3.0m	44	−26.0	17.0
NHL	168	66	94	$53m	33%	$1.4m	79	−18.5	6.4
MLS 2007	36	5	13	$3.3m	25%	$126,000	4	(4.5)	(1.6)
MLS 2022	53	39	46	$10m*	21%	$300,000	33	19.0	26.0

Note: Average salaries for MLS exclude Beckham's $6.5m.

Source: compiled from *Forbes Magazine* online reports for the 2008–9 of season plus MLS estimates.

ultimately have a mix of venues based on existing infrastructure; the Home Depot Center in LA would not be classed as "urban" but generates significant profit. However assuming sites are found in the major cities and a 24-team one or two division league created, what might the clubs be worth? Those in unworkable stadium scenarios will never realize their full potential and may have to move and equally those that have lost touch with their fan bases or are just "tired" will have to either "reconnect" or assess their options. Clubs that are new to the league or older teams that build new stadiums in the right place will see values that could exceed $150m. Profitable soccer will represent excellent value and attract a host of domestic and international suitors (Table 13.9).

The following is a list of 20 factors that might influence the value of MLS clubs:

1 Teams owning their own soccer stadiums and/or revenue streams.
2 The emergence of a new breed of American Soccer fan.
3 Attracting the 18–34 young adult (critical to sponsors) and real fans.
4 With a national footprint of 24 teams the league will have stature and gravitas.
5 Control of the player costs.
6 Strength as a Hispanic Sport: 1 in 4 Americans will be Hispanic by 2050.

Table 13.9 Average revenue and income for USA Professional Sports Leagues compared to MLS

MLS teams become valuable

League	Revenue	Income	Team Salary	%	Avg Player	Team Value
NFL	234	32.0	142.0	50.7	1.1	$678m
NBA	126	7.7	78.0	37.5	5.4	$360m
MLB	194	17.0	146.0	44.6	3.0	$451m
NHL	94	6.4	53.0	33.0	1.4	$222m
MLS 2007	13	−1.6	3.3	25.0	104,000	$37m
MLS 2022	46	26.0	10.0	21.0	300,000	$100–$150m

Source: Current averages for NFL,NBA,MLB,NHL 2008: compiled from Forbes 9/9/2009 Article Projected numbers for MLS.

7   Plenty of upside remaining on television rights.

8   Beckham and the likes thereof.

9   Fox Soccer/ESPN/Univision/Gol TV battling for rights.

10   The increasing likelihood of the MLS and Mexican Soccer leagues getting closer.

11   Strength of international game, and education of fans to it.

12   Interest from international teams and investors in conquering the USA.

13   Huge participation levels to draw upon and nurture as fans.

14   Growing interest in World Cup Soccer and the USA National team in it.

15   Rise in World Cup television ratings and importance as major sports event in USA.

16   The internet and social media level the playing field in the battle for fans.

17   Globalization and strength of soccer world wide to support the USA.

18   Development of young valuable American talent.

19   Leading Mexican players coming into the league.

20   PROFITABILITY.

The "x" value multiplier in all of the above is FIFA's decision to grant either the 2018 or 2022 World Cup to the USA, the impact of which would be immense and ensure all of the above is achieved and exceeded.

50 million soccer-mad Hispanics: let's do the math

There is something a little too obvious here: by 2025 MLS will have 24 teams and America will have 50 million soccer Hispanics. Soccer needs 20,000 fans at each game to become a very valuable and profitable investment. Let's assume that half the population is male and focus on just winning their support. Each week MLS needs 240,000 fans to fill its 12 home-team stadiums. That's less than 1 percent of the male Hispanic population. Surely 15 years of embracing them in their markets, supporting their grass-roots youth players, creating culturally appropriate marketing events, and raising the quality of play with top European and maybe Mexican talent might just convince 1 percent to become fans. It's simplistic math of course and a little naïve, but you get my point. I am not advocating turning MLS into a totally Hispanic-focused league but the numbers are too compelling to ignore.

Every team needs a Beckham?

Some teams will far exceed these numbers and blast through the salary cap models presented. LA Galaxy for example already spends close to $9m on players in 2009 but still makes money. Each team needs to finds its own path but the league should ensure that all of its teams are in a position to achieve profitability and if not, options should be reviewed. The ultimate goal of course is to drive revenue and profitability, which the LA Galaxy has been very successful in achieving. Spending $6.5m per year over five years for David Beckham was not a financial commitment made lightly, but for the Galaxy it has paid off in spades with profitable new revenue streams generated from shirt sponsorship, local broadcast revenues, overseas tours, increased attendances and increased marketing partners. Before Beckham even set foot in the USA, a clear well-thought-out business plan had been put in place to recoup and profit from the "investment". But this was Beckham, Los Angeles and a perfect storm. There is no other player in the world that brings with him so much star power and media "equity" and it's impossible to find a second. Another $6.5m spent acquiring "non Beckhams" will not generate a profitable return. The league needs more quality players and indeed stars, but at the right price for the right market.

The commercial growth of soccer in the USA is clearly being driven by Major League Soccer and Soccer United Marketing, who between them account for most of the significant professional programs being delivered in the US market. There are of course other forces at play in the country that are shaping and will continue to shape soccer.

1 **The Yanks are coming ... love them or hate them**
   American investors have now actively identified soccer as a valuable investment opportunity and many of them have taken

the opportunity to acquire English clubs. Stan Kroenke, owner of the Colorado Rapids, is also a now a 29 percent stakeholder in Arsenal. The Glazers own Manchester United, Gillette and Hicks own Liverpool, Randy Lerner owns Aston Villa and Ellis Short owns Sunderland, and Jeff Mallett and partners own Derby County rounding off a new and sure-to-be-continued trend of American investors owning English and European soccer teams.

2 "Girls still rule" (so my daughters tell me)

Women are a critical part of soccer's future in the USA both as players and fans as well as future business executives. The USA is the beacon for the development of the women's game world-wide and much rests on its commitment and success. The country will continue to develop great players and will win its share of Olympic Gold Medals and World Cups. It will also be the training ground for those players and countries that will challenge the USA for supremacy. The success of the new Women's Professional League will depend very much on the patience and tolerance for losses of the investors involved for as MLS know only too well, it's a long road to profitability for any new league. This book has devoted an entire chapter to their importance and the incredible role they have and will continue to play in American soccer and the long road they have taken to earn their just rewards. Commercially however it is just a simple fact that the world of women's soccer lags way behind the men's game. To prove the point the prize money for the men's 2006 World Cup in Germany was estimated to be \$332m; and in 2010 in South Africa \$420m the prize money for the Chinese 2007 Women's World Cup – just \$6m.

3 It's like the mail, they just keep coming

Whether professional leagues thrive or fail, the USA team wins or loses, it seems the never-ending procession of kids to American soccer fields will continue. This is of course great for the sport and healthy for the kids but everyone in soccer is doing them a great disservice if they do not offer them clear pathways to develop as professional players, coaches, officials or even business executives. The NFL, NBA, and MLB offer all of these and soccer should be no different. Every "football" kid wants to be quarterback and throw the winning touchdown in the SuperBowl, every baseball kid the home run that wins the World Series and every basketball kid the buzzer beating three pointer in game seven of the NBA finals. Soccer hasn't instilled this dream or aspiration in American kids yet and needs to. It is of course a last minute 30-yard volley to win the World Cup for the USA.

4 Just a click away

I am sure that the internet was designed with soccer in the USA in mind. Soccer still does not get tremendous print or televised media coverage (except in dedicated channels) and so soccer fans flood to the internet to communicate and interact and get their soccer with a depth and immediacy impossible 10 years ago. A new generation of American kids are growing up that do not relate to 30-second commercials, newspaper articles and forced television. They get their news, watch their shows and plan their lives online, and at times of their choosing. Soccer could never buy its way onto the media landscape or compete economically in the expensive television and print market. It can however compete just as well as the "big leagues" online. Soccer can literally talk one-on-one with its key fan base and build sophisticated databases that will allow them to engage one-on-one. Soccer also controls exciting and valuable content that will only get more valuable as the TV networks lose "eyeballs" and advertisers seek a direct and focused reach to fans. For the near future however the internet is the perfect tool to develop and foster the personalized interaction with its core fans that will be the bedrock of its success. The internet alone however is just a tool and no substitute for ensuring that the fan experience at games and quality on the field is there, but it can help speed up the rate at which the sport is adopted, understood and shared.

5 The University of EA

This might sound slightly forced but a generation, being raised on computer games, has in EA Sports FIFA 2010 one of the most popular titles in the world. American kids interested in soccer are by osmosis being educated to the game.

They relate to the global scope of the game because in their bedrooms they play Inter Milan versus Real Madrid, they buy and sell Ronaldo and Rooney and devise tactics for Barcelona and Liverpool. In the 1990s these teams were just names in a soccer magazine or results in a paper, completely alien and without meaning or reference. Today they are alive in plasma on computer screens and TV sets throughout the country. American soccer kids can name you teams, starting line-ups, colors, nicknames, stadiums, and players. It's still a relatively small group but soccer does not need mass-market coverage to be successful, it needs to reach, support and nurture a focused soccer-educated audience, and EA sports kids have PHds.

6 The North American Soccer League returns
Not the one with Pele and Beckenbaur but the semi-professional version formulating as this book goes to press (quite why they resurrected the old name is unknown). Applying for second division professional status, they may well develop over the next decade to become a strong feeder league to the MLS and who knows maybe a foretaste of relegation and promotion. Not in my lifetime however.

7 The global game
Soccer's greatest weapon in the USA is the power and strength of the international game and all it brings with it. On its own, American soccer cannot breakdown all the barriers and competition, nor can it alone compete for the hearts and minds and eventual wallets of America's sports fans. It's American Soccer competing in the World Cup, it's MLS bringing in international players, it's Barcelona, Manchester United and Real Madrid on American television and in American stadiums, it's USA versus Mexico in Los Angeles and Colombia versus Argentina in New York, it's Mexican soccer on Univision and Italian soccer on Fox. It is accepting, embracing and integrating the global game into the fabric of American soccer while building a sport that speaks to and serves the American player and fan and the unique attributes that make America great. It comes of course with challenges but the global game if used correctly can be American soccer's greatest asset.

CHAPTER 14

The World Cup Returns

Flash forward!

Stop the world for three weeks in June of 2022 and send every 16–30 year-old in America to a World Cup Soccer match in the USA and nothing would ever be the same in American sports again. A nation of kids brought up on soccer and then experiencing the greatest atmosphere of any sports event they have ever seen would be enough to make them fans for life and relegate the experiences of baseball and football to their father's scrapbook. The impact of bringing back the World Cup to the United States is that big.

Everything changed for soccer in the USA on 4 July 1988, the day the World Cup was granted and hopefully this book has helped you understand the impact and influence it had and the long and often perilous journey the sport has taken to establish a foothold in America. The journey is by no means over and equally by no means certain that it will ultimately succeed to the level those of us in soccer would like. The American sports market is, as ever, brutally tough and unwaveringly unforgiving. The dominant sports are not going to give up their positions easily, their sponsors willingly or their fans without a tough "street fight". Soccer is going to have to continue to battle as it has always done, for everything it gets. The event however that kicked it all off, can ultimately be the same one that propels it to levels it could never have dreamed of in the late 1980s. There is no doubt in my mind that the World Cup represents the galvanizing force in US Soccer's current and future development. From a standing start in 1988 the World Cup stimulated soccer's commercial development providing the funding and motivation that staged the best-attended World Cup in history, a new Men's Professional League launched, nine new soccer stadiums built, a host of new investors amassed, two professional women's leagues launched, a 24-hour soccer television network established, and a 60 percent increase in youth soccer participation achieved, all from an insolvent Federation's dream.

There is a growing love affair building between soccer in America and the World Cup. Seventeen million Americans watched the 2006 final between Italy and France, an enormous increase over the 2.3 million who switched on in 1990. Incredibly, according to Nielson ratings, 90 million Americans, almost one-third of the US population, watched all or part of a World Cup game from Germany in 2006, which would have been unimaginable as LeTellier flew home from Zurich in 1988.

Soccer in the USA has come a tremendous distance since that time and is well on its way to establishing itself on the sporting landscape, but the re-appearance of a World Cup, in either 2018 or 2022 would put it on an accelerated trajectory that would simply explode soccer in the USA. Another World Cup in the USA would "finish off" the work FIFA started in 1988 and establish a position in the sporting landscape that could never be unseated. Here are six important factors that would come into play should the USA win the bid:

1 Current and future potential investors in MLS would have the confidence to further invest in both their teams and stadiums knowing that an event of such magnitude was coming back. MLS needs a bigger national footprint and the arrival of the World Cup would be a huge motivator. It was the success of the World Cup in 1994 that convinced Phil Anschutz, the Krafts, Hunts and other investors to get behind the launch of a high-risk professional league in the USA at a time when the future landscape was still uncertain. A returning World Cup in 2018 or 2022 would offer investors a whole new level of opportunity in a far more sophisticated, mature and expansive soccer landscape.
2 The World Cup already has a proven track record in the USA and its impact on a sport that has spent 20 years trying to "break through" would be immense.
3 Cities that are keen to bid for, and enjoy the financial benefits of hosting a World Cup match, could be requested to support either the establishment of an MLS team or develop inner-city soccer facilities that could benefit the sport – there is nothing

like leverage. My discussion with Sunil Gulati, Chairman of the World Cup bid, led me to believe there will be a quid pro quo required to the benefit of the game.

4 Television contracts for both the US National Team and MLS would improve. This would make more money available for acquiring or developing players and teams. The World Cup is the ultimate leverage tool for driving television revenue for soccer in the USA.

5 This time round, the sport will not only be ready and waiting to capitalize on every ounce of equity the World Cup can deliver, it would equally have had 8–10 years of using the event to build fans bases, entrench professional teams, develop better players and continue to drive critical marketing and sponsorship money into the sport. A successful World Cup this time would instantly drive millions of new fans to Major League Soccer, a league ready and prepared to absorb them and create an explosion in professional soccer that would stun America.

6 However, the single and most important impact the arrival would have would be on the fans. The USA came alive to soccer in 1994 with an explosion of interest and support that shocked both the world and the country. World Cup 1994 represented soccer's coming out and America was "blown away" by the size of the crowds and the passion that fans had for their teams. World Cup 1994 was the breeding ground and first taste of top-level soccer for millions of Americans. A whole new generation started to pay attention to soccer and in particular World Cup soccer following 1994 and its return would cement this passion for generations to come. The transition of soccer has been from a participatory sport played by young kids and soccer moms to a fully rounded professional sport both on and off the field on par with leading American sports.

The marketing message being adopted by the United States bid committee for it global campaign to win the right to host the World Cup is "*the Game is in US*": smart and catchy and actually accurate, for soccer in the USA is as much a part of American culture in 2010 as baseball, football or basketball. It may not be as big and not as intensely supported, but soccer is here, it is staying and it's growing in depth. Youth soccer helps it grow, MLS helps it grow, the USA National teams help it grow, Mexico helps it grow, Barcelona and Manchester United help it grow, Fox Soccer, ESPN and Univision help it grow, agents (yes, agents) and soccer business executives help it grow and a myriad of sponsors and other forces play their role in moving the sport forward each year. Ultimately however it will be the fans who decide if the sport succeeds or not in the USA and there is nothing that will excite and cement the current fan base in American and create millions of new ones than the return of a World Cup. And this is not solely because of the financial success it will assuredly deliver, or the economic impact it will have on host cities or even the millions of corporate dollars that will pour into the sport. For me, it is about the arrival on American soil, both in the years before and the event itself, of the world's greatest players and teams and the excitement this will generate for fans throughout the country. Anyone who has ever been to a World Cup will know what I mean and the thought of tens of millions of American teenagers and young adults being exposed to the world's best players, teams and fans salivates the palate for the future of soccer in the USA and would provide sleepless nights for every competitive sports league in the country.

The end of the beginning

It's been a long hard road for soccer in the USA and it has had to fight for every scrap of respect it has gained over the past 25 years and even today, with all of its successes, it still battles to maintain its first foothold on the American sports landscape. Over the past decades it has had to fight against a nation of soccer skeptics, battle a cynical and disinterested media, overcome corporate indifference and go head-to-head with some of the toughest and most professional sports organizations in the world. It has equally had to fight internally with disparate and competing soccer groups to gain consensus on a common purpose and direction for the sport, possibly its biggest battle yet and one far from being won.

The premise of the book however is that a single event, the 1994 World Cup, changed the direction and fortunes of soccer in the USA forever and set it on a course from which it would never look back. A premise that hopefully by now you can see to be true.

It would be a mistake though to believe that the "simple" act of acquiring and staging the event was all that was needed (a sort of light the touch paper and step back solution to all soccer's woes), which could not have been further from the truth.

What gaining the 1994 World Cup actually did was to place American soccer under the intense scrutiny and harsh spotlight of not only the world governing body of soccer FIFA but also the cynical and watchful eyes of the global soccer community. A community that had, in its mind, just entrusted it's most important and precious event to the land of Hollywood, Disneyland and Las Vegas and were seriously questioning the wisdom of doing so, probably with good reason. For in 1990 it was clear that the USA was not ready to host the world's greatest sporting event and lacked the necessary resources both personally or financially to deliver on what it had promised. It took bold moves, tough choices, strong characters and the unyielding optimism and belief, almost genetically imprinted in the American psyche, to make the event happen, but happen it did and the rest, as they say, is history. People can and do change the course of events and I have spoken to few in American soccer who do not believe that Alan Rothenberg's contribution to changing the professional face of US Soccer was immense, his FIFA orchestrated election a catalyst for revolutionary change. Payback for FIFA of course (apart from the millions in World Cup profits) was the promise that the USA would establish a Division One Professional League, giving soccer a window into one the wealthiest and most prosperous countries in the world. This of course has been a much tougher promise to deliver and one that would take more than the warm fuzzy glow of a great World Cup to crack. It was however the millions of flag waving, passionate and engaged fans flooding into stadiums around the country that convinced investors launching a professional soccer league could be an exciting and profitable venture.

If Rothenberg was the driving force of soccer in the 1990s it has been Major League Soccer, its owners and in particular Phil Anschutz who have shaped the growth of the sport in the past decade and underpin it still today. It has been Phil Anschutz's unwavering commitment to professional soccer along with the support of Lamar Hunt and the Kraft family (who stepped up to the plate when it mattered most) that has secured soccer's professional future. It has allowed the league to survive long enough to succeed and prosper, seeing stadiums built, fan bases created, sponsors arrive and television contracts pay. It is quite a turn-a-round from the dark days of 2001, representing one of the great sports business stories of the decade.

On the back of World Cup 1994, and the steps subsequently taken, millions of fresh dollars have come into the sport supporting its development at all levels. The once bankrupt Federation that bid for the games now has $50m in reserves, and a $10m plus a year sponsorship contract with Nike. The US Soccer Foundation, recipient of the World Cup 94 profits, a further $60m, distributing millions a year in grants. The US Women's National Team are now the highest paid female players in the world (the men are not), and motivated investors have poured millions into trying to establish a professional league for them to play in. These are investment levels no other country in the world would dream of committing to women's soccer. American youth soccer registration rose 82 percent during the World Cup decade and continues to prosper today with millions of players and thousands of coaches on the fields each week. They also fuel a $2b dollar registration business. The fierce rivalry between the USA and Mexico brings to a point the incredible growth and amazing influence the soccer-rabid American-Hispanic community has on all aspects of the game.

It is however, not the past that soccer needs to look to now, but the future and I firmly believe soccer's greatest days in the USA are still ahead of it. The platform for exponentially expanding the sport has never been stronger, stadiums are up (or going up), investors are wealthy and committed, fans are knowledgeable and soccer educated, television coverage is improving and extensive, sponsors excited and numerous and the power and personality of the global game is starting to have a real influence in delivering the excitement and intensity that sets soccer apart from all other sports.

In 2010 and for soccer in America, Winston Churchill said it best … "Now this is not the end. It is not even the beginning of the end. But it is, perhaps, the end of the beginning".

The first 25 years are over … American soccer is off the beaches and heading inland.

The Future of Soccer in the USA

2010–20: The decade of the American Player

"Everything begins and ends with the quality of product on the field"

With the number of players participating, its sporting pedigree, and the financial and human resources available to anything that it puts its mind to, the USA should produce players the world demands and have a national team capable of competing for honors at the World Cup. The USA over the next ten to 15 years, should develop players worth tens of millions of dollars in transfer fees for MLS teams to underpin their finances or to elevate the leagues' quality, and players that populate top leagues and progress in the World Cup. The ideas that follow should still allow everyone in the game to continue to "make their living" in the sport but to do so in a way that ensures that the game progresses at the pace of the global game of which it is a part. Winning a World Cup and having a top-class Division One Professional League will make the soccer pie bigger for everyone and only enhance the financial prospects for all. Once again, I am no coach but there are great USA coaches out there that can work this out if given the chance, and a 30,000-member NSCAA coaching organization that should be able to drive it to grass roots. American soccer owes it to the millions of kids playing the sport to ensure they receive training and coaching on a par with the rest of the world (and, ultimately, better) and to provide them with a clear roadmap to a future in soccer. This can only be achieved if soccer comes together as a sport to define exactly what this is.

1 **Reduce emphasis on "winning"**
   From the ages of 6–12 there should be no score kept or league tables calculated for youth team games in the USA. All the focus should be on skill development. It's un-American, but winning

is irrelevant and often counter-productive at this age. We need more "pick up" and "casual soccer" and less organized play.

2 Define the "American Player"

To support this, a national "coaching symposium" should be held with leading coaches from US Soccer, MLS, US Youth Soccer, College, NSCAA, US Club Soccer and AYSO. Out of this symposium should emerge a National set of age group-specific "skill sets" and coaching guidelines for American players. Every coach I have spoken to feels that, at 16–18, USA players have "missed" key critical steps in their soccer education, steps that stop them progressing to the next level. The USA needs to establish what these steps are and ingrain them throughout the USA youth system, and include coaches from all sectors of US Soccer: "What is the American player?"

3 Coaches "Proclamation"

Parents, players and youth soccer coaches listen to college coaches. They need to get behind it and embrace the philosophy. It will improve their teams, and ultimately their players and the game at the college level. If the parents "buy in", the coaches will. The parents will buy in if college coaches and MLS coaches tell them it is so.

4 Coaching the coaches

America probably has more enthusiastic, committed and involved coaches than any country in the world. The Soccer Foundation/ US Soccer/MLS should introduce a soccer coaches loan program that US coaches can use to take leading "world" coaching certifications. To beat the best you need coaches that are as qualified as the best. All MLS coaches should have EUFA/Spanish/ Brazilian or similar certification and should be helped financially to achieve this. Bring the schools over here if necessary. Soccer needs to use this phenomenal grass-roots movement.

5 Professional development

Developing professional quality players needs to be done by professional clubs and in conjunction with the USA National Team, to which every US kid should aspire. MLS should be the vehicle and tie in with local youth clubs and international clubs. Players should spend time with MLS teams and "apprenticeships" with foreign clubs; youth teams benefit financially from any sale. There is the practical issue of competing sponsors with

Adidas (sponsoring MLS) and Nike (sponsoring US Soccer), but both are smart enough to realize the importance of developing world-class American players and the impact it will have on the game and their business. Developing players to help the USA win a World Cup should be brand agnostic.

6 Diversity

Suburban America will not win the USA a World Cup. Look at Brazil, France, Argentina, Germany and England. America's diversity is one of its greatest strengths; American soccer's lack of diversity its greatest weakness. American demography is changing and American soccer needs to change with it.

Soccer aficionados, coaches, organizations and businesses know most of the above but the inherent "silos" that soccer has created over the past 25 years inhibits communication and the ability for the sport to act as one (as the NBA, NFL, MLB and NHL seemingly do). Individually and privately, many I have spoken with fully agree with the need for change and that the sport needs a common shared purpose in the development of players. It's not criticism or a negative; it's just progress – maintaining status quo is not good enough. The US Soccer Developmental Academy is a good step forward, but more is needed.

If the sport of soccer is to go the next level in the USA and the American soccer player is to become a sought after MLS and global commodity, then it must adapt and change. All of us in American soccer owe it to the next generation of soccer kids to make it so.

Appendix 1

Soccer in the USA "Organizational Chart"

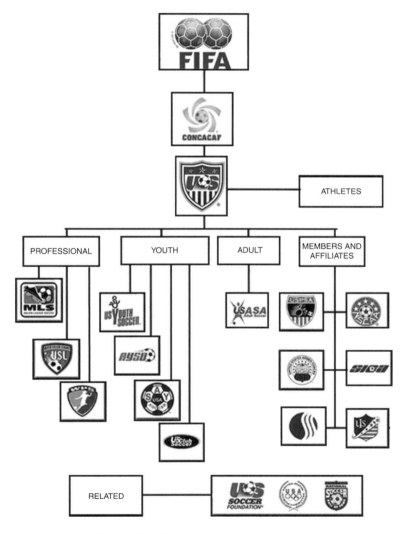

Source: adapted from Organizational Structure, which appears on www.ussoccer.com

Appendix 2

USA World Cup television ratings English and Spanish language 1990–2006

Broadcast	Italy 1990*	USA 1994	France 1998	Korea Japan 2002	Germany 2006
Television Universe Estimates					
Television Universe Estimates	49,300,000	94,200,000	98,000,000	105,500,000	110,200,000
ESPN 1 Universe (JUN–JUL)	N/A	63,147,000	73,899,000	86,423,000	90,872,000
ESPN 2 Universe (JUN–JUL)	N/A	12,894,000	58,128,000	83,702,000	90,379,000
Univision*	2,500,000	6,520,000	7,000,000	10,000,000	12,000,000
Number Games Covered	TNT	ABC/ESPN	ABC/ESPN	ABC/ESPN	ABC/ESPN
Total Games Available	52	48	64	68	64
Games Aired on Network	23	11	14	10	12
Games Cable ESPN 1 (only Live games)		29	27	24	21
Games Cable ESPN 2 (only Live games)		8	23	34	31
Spanish Language	52	52	64	64	64
English Language Ratings	TNT	ABC	ABC	ABC	ABC
World Cup Final Viewers	1,518,440	14,509,777	8,623,943	3,932,338	11,961,318

	1990*	1994	1998	2002	2006
World Cup Final Households	1,084,600	8,949,000	5,604,484	2,669,678	7,755,871
World Cup Final Rating	2.2%	9.5%	5.72%	2.53%	7.04%
Regular Game Viewers		7,527,638	3,559,868	1,977,990	4,790,743
Regular Game HH		4,953,286	2,535,359	1,463,229	3,450,412
Ratings		5.26%	2.59%	1.39%	3.13%
English Language Cable Ratings	TNT	ESPN 1	ESPN 1	ESPN 1	ESPN 1
Regular Game Viewers	713,750	1,969,417	830,170	1,302,732	2,313,370
Regular GamesHH	571,000	1,357,626	691,329	963,193	1,748,799
ESPN 1 Coverage Ratings		2.15%	0.94%	1.11%	1.93%
		ESPN 2	ESPN 2	ESPN 2	ESPN 2
Regular Game Viewers		177,913	403,278	651,330	1,147,062
Regular GameHH		103,966	322,911	488,556	918,685
Coverage Ratings		0.81%	0.56%	0.58%	1.02%
Spanish Language Ratings	Univision	Univision	Univision	Univision	Univision*
	1990*	1994	1998	2002	2006
World Cup Final Viewers	1,200,000	3,551,000	4,346,000	2,882,000	5,041,000
World Cup Final Households	600,000	1,617,000	2,004,000	1,918,000	2,915,000
World Cup Regular Games	680,000	1,308,000	1,243,000	846,000	2,002,000
World Cup Regular Games HH	400,000	767,000	843,000	610,000	1,338,000

(Continued)

Broadcast	Italy	USA	France	Korea Japan	Germany
	1990*	1994	1998	2002	2006
Combined World Cup Final					
Total Viewers WC Final	2,718,440	18,060,777	12,969,943	6,814,338	17,002,318
Total Households WC Final	1,684,600	10,566,000	7,608,484	4,587,678	10,670,871
Combined WC Regular Games					
Total Viewers Regular Games	1,393,750	6,261,286	3,778,359	2,309,229	5,452,412
Total Households Regular WC	971,000	5,720,286	3,378,359	2,073,229	4,788,412

Note: Univision Universe Estimates not confirmed.

Source: ESPN and Univision Research Departments.

Appendix 3

Grass-roots participation statistics for five major professional sports in the USA

Category	Soccer	Ice Hockey	Football Tackle	Football2 Touch	Baseball	Basketball
Total Players	16,000,000	1,800,000	9,000,000	12,000,000	16,000,000	24,700,000
Casual	6,200,000	700,000	3,200,000	5,300,000	3,900,000	5,900,000
Regular	4,800,000	200,000	2,000,000	2,300,000	1,900,000	4,100,000
Frequent	3,700,000	900,000	4,000,000	4,400,000	1,030,000	14,700,000
Core Player*	9,500,000	1,100,000	6,000,000	6,700,000	12,100,000	18,800,000
High School Boys	377,999	35,955	1,131,484		478,842	556,269
High School Girls	337,632	7,350				456,967
High School Total	715,631	43,305	1,131,484		478,842	1,013,236
College Men	19,793	3,973	61,252		28,767	16,571
College GIrl	21,709	1,727				15,091
College Total	41,502	5,700	61,252		28,767	31,662
Total Youth Organized	4,000,000	355,156			4,136,000	240,720
Youth Clubs Boys	3,200,000	313,317	225,721		4,136,000	131,962
Youth Clubs Girls	1,200,000	41,839				108,758
Club Youth Program	4,400,000	355,156	225,721		4,136.000	240,720

(Continued)

Category	Soccer	Ice Hockey	Football Tackle	Football2 Touch	Baseball	Basketball
Type of Play						
League	54%	42%	16%	12%	54%	24%
School	21%	7%	44%	21%	17%	27%
Casual Pick Up	21%	47%	37%	65%	25%	45%
Age Group						
Age 6–12	55%	13%	26%	36%	51%	34%
Age 13–17	18%	22%	54%	31%	37%	27%
18+	27%	65%	20%	33%	12%	39%
Household Income						
100,000+	28%	39%	28%	28%	27%	28%
75–100	19%	19%	17%	17%	20%	16%
50–75	26%	18%	20%	20%	23%	22%
25–49	17%	15%	22%	22%	19%	21%
less 25	10%	9%	13%	13%	11%	13%
Average Household Income	$76,000	$83,600	$66,900		$73,200	$72,800
Annual Attendance	3,588,380	21,200,000	17,500,000		78,000,000	36,000,000
Pro-League						
Games Per Regular season	220	1230	256		2,430	2,430
Average Attendance	16,311	17,236	68,359		32,099	14,815
	37.8%	1927.3%	137.8%		644.6%	191.5%

Note: * Core player defined as playing 25+ days per years.

Source: Compiled from the Sporting Goods Manufacturers Association 2007 Insight report.

Glossary

American Soccer is littered with acronyms that can confuse even the most committed reader. Hopefully this (in order of "importance" rather than alphabetically) will help.

USSF: United States Soccer Federation.
The governing body of soccer in America (also often referred to as US Soccer).

MLS: Major League Soccer
Division One Men's Professional Soccer.

SUSAP: Soccer USA Partners.
Sports Marketing Company that acquired the commercial rights to represent US Soccer between 1990 and 1998.

API Soccer: Sister Company of SUSAP.
Represented US Soccer Rights between 1995 and 1998, and US Youth Soccer Rights between 1995 and 1998.

Octagon: Global Sports Marketing Company (part of the Interpublic Group).
Acquired API /SUSAP in 1997.

World Cup USA, 94 Inc: (WCOC)
Organizing Committee for the World Cup hosted in the USA in 1994 (often referred to in this book as World Cup 94).

FIFA: Federation Internationale de Football Association
The world governing body of soccer.

CONCACAF: Confederation of North, Central America and Caribbean Association Football.
The Confederation under which the USA competes.

USYSA: United States Youth Soccer Association

A 3-million member youth association sanctioned by the USSF. Comprises 55 state associations, run state, regional and national champion for teams at the under-19 level. Also referred to in the book as US Youth Soccer.

AYSO: American Youth Soccer Organization.

A 600,000+ youth soccer organization sanctioned by the USSF. Regarded in the USA as primarily a recreational soccer program, their ethos is that every player is guaranteed to play at least 50 percent of each game.

NASL: North American Soccer League

Home to the likes of Pele, Beckenbauer, George Best and the New York Cosmos. The league was formed in 1968 and folded in 1984.

WUSA: Women's United Soccer Association.

Division One Professional League; formed in 2000, folded in 2003.

WPS: Women's Professional Soccer

Second Attempt at launching Division One Soccer. Launched in 2009.

NSCAA: National Soccer Coaches Association

30,000-member soccer coaching organization. Most top coaches in American Soccer are members.

MLB: Major League Baseball

NFL: National Football League

NFLPA: National Football League Players Association.

Union for NFL players.

NBA: National Basketball Association

NHL: National Hockey League

MLSPU: Major League Soccer Players Union
  Union representing MLS Players

USNTSPA: United States National Team Players Association
  Union representing the USA Men's National Soccer Team Players.

SUM: Soccer United Marketing
  Company formed by Major League Soccer owners to generate additional revenue by representing properties and rights.

US Club Soccer
  Sanctioned youth soccer organization comprising the leading club teams in the USA. 200,000 associated players and most major youth teams are members.